Essential C

An Introduction for Scientists and Engineers

**P. K. Andersen,
G. Bjedov, and
M. G. Scarbrough**

Purdue University

SAUNDERS COLLEGE PUBLISHING

Harcourt Brace College Publishers

Fort Worth   Philadelphia   San Diego   New York   Orlando   San Antonio
Toronto   Montreal   London   Sydney   Tokyo

Text Typeface: Melior
Compositor: York Graphic Services
Executive Editor: Emily Barrosse
Senior Developmental Editor: Alexa Barnes
Managing Editor: Carol Field
Project Editor: Linda Boyle
Copy Editor: Andrew Potter
Manager of Art and Design: Carol Bleistine
Art Director: Anne Muldrow
Text Designer: Merce Wilczek
Cover Designer: Lou Fuiano
Text Artwork: Academy Artworks, Inc.
Director of EDP: Tim Frelick
Production Manager: Joanne Cassetti

Printed in the United States of America

ESSENTIAL C: An Introduction for Scientists and Engineers

The programs presented in this book have been included for their instructional value. The publisher does not offer any warranties or representations, nor does it accept any liabilities.

ISBN 0-03-004158-9

Library of Congress Catalog Card Number: 94-067128

4567890123   042   10 987654321

This book was printed on acid-free recycled content paper, containing **MORE THAN 10% POSTCONSUMER WASTE**

To our parents

Detailed Table of Contents

Preface

This book provides a simple and brief introduction to programming in standard C, suitable for a one-semester course for beginners. It presents the bare minimum—the essentials—that a student must know to produce useful C programs, paying special attention to the needs of students in the sciences and engineering.

Why C?

In recent years, C has become the programming language most often chosen by "serious" programmers—those who program for a living. It is not hard to see why:

- *Power.* C possesses a rich set of operators and library functions that allow the programmer to write powerful, concise, and elegant code.
- *Availability.* C compilers are found on nearly every type of computer, from microcomputers to supercomputers.
- *Portability.* C makes it possible to develop a program on one type of computer, and port it to another type of computer with minimal or no alteration.
- *Efficiency.* C compilers tend to produce highly efficient machine code.
- *Versatility.* This is what really sets C apart from other languages. On the one hand, C is a powerful general-purpose language that supports structured and modular programming methods. In this respect, it compares favorably with other high-level languages such as Pascal or Modula-2. At the same time, C provides access to lower-level facilities that most other languages hide from the pro-

grammer; this has made C useful for creating compilers and operating systems. (The UNIX operating system is written in C.)

C is not perfect. It has been criticized as being overly terse, tempting the programmer to write dense, hard-to-read code. Its operator set is too rich for some tastes. (There are at least four different ways to add 1 to an integer variable, for example.) In general, C does not prevent the programmer from making mistakes because it is assumed that the programmer knows what he or she is doing—a dangerous assumption when the programmer is a beginner.

● ━━━━ Who Should Read This Book?

Essential C is intended for students who have had no prior programming experience. Although it is especially written with the needs of science and engineering students in mind, it should be suitable for students in other disciplines as well. A knowledge of algebra and trigonometry is assumed.

● ━━━━ What Is Covered?

We have selected topics that will be most useful to beginning science and engineering students:

- *The preprocessor.* The reader is shown how to use the **#define** preprocessor directive to creative symbolic constants, as well as how to use **#include** with the standard header files *stdio.h*, *limits.h*, *math.h*, *stdlib.h*, *ctype.h*, and *string.h*.

- *Arithmetic data and variables.* The **int** and **double** data types are stressed, although **long** and **float** types are mentioned as well (Chapters 2 and 3). Students learn to use the information contained in *limits.h* and *float.h* to find the integer and floating-point limitations of their computers. They also learn how to use typecasts in arithmetic operations, assignments, and function calls.

- *The Standard Mathematics Library.* An entire chapter (Chapter 4) is devoted to the standard mathematical functions because of their importance in scientific and engineering work.

- *Control structures.* The most common selection structures (**if** and **if/else**) and repetition structures (**for** and **while** loops) are presented in Chapters 5 and 6.

- *Functions and call by value.* Students are shown how to write, compile, and test their own functions. The importance of modularity and top-down design is stressed. Students are shown how to compile and link code from multiple source files (Chapter 7).

- *Functions, pointers, and call by reference.* Our treatment of functions and pointers is unique and especially clear to beginners (Chapter 8).

- *Arrays.* In Chapter 9, the reader is shown how to process sets of related data using **int** and **double** arrays. Subscript notation is used because it is easier for most beginners to understand than pointer access.

- *Two-dimensional arrays.* Because of their usefulness in science and engineering, two-dimensional arrays are treated in greater detail than in most C texts. Higher-dimensional arrays are presented as well (Chapter 10).

- *Character data and strings.* The ASCII and EBCDIC character codes are discussed in detail. Variables and arrays of type **char** are introduced, as are the standard character- and string-processing functions (Chapters 11 and 12).
- *Sequential file I/O.* Students are shown in Chapter 13 how to use the file-processing functions **fopen()**, **fclose()**, **fscanf()**, and **fprintf()** to perform sequential reading and writing of data files.
- *C shortcuts and idioms.* Increment and decrement operators (++ and −−), the compound assignment operators (+=, −=, *=, /=, and %=), and the use of **scanf()** in loop conditions—are postponed to the last chapter of the book (Chapter 14).

What Is Omitted?

Just as important as what is included is what has been left out. We have omitted topics that are either too advanced for beginners, or not sufficiently useful for the kind of programming that most scientist and engineers will do:

- *Data types.* C offers a bewildering variety of data types, storage classes, and qualifiers that are not needed by the beginning programmer. Thus, we have omitted any reference to the C keywords **short, unsigned, auto, extern, register,** and **static.**
- *Structures, typedefs, and unions.* These are intermediate or advanced topics, unsuitable for the beginning programmer.

  Pointers. Much of the power of C can be attributed to its heavy use of pointers. However, this power comes at a price: it is difficult for beginners to use pointers properly. In this text, pointers are used only to achieve call by reference.
- *Memory management.* Dynamic memory management functions such as **malloc()**, **calloc()** and **free()** are notoriously error-prone. Fortunately, they are also unnecessary for most beginning programmers.
- *Random-access file I/O.* This is an intermediate or advanced topic that is rarely covered in beginning programming courses.
- *Bitwise operators.* Few scientists or engineers have any need to use bitwise operations.
- *Recursion.* Despite its importance in systems programming, recursion is less useful in most general scientific and engineering work.
- *Risky or unusual control structures.* Control structures that are dangerous or difficult for the beginner are omitted. These include the **goto, break,** and **continue** statements. Also omitted are the **switch/case** and **do-while** statement, and the ternary operator (?:).

Pedagogical Features

We have included a number of features intended to help the student learn to program in C:
- *Programming examples.* In the beginning, we all learn by imitation. With that in mind, we have provided many sample programs, carefully chosen to illustrate important elements of programming.

- *Program dissections.* Each sample program is accompanied by a "dissection," which provides a close analysis of key parts of the program.
- *Helpful hints.* Based on our extensive teaching experience, we have been able to provide a number of hints and warnings that can help the beginning programmer avoid the most common pitfalls.
- *Chapter summaries.* Every chapter includes a table of new language features, as well as a brief summary of the programming concepts presented in that chapter.
- *Exercises.* To become a competent programmer, it is necessary to practice programming. For this reason, we have provided a variety of exercises at the end of each chapter.
- *Instructor's manual.* Solutions to all end-of-chapter exercises are available in an instructor's manual.

Acknowledgments

Many persons assisted in the preparation of this book. The following reviewers provided valuable comments and suggestions:

Dorothy Attaway—Boston University
Nelson Baker—Georgia Institute of Technology
Daniel Berleant—University of Arkansas
H.C. Brearley—Iowa State University
Frank Coyle—Southern Methodist University
Vijay Kumar Garg—University of Texas at Austin
Kathi Hogshead Davis—Northern Illinois University
Norman Jones—Brigham Young University
Joseph Konstan—University of Minnesota
Leon Levine—University of California at Los Angeles
C. Dianne Martin—George Washington University
Steven McLaughlin—Rochester Institute of Technology
Daniel Rehak—Carnegie Mellon University
Stephen Schach—Vanderbilt University
Bala Swaminathan—Washington University
Gregory Tonkay—Lehigh University
Robert Walker—Rensselaer Polytechnic Institute
Jerry Weltman—Louisiana State University
Sudhakar Yalamanchili—Georgia Institute of Technology

The accuracy of the program listings and exercises was carefully checked during manuscript and galley stages by Kathi Hogshead Davis, Joseph Konstan, and Jay Perry (Purdue University). Their careful and diligent work is greatly appreciated.

We are also grateful for the help and dedication of the Saunders staff, especially Emily Barrosse, Executive Editor; Alexa Barnes, Senior Developmental Editor; Linda Boyle, Project Editor; Anne Muldrow, Senior Art Director; and Joanne Cassetti, Production Manager.

P. K. Andersen
G. Bjedov
M. G. Scarbrough
October 1994

Chapter

1.

Introduction

In this chapter you will see how to create and run C programs. You'll also become acquainted with some tools that will help you in programming, and you will learn some useful computer terminology.

Programs and Programming Languages

A *computer program* is a set of instructions that tell your computer how to complete a task. Computer programs are often referred to as *software*, to distinguish them from the physical components of the computer, which are called *hardware*.

You cannot write programs in your native language; computers respond only to instructions written in what is called *machine language* (or *machine code*). Machine language is a kind of *binary code*—in other words, it consists entirely of 0s and 1s. For an idea of what machine language is like, consider how a simple English sentence might appear when written in a binary code:

```
01010000  01110010  01101111  01100111  01110010  01100001
01101101  01101101  01101001  01101110  01100111  00100000
01101001  01101110  00100000  01100010  01101001  01101110
01100001  01110010  01111001  00100000  01101001  01110011
00100000  01110100  01110010  01110101  01101100  01111001
00100000  01110100  01100101  01100100  01101001  01101111
01110101  01110011  00101110
```

This says, "Programming in binary is truly tedious." And it is. Fortunately, there is an alternative: write your programs in a high-level programming language. A *programming language* is a notation that aids humans in creating programs that the computer can translate into machine code. Although it does not necessarily make programming easy, a language such as C reduces the effort considerably.

Syntax

Natural languages such as English, French, Chinese, and Russian follow certain rules of usage, called *syntax* rules. These rules determine how the elements of the language should be put together to make grammatical sense.

Programming languages also follow syntax rules. This book will teach you the syntax of the ANSI C language. As you learn, keep in mind that the syntax of a programming language is very limited and very strict. It may seem to you that the rules are also arbitrary and unreasonable. We are sympathetic to that point of view, but the truth is that you must follow the rules if you are to program successfully. In that respect, learning a programming language is not so different from learning a foreign language such as French: You can complain all you want about French spelling, grammar, or punctuation, but if you want to be understood in France, you must follow the rules.

When you break one of the syntax rules of a human language, a native speaker can usually figure out what you mean. Computers are not so forgiving. The computer cannot figure out what you mean when you misspell a word, omit some required punctuation, or make some other syntax error. *Computers don't think; they don't reason; they don't understand anything.* It is up to you to get the program right. (It might help to remind yourself occasionally that a computer has all the intelligence of a lawn mower or golf club.)

Tools You Will Need

Before you start writing C programs, make sure you have the right tools. Throughout this book, we will assume that your computer runs either the UNIX or MS-DOS operating system, although most of what we say applies to other systems as well. We will also assume that you know the basics of running your computer, including such things as how to find, create, modify, copy, and delete files and directories.

You will need two essential programming tools to write C programs and translate them into machine code. The first is a *text editor*, a program used to create and modify computer files. You will use the text editor to create files containing C code.

The second essential tool is a *C compiler*—software that translates C code into machine code. UNIX operating systems almost always come equipped with a C compiler that is invoked by the **cc** command; however, many other C compilers are available for UNIX and DOS systems. Here is a partial listing:

Command	Compiler	System	Vendor
acc	ANSI C	UNIX	Sun Microsystems
cc	C	UNIX	(various)
cl	Microsoft C	DOS	Microsoft Corporation
gcc	GNU C	UNIX	Free Software Foundation
hc	High C	DOS	MetaWare
qc	QuickC	DOS	Microsoft Corporation
tcc	Turbo C	DOS	Borland International
ts	TopSpeed C	DOS	Jensen & Partners

Usually, when we speak of the "compiler" we are actually talking about three programs that are used together:

- **Preprocessor.** As its name implies, the preprocessor prepares a C program for translation into machine language.
- **Compiler.** The compiler translates your C code into machine language.
- **Linker.** Most C programs use machine code from more than one source. The linker combines code from different files into a complete program.

Some C compilers are actually "integrated programming environments" that combine the text editor, preprocessor, compiler, and linker into one package. These packages often include other useful tools that can make programming much more efficient and convenient.

Whichever C system you use, be sure that it conforms to the standards set by the American National Standards Institute (ANSI). Most C compilers on the market today *are* "ANSI C," but you may occasionally come across a pre-ANSI compiler (especially on UNIX systems).

Your First Program

You are now ready to create your first C program. Open a new file named ***proverb.c*** using your text editor. (Do not omit the *.c* ending on the file name.) Enter the lines shown in Listing 1–1. Make sure you enter the lines *exactly as shown*, then save the file.

Listing 1–1. *proverb.c*

① `/* Print a proverb. */`

② `#include <stdio.h>`

③ `main()`
④ `{`
⑤ `    printf("Time flies ");`
⑥ `    printf("like the wind;\n");`
`    printf("fruit flies ");`
`    printf("like bananas.\n");`
⑦ `}`

Dissection of *proverb.c*

Let's examine this program in detail:

① `/* Print a proverb. */`

Any text appearing between the `/*` and `*/` is considered a *comment* and is ignored by the compiler. Comments are included for the benefit of the programmer. As you will see, comments can extend over several lines.

② `#include <stdio.h>`

The first stage of the C compiler is a preprocessor that prepares the program for compiling. Lines that begin with a pound sign (**#**) are treated as instructions to the preprocessor. In this case, the preprocessor is to include the contents of the file ***stdio.h*** (***st***andard ***i***nput/***o***utput ***h***eader file), which contains information about the **printf()** function. The angle brackets around the file indicate that this file is to be found "in the usual place." Exactly where that is depends on your particular system—the preprocessor will know where to look.

③ `main()`

C programs consist of one or more units called *functions*. Every program has one main function, which is named, appropriately enough, **main()**. The parentheses indicate that **main()** is the name of a function. Although there is nothing inside the parentheses, they are required here.

④ `{`

An opening (left) brace is used to mark the beginning of the function body.

⑤ `printf("Time flies ");`

Note the semicolon (**;**) that terminates this line. In C, a semicolon is used to mark the end of a program *statement,* which is simply a complete instruction to the computer. This statement calls the **printf()** function to print a message on the computer screen. The message itself is enclosed in double quotes (**"..."**). We will have more to say about **printf()** later.

(6) `printf("like the wind;\n");`

This is another **printf()** function call. The principal difference to note is the **\n** (read "backslash n"). This tells the computer to start a new line of text in the output.

(7) `}`

A closing (right) brace is used to mark the end of the function body.

Compiling *proverb.c*

Now you are ready to compile the program. How you do this depends on the compiler you are using. (Check your manual for details.) For example, we use the GNU C compiler (**gcc**) from the Free Software Foundation. We would type *gcc*, the name of the file containing the C code, and press the RETURN key:

`gcc proverb.c` `RET`

The preprocessor takes a copy of the C code from *proverb.c* and inserts the contents of the *stdio.h* file. The modified code is then sent to the compiler, which checks it for syntax errors.

If the compiler detects no syntax errors, it will translate your C code into machine language and place the resulting program into an *executable file*. This file will be named *a.out* on most UNIX systems; it will be named *proverb.exe* on most DOS systems. (You can choose another name for the executable file—see the exercises.)

What if there is a syntax error in *proverb.c*? If the compiler finds an error, it will give you some indication of where the problem is. For example, you might see an error message that looks something like this:

```
proverb.c: In function 'main':
proverb.c: 10: parse error before 'printf'
```

The first line of the error message tells us that the compiler found an error in the **main()** function; the second line tells us that it occurred on line 10 somewhere before the **printf()** function call. If you see an error message, you will have to use your text editor to correct the error, then start the translation process over again. When searching for an error, remember:

The error might not be on the line indicated by the error message.

Often the compiler discovers an error, but cannot determine its exact location in the file. If you do not find the error on the line indicated by the compiler, examine the preceding line. If you cannot find the error there, look at the next line up, and so on. Also, when confronted by multiple error messages,

> *Fix the first error first.*

One error can trigger a long list of error messages. Correcting the first error in the list may be enough to satisfy the compiler.

Running *proverb.c*

On UNIX and DOS systems, you can run an executable file simply by typing its name and pressing the RETURN key. On a UNIX system, type *a.out* and RETURN:

```
a.out RET
```

On a DOS system, type *proverb* and RETURN:

```
proverb RET
```

If you have done everything correctly, the message should appear on the screen:

```
Time flies like the wind;
fruit flies like bananas.
```

Library Functions

As we said, C programs consist of one or more functions. A *function* is a self-contained collection of statements that are grouped together to perform a task. Your first program was composed of two functions, **main()** and **printf()**. (Every C program must have a **main()** function.) You wrote the code for **main()** yourself, but you did not write **printf()**. Where did **printf()** come from?

The answer is that many useful functions such as **printf()** are supplied as a part of the C system. These functions—called *library functions*—handle such common tasks as data input and printing, mathematical computations, and so on. Collectively, these functions make up what is called the *standard C library*.

The printf() Function

Let's examine the **printf()** function more closely. The name **printf()** is short for "***print-f***ormatted." This is a standard C library function that enables programs to print to the *standard output*, which by default is the terminal screen. Consider the statement

```
printf("like the wind;\n");
```

Items appearing inside the parentheses of a function call are the *arguments* of the function. In this case, there is one argument, called the *control string* or *format string*:

```
"like the wind;\n"
```

A group of characters enclosed by double quotes (**"**) is called a *string constant* or *string literal*.

The **\n** ("backslash n") in the control string starts a new line in the output. This is an example of an *escape sequence*. Escape sequences are used to represent special characters:

Escape Sequence	Special Character
\a	Audible alarm
\b	Backspace
\f	Form feed
\n	Newline
\r	Carriage return
\t	Horizontal tab
\v	Vertical tab
\\	Backslash (\)
\'	Single quote (')
\"	Double quote (")

The carriage return (**\r**), form feed (**\f**), newline (**\n**), horizontal tab (**\t**), and vertical tab (**\v**) are *nonprinting characters*—that is, they affect spacing in the output, but otherwise do not cause anything to be printed on the screen. These characters, along with blank spaces and comments, are often referred to as *white space*.

Keep in mind that the compiler treats an escape sequence like **\n** as a single character. Be careful not to put a space between the **** and the **n**.

The Programming Process

Figure 1–1 summarizes the process of creating a C program. There are four steps in the process:

1. ***Creating the source code.*** The first step is to prepare a file containing the C code. This file is called the *source file;* it contains *source code.* Almost all C compilers require that the name of the source file end in a *.c* suffix (e.g., ***proverb.c***).

2. ***Preprocessing the code.*** The first stage of the C compiler is the preprocessor. The preprocessor searches through the source file for lines that begin with a pound sign (**#**). In ***proverb.c***, there is one such line:

```
#include <stdio.h>
```

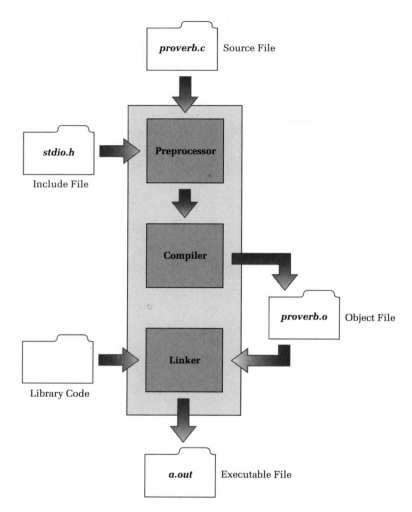

Figure 1–1 Creating a C program and translating it into executable code on a UNIX system. The process is very similar on a DOS system—only the file names are different.

This tells the preprocessor to copy the contents of the standard header file **stdio.h** into the source code. (Later, we will see how the preprocessor can make other changes in the source code.)

3. **Compiling the program.** The compiler takes the output from the preprocessor and checks it for syntax errors. If it finds none, it translates the C code into machine code. The output from the compiler is called *object code*; it is put in a file called the *object file*. Most compilers on UNIX systems give this file a **.o** suffix (e.g., **proverb.o**). Compilers on MS-DOS systems give this file a **.obj** suffix (e.g., **proverb.obj**).

4. ***Linking the object code.*** Almost all programs use precompiled code from the C libraries. In the first program, you used the **printf()** function. Library code is added to your object code by the linker to make a complete program. The output from the linker is put into the *executable file* (***a.out*** or ***proverb.exe***).

Some beginning programmers confuse steps (2) and (4) of this process. That is, they believe that the preprocessor instruction

```
#include <stdio.h>
```

inserts the code for the library function **printf()**. This is not true. The header file ***stdio.h*** only describes the **printf()** function. The actual code for the function is brought out of the standard library and combined with your object code by the linker.

Speaking of object code, you may have noticed that there was no file named ***proverb.o*** or ***proverb.obj*** in your directory when you finished compiling the first program. On many systems, the linker normally deletes the object file when it creates the executable file. (Most compilers have an option that allows you to save the object file, but at this point, you should not need to do so.)

Output Redirection

Normally, the standard output is connected to the terminal screen. However, both the UNIX and DOS operating systems permit you to redirect the standard output into a file using the *redirection operator* (>). If you are working on a UNIX system, try this command line:

```
a.out > outfile RET
```

If you are working on a DOS system, try this command line:

```
proverb >outfile RET
```

The program will run, but you should not see its output on the screen. Instead, the output goes into ***outfile***. (If there is no file of that name in your directory, the operating system will create one.) Examine the contents of this file; you should see the message

```
Time flies like the wind;
fruit flies like bananas.
```

Output redirection is very useful, but be warned: When you redirect the output into an existing file, the original contents of the file are wiped out and replaced by the new output. To keep whatever was already in the file, use the *append operator* (>>). On a UNIX system, enter the command

```
a.out >> outfile RET
```

On a DOS system, enter the command

```
proverb >>outfile RET
```

Examine *outfile* now and you will see that the new output was added to the end of the file:

```
Time flies like the wind;
fruit flies like bananas.
Time flies like the wind;
fruit flies like bananas.
```

First Program—Revised

We're going to make some changes to the first program just to emphasize a point. Create a copy of the file **proverb.c** and give the name **mixup.c** to the copy. (Refer to your UNIX or DOS system manual if you do not know how to copy files.) Now open **mixup.c** and switch the order of the **printf()** function calls, as shown in Listing 1–2.

Listing 1–2. *mixup.c*

```c
/* Print a mixed-up proverb. */

#include <stdio.h>

main()
{
    printf("like the wind;\n");
    printf("fruit flies ");
    printf("Time flies ");
    printf("like bananas.\n");
}
```

Compile and execute the program as you did before. You should see output that looks like this:

```
like the wind;
fruit flies Time flies like bananas.
```

The point to note—a point sometimes missed by beginning programmers—is this:

> *The statements in a C program are executed in the order in which they are written.*

The computer does not think; it does not realize that the output from the revised program doesn't make sense. The computer simply follows the program as you wrote it. If you don't like the result, it is up to you to change the program.

STYLE

In programming, *style* refers to layout of the program—the use of blank lines, indentation, spacing, and so on—to improve readability. In laying out the programs in this chapter, we have observed the following guidelines:

- Begin every program with a comment describing what the program does. This is called a *comment heading*.
- Group preprocessor directives together near the top of the file below the comment heading. Preprocessor directives should not be indented.*
- Do not indent the function name **main()**. Place the opening and closing braces of **main()** in the first column, aligned with the first letter of **main()**.
- Indent statements in the body of the **main()** function 3 spaces. (Other programmers prefer 2, 4, 5, or 8 spaces, or a tab stop. Whichever you choose, be consistent.)
- Use one or more blank lines between major parts of the file—such as between the comment heading and the **#include** line, and between the **#include** line and the **main()** function.
- Write just one statement per line.

The purpose of these guidelines is to make your programs more readable, in much the same way that punctuation and spacing make ordinary text more readable. The guidelines make little difference to the C compiler, which ignores most white space. Thus, as far as the compiler is concerned, we could just as well have run everything together like this:

```
/* Print a proverb. */ #include <stdio.h>
main(){printf("Time flies ");printf("like the wind;\n"
);printf("fruit flies ");printf("like bananas.\n");}
```

Programs laid out this way are painful to read. Make life easier for yourself—and for anyone else who may have to read your code—by following reasonable style guidelines.

---

* In traditional C, preprocessor directives *had* to begin in the first column. This is no longer the case in ANSI C—you can indent preprocessor directives—but it is still a good rule to follow.

● ▬▬▬▬▬   **HELPFUL HINTS**

Good organization of your file system can also make your life easier. We offer two suggestions for reducing clutter and saving disk space:

- Create a separate directory to hold the files for each chapter (e.g., *Chap01*, *Chap02*, etc.). Within each chapter directory, create a subdirectory to hold the exercises for that chapter.
- Delete any executable files that you are not currently using, but keep the source files. (You can always recompile the program later if you need to.)

Some beginning programmers heave a sigh of relief when their program finally compiles. Although we sympathize, it is important to realize that the successful compilation of a program is not enough. Your program must also run and produce the correct results. Hence,

- Always run the program to see that it produces the correct results.
- If you ever make a change in your program, even a minor one, always compile and run the code to be sure that it is correct.

● ▬▬▬▬▬   **SUMMARY**

Comment

```
/* This is a comment */
```

Provides information for human readers of the code. The compiler treats text between /* and */ as if it were white space.

Preprocessor Directive

```
#include <stdio.h>
```

Instructs the preprocessor to insert the contents of the standard input/output header file, *stdio.h*. Angle brackets, < and >, tell the preprocessor to look in the "usual place," which is system-dependent.

Definition of main()

```
main()
{
  /* Function body goes here. */
}
```

Defines the **main()** function. The first line of the definition is the header. Braces, { and }, mark the beginning and end of the function body.

Function Call

```
printf("Gone fishing!\n");
```
Calls the library function **printf()** to print `Gone fishing!` on the standard output. Text enclosed by double quotes is called a string constant or string literal. The escape sequence `\n` causes a new line to be printed. A semicolon marks the end of a statement.

- A computer program (also called software) consists of instructions to be carried out by the computer. Computers respond only to a binary code called machine language or machine code.
- C is considered a high-level programming language because its syntax is relatively easy for humans to interpret. C programs must be translated into machine code by the compiler before they can be run.
- Programming languages follow very strict syntax rules. If you violate these rules, the compiler cannot translate your code. Instead, it will try to inform you of the nature and location of the error(s).
- The creation of a working program is a four-step process. First, you use the text editor to make a source file containing C code. Second, the preprocessor prepares the C code for compiling. Third, the compiler takes the preprocessed code and translates it into machine code, which it places into an object file. Fourth, the linker combines the contents of your object file with code from the C libraries to make an executable file. (Some linkers also delete your object code.)
- C programs consist of functions such as **main()** and **printf()** that work together to perform a task. Some functions, like **main()**, you will write yourself. Others, like **printf()**, are made available to you as a part of the standard C library. You must write a **main()** function for every program.
- When fixing compiler errors, begin with the first error listed by the compiler. The actual location of an error might not be on the line indicated by the error message; if you cannot find the error on that line, it may be on one of the preceding lines.
- The computer will follow your instructions exactly. Computers do not think, reason, or understand anything. It is important to test your programs to make sure they work correctly. If a program does not produce the proper results, you may need to revise it.

EXERCISES

Note: Many of these exercises depend on your ***proverb.c*** program being correct. If it is not, take a moment now and correct it before going on.

1. *Define:* **a.** computer program;   **b.** software;   **c.** hardware;   **d.** binary code;   **e.** machine language;   **f.** programming language;   **g.** syntax;   **h.** text editor;

i. preprocessor; **j.** compiler; **k.** linker; **l.** source file; **m.** object file; **n.** library function; **o.** executable file; **p.** comment; **q.** function; **r.** standard output; **s.** statement; **t.** string literal; **u.** control string; **v.** function argument; **w.** escape sequence; **x.** style; **y.** comment heading; **z.** white space.

2. *Errors.* This exercise is designed to acquaint you with the error messages produced by your compiler. Familiarity with the error messages will help you debug your programs. Create a copy of ***proverb.c*** called ***errors.c***, and introduce into the file the first syntax error listed below. Run your compiler on the file. Does it catch the error? If so, write down both the error and the error message; if not, run the program and make a note of any unexpected results. Correct the file and repeat the process for the next error on the list. Continue until you have tried all of the errors. When you are finished, you should have a list of error messages and their causes. Save this list for future reference.

    a. Remove the **/*** from the comment heading.

    b. Remove the ***/** from the comment heading.

    c. Omit a semicolon at the end of a **printf()** call.

    d. Remove the closing parenthesis from **main()**.

    e. Remove both parentheses from **main()**.

    f. Misspell **printf()**.

    g. Omit the closing brace from the end of the program.

    h. Omit the **#** sign from the **#include** directive.

    i. Omit **#include <stdio.h>** from the top of your program.

    j. Put a blank space between **** and **n** of the newline escape sequence.

    k. Omit the opening double quote from the control string of the first **printf()** call.

    l. Omit the closing double quote from the control string of the first **printf()** call.

3. *More errors.* Repeat Exercise 2, but put all of the errors into the file at the same time.

4. *The .c extension.* Many C compilers require that the names of C source files end in the *.c* extension. Change the name of your ***proverb.c*** file to ***proverb*** and try to compile it. What happens?

5. *One* **printf()** *call.* Make a copy of the ***proverb.c*** file and give the name ***oneprint.c*** to the copy. Modify the new file to use a single **printf()** function call in place of the four **printf()** calls in the original. Be sure to insert new lines where needed to make the output the same as before.

6. *Escape sequences.* Thus far, the only escape sequence we have used is the newline. Try out the other ones. Make a copy of the ***proverb.c*** file and give the name ***escapes.c*** to the copy. Open the new file and introduce the escape characters **\a, \b, \f, \r, \t,** and **** into the **printf()** control strings. Describe what each escape sequence does. What is the difference between the form feed, the carriage return, and the newline characters?

7. *The newline character.* This exercise is intended to help you see how the newline character works. Write a program named ***prdown.c*** that prints the following vertically and diagonally down the screen:

```
D
    o
        w
            n
                s
                    t
                        a
                            i
                                r
                                    s
```

8. *Centering text.* Write a program named ***aphorism.c*** that prints out the following messages:

```
                To the computer,
         everything is a binary number.

              Computers don't think.

            Garbage in, garbage out.

     If you can tell good advice from bad advice,
              you don't need advice.
```

Use tabs and spaces to center these messages on the screen and newlines to introduce blank lines between the messages.

9. *Double quotes.* Modify ***aphorism.c*** from the previous exercise so that it also prints the line

```
     "Go ahead, make my day", he snarled.
```

Remember to use the escape sequence \" to print the double quotes.

10. *Comments.* Consider these three lines:

```
/* printf("This is the first line.");*/
printf("/* This is the second line.*/");
printf(/*"This is the third line."*/);
```

What do each of these lines do in a C program? Write a short program to check your answer.

11. *The **system()** function.* The library function **system()** allows you to run operating system commands from C programs. For example, if your operating system is UNIX, the C statement

```
system("ls");
```

will run the UNIX command **ls**, which lists the names of the files in the current directory. Note the double quotes; these are required. On a DOS system, the same effect is produced by the statement

```
system("dir");
```

Write a program that uses the **system()** function to carry out the following tasks:

a. List the files in the current directory.

b. Display the contents of the files in the current directory (using **cat *** or **type ***).

c. Display the current date on the standard output.

d. Put the current date into the file **now**.

e. Print the file **now**.

12. *Compiler options.* Most C compilers offer various options. Check your C manual to see what (if anything) each of the following options does with your compiler:

```
-c
-g
-o
-O
-E
```

13. *Renaming the executable file.* As we have seen, the default name for an executable file on a UNIX system is **a.out**; on most DOS systems, it is the name of the source file but with the **.c** suffix replaced by **.exe**. Most compilers allow you to select another name for the executable file using the **–o** option. For example, the command

```
gcc -o flies proverb.c RET
```

instructs the GNU C compiler to compile the program in **proverb.c** and put the executable code into the file **flies**.

   Check your C manual for the option that allows you to select a different name for the executable file, and try out the option on your version of the **proverb.c** file.

14. *Printing with* **fprintf().** In addition to **printf()**, the C library includes an output function named **fprintf()**, which can print to files as well as the standard output (**stdout**). The statement

```
fprintf(stdout, "like the wind;\n");
```

is exactly equivalent to

```
printf("like the wind;\n");
```

Make a copy of **proverb.c** named **testprnt.c** and modify the copy to use the **fprintf()** function instead of the **printf()** function.

Chapter

2.

Integer Data

Printing messages on the standard output might be entertaining, but there are better uses for the computer. You might reasonably expect the computer to be used to *compute* something, and that implies processing of numerical data. In this chapter and the next one, we will see how C handles numbers.

Numerical Data Types

To most of us, a number is just a number. However, in C programming you have to get used to thinking about two categories or types of numbers. The first are the *integers*, or whole numbers:

$$\ldots, \; -4, \; -3, \; -2, \; -1, 0, 1, 2, 3, 4, \ldots$$

The second category is composed of the so-called *floating-point* numbers. These are numbers having a decimal point. For example, the following are all floating-point numbers:

$$0.000 \quad -147.253 \quad 76.13908 \quad 3.1 \times 10^5 \quad -0.00174 \quad -3. \quad 1.0$$

The thing to keep in mind is that C treats integers and floating-point numbers differently. Although we tend to think of 1 and 1.0 as the same, 1 is an integer and 1.0 is a floating-point number.

Integers vs. Floating-Point Numbers

Why have two types of numbers? The answer is that integers and floating-point numbers serve different purposes. Integers are used primarily for *counting* things; floating-point numbers are used for *measuring* rather than counting. For example, the following are all integer quantities:

Number of pages in this book
Number of persons in a room
Number of classes taken by a student

On the other hand, the following are all floating-point quantities:

Size (in centimeters) of the pages in this book
Average weight (in kilograms) of the persons in a room
A student's grade-point average

We will discuss integers in this chapter and floating-point numbers in the next chapter.

Integer Variables

In mathematics, a *variable* is a symbol that represents a value. In computer programming, a *variable* is a data storage location. Figure 2–1 shows how we will represent integer variables. Each variable has three important parts:

- *Storage.* Think of a variable as a box for storing a value. An integer variable is a box with enough space to hold one integer.
- *Name.* In C terminology, this is called an *identifier.* We will show you how to choose an appropriate identifier for any variable that you create.

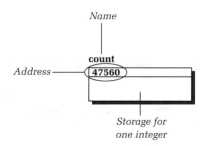

Figure 2–1 An integer variable. In general, a variable is a storage location that has a name and an address.

- ***Address.*** Each variable has its own location in memory. The computer keeps track of this location by giving it a unique address. Whereas you choose the names for your variables, you cannot choose or alter their addresses.

Declaration of Variables

You create a variable with a *declaration*. For example, the following declaration tells the C compiler to reserve space for an integer variable and give it the name `count`:

```
int count;
```

As you probably guessed, `int` is short for "integer." You must declare all integer variables this way before you can use them.

It is important to realize that declaring a variable does not automatically put a value in it—although it is possible that some "garbage" value might be left in that space from some previous program.

Variable Names

You must give every variable a name when you declare it. In C, a variable name or identifier consists of the following characters:

- Uppercase letters (**A** to **Z**)
- Lowercase letters (**a** to **z**)
- Numerals (**0** to **9**)
- Underscore (**_**)

There are some rules to keep in mind when naming a variable:

- ***Do not use white space or punctuation characters.*** The only characters allowed in variable names are letters (**A** to **Z**, **a** to **z**), digits (**1** to **9**), and the underscore (**_**). Hence

`time_of_flight`	OK
`stage2`	OK
`IceAge`	OK
`who_knows?`	Illegal; the question mark (**?**) is not allowed
`break up`	Illegal; the space is not allowed
`his+hers`	Illegal; the plus sign (**+**) indicates addition
`$#@?!<*~@.&`	Illegal; none of these characters is allowed
`proverb.c`	Illegal as a variable name; OK as a file name

- ***Begin with a letter, not a digit or underscore.*** A digit is never allowed as the first character in an identifier. Thus, the following would all be illegal names:

```
1_too_many    2on1    4by4    54_40_or_Fight
```

Underscores at the beginning of a variable name are technically legal, but they may conflict with other names already used by your system. To avoid problems, do not create names that begin with an underscore.

- ***Be case-sensitive.*** C compilers distinguish between uppercase and lowercase letters—in other words, they are *case sensitive*. Thus, the following are all different names:

```
velocity    Velocity    VELOCITY
```

(However, it would be considered bad programming style to use these three variables in the same program: Names that differ only in case are too easily confused.)

- ***Observe the 31-character limit.*** Some C compilers accept names having more than 31 characters, but ignore any characters beyond the first 31. Such a compiler would consider these to be the same:

```
a_truly_long_variable_identifie
a_truly_long_variable_identifier
a_truly_long_variable_identifier_TOO
```

Other compilers, however, recognize more than 31 characters in a name, and would treat these as three different variables. To be safe, do not make variable names longer than 31 characters. (You should never need that many. Names that are more than a dozen characters long can be awkward to type and to read.)

- ***Do not use any C keyword as a variable name.*** A *keyword* (also called a *reserved word*) is a special word that already has a strictly defined meaning to the C compiler. There are 32 keywords in ANSI C:

auto	double	int	struct
break	else	long	switch
case	enum	register	typedef
char	extern	return	union
const	float	short	unsigned
continue	for	signed	void
default	goto	sizeof	volatile
do	if	static	while

You will learn about many of these keywords as we go along.*

---

* Some systems define additional keywords, including `asm`, `far`, `fortran`, `huge`, `interrupt`, `near`, and `pascal`. When in doubt, avoid using these as variable names.

- ***Do not use the name of any C function.*** Treat all names in the standard C library as reserved words. Thus, you should never name a variable **printf**. Likewise, because every program must have a **main()** function, you should never name a variable **main**.

A bit of advice about naming variables: *Always choose names that are meaningful.* A variable's name should convey information about the variable's purpose. Few things are more frustrating than trying to read a program that contains a lot of short, cryptic variable names.

The Assignment Operator

We know how to set up an integer variable; now how do we put integers in it? One way is to use the *assignment operator*, which looks just like an equals sign (=). Figure 2–2 shows how this works. First, suppose we have declared **a** and **b** to be **int** variables:

```
int a, b;
```

This declaration creates two variables, but does not put any particular values in them. The following assignment statement puts the integer value 5280 into the variable **a**:

```
a = 5280;
```

We say that the value 5280 is "assigned" to the variable box **a**, or that "**a** gets 5280." Once **a** has been assigned a value, this value can be assigned to another **int** variable:

```
b = a;
```

This takes a *copy* of the contents of **a** and assigns it to **b**. The value in **a** is not altered.

Always remember that the assignment operator is not the same as the equals sign used in mathematics. Consider this statement:

```
b = b + 1;
```

This would be a contradiction in algebra because there is no number that will satisfy the equation. In C, however, this statement tells the computer to take a copy of the contents of **b** (5280), add 1 to it (5280 + 1), and put the result (5281) back into **b**. This is a common operation in computer programming.

In mathematics, $a = b$ means the same thing as $b = a$. However, in C programming, the statements

```
a = b;
b = a;
```

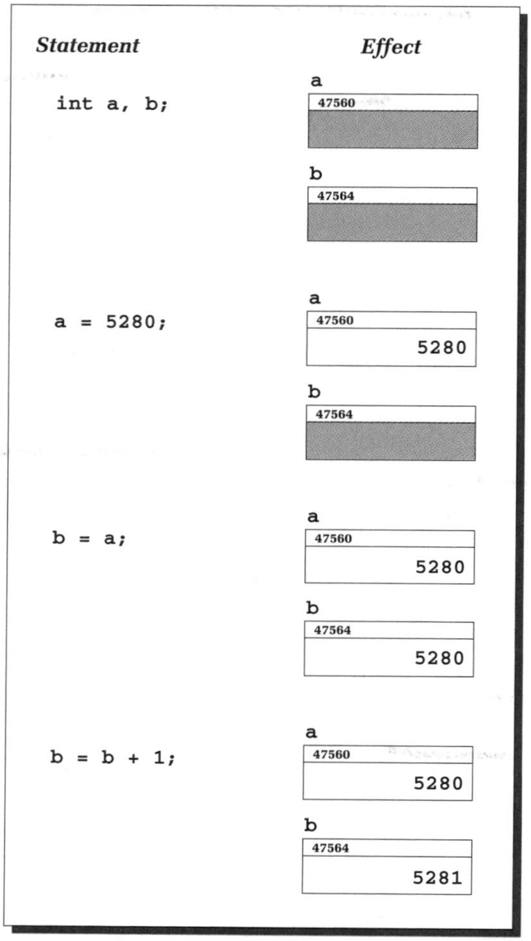

Statement	*Effect*
`int a, b;`	**a** 47560 ▨▨▨ **b** 47564 ▨▨▨
`a = 5280;`	**a** 47560 5280 **b** 47564 ▨▨▨
`b = a;`	**a** 47560 5280 **b** 47564 5280
`b = b + 1;`	**a** 47560 5280 **b** 47564 5281

Figure 2–2 Declaration and assignment. Note that when the variables are first declared, they hold no value (except perhaps some value left over from a previous program). We show this by shading the boxes.

are definitely *not* the same. The first statement copies the contents of **b** into the variable **a**, whereas the second statement copies the value of **a** into **b**. Similarly, in algebra it makes no difference whether you write $a = 5280$ or $5280 = a$. But in C programming, the following are different:

```
a = 5280;
5280 = a;    /* Illegal assignment */
```

The second statement would not be allowed. The assignment operator is used to put values into variables; therefore, *a variable must always appear on the left-hand side of an assignment operator.* The value 5280 is a constant value, not a variable, and we cannot change the value of a constant. (That is why it is called a constant.) Likewise, these statements are different:

```
b = b + 1;
b + 1 = b;    /* Illegal assignment */
```

The second statement is illegal because **b + 1** is not the name of a variable.

Integer Input with scanf()

We have seen how to put values into variables using the assignment operator. There is another way to fill a variable: obtain a value from the keyboard. The library function **scanf()** will do this for you. Consider the following statement:

```
scanf("%d", &a);
```

In this example, the **scanf()** function takes two arguments. The first is a control string, which tells the function what type of value it is supposed to get from the keyboard:

```
"%d"
```

Here **%d** is a *format or conversion specification,* which directs **scanf()** to read a decimal (base-10) integer.* The second argument tells **scanf()** where to store the integer:

```
&a
```

Here, the ampersand (**&**) is the *address operator.* Thus, **&a** produces the "address of **a**." The **scanf()** function always refers to variables by their addresses. (You will find out why in Chapter 8.) *The most common error that beginners—and experienced programmers—make when using* **scanf()** *is to omit the address operator.*

Integer Output with printf()

You can print integers with the same **printf()** function that you used in the first chapter. Consider an example:

```
printf("The value of a is %d.\n", a);
```

---

* In addition to decimal integers, C gives the experienced programmer the option of working with octal (base-8), and hexadecimal (base-16) integers.

Here, **printf()** takes two arguments. The first is a control string:

```
"The value of a is %d.\n"
```

This string contains the format **%d**, which tells the computer "put a decimal integer here." The value that will be printed comes from the second argument, the variable **a**:

```
a
```

Suppose that **a** contains the value 1765, an integer. The **printf()** statement would then produce the following line on the standard output:

```
The value of a is 1765.
```

Program: *intarith.c*

Our first sample program will make use of the concepts we have discussed thus far, and it will illustrate the use of integer arithmetic as well. This program will compute the sum, difference, product, quotient, and remainder of two numbers entered by the user. Let's plan the program first using *pseudocode*, a kind of abbreviated English that is structured to resemble the final program:

prompt the user for two integers
read two integers
compute the sum, difference, product, quotient , and remainder
print the results

The C program that implements this plan is set out in Listing 2–1. Create a file named ***intarith.c*** and enter the program exactly as shown in the listing.

Listing 2–1. *intarith.c*

```
①  /*******************************

        Try out integer arithmetic.

    *******************************/

    #include <stdio.h>

    main()
    {
②      int first, second;          /* Data entered by user. */
        int sum;
        int prod;
        int diff;
        int quotient;
        int remainder;

③      printf("Please enter two integers: ");
④      scanf("%d %d", &first, &second);

⑤      sum = first + second;
⑥      diff = first - second;
⑦      prod = first * second;
⑧      quotient = first / second;
⑨      remainder = first % second;

⑩      printf("%d + %d = %d\n", first, second, sum);
        printf("%d - %d = %d\n", first, second, diff);
        printf("%d * %d = %d\n", first, second, prod);
        printf("%d / %d = %d\n", first, second, quotient);
⑪      printf("%d %% %d = %d\n", first, second, remainder);
    }
```

Dissection of *intarith.c*

```
①  /*******************************

        Try out integer arithmetic.

    *******************************/
```
Comments can extend over several lines, such as in this example, which shows one common way to write a comment header. Remember, comments are treated as white space by the compiler.

```
② int first, second;          /* Data entered by user. */
  int sum;
  int prod;
  int diff;
  int quotient;
  int remainder;
```

These declarations tell the compiler to reserve space for seven integer variables. We could have accomplished the same thing with just one declaration:

```
int first, second, sum, prod, diff, quotient, remainder;
```

This would save space, but would also make our program harder to read and to edit. Note that we have chosen variable names that are descriptive of the values they will hold (**sum**, **prod**, etc.).

③ `printf("Please enter two integers: ");`

Our program is designed to receive data typed by the user at the keyboard—in other words, we would say that the program is *interactive* with the user. This statement prompts the user when it is time to enter the data required by the rest of the program.

④ `scanf("%d %d", &first, &second);`

Here we are using the **scanf()** function to read two decimal integers (**"%d %d"**) that will be stored in the variables **first** and **second**. The order in which the variables are listed is important: the first number will be stored in **first**, the second in **second**. Note the address operators placed before the variable names—remember, the most common mistake beginners make when using **scanf()** is to omit the ampersands.

⑤ `sum = first + second;`

This statement instructs the computer to take copies of the values stored in **first** and **second**, add these values together, and store the result in **sum**. The contents of **first** and **second** are unchanged by this operation, so we can use these values again in the next statement.

⑥ `diff = first - second;`

Here, − is the subtraction operator. This statement subtracts a copy of the value contained in **second** from a copy of the value in **first** and stores the result in **diff**.

⑦ `prod = first * second;`

In C, multiplication is indicated by an asterisk (*****). This statement takes copies of the values contained in **first** and **second**, multiplies these values together, and stores the result in **prod**.

⑧ `quotient = first / second;`

C uses a slash (/) to indicate division. As you will see later in this chapter, integer division is a bit peculiar because the result must be an integer.

⑨ `remainder = first % second;`

As used here, the percent sign (%) is the *remainder operator*. The operation **first % second** produces the remainder that is left over when the value of **first** is divided by the value of **second**. The remainder operator is also called the *modulus operator*.

⑩ `printf("%d + %d = %d\n", first, second, sum);`

This is the first of five **printf()** function calls that will display the results of the computations on the standard output. Wherever the format **%d** appears in a format string, the value of the next variable in the argument list will be inserted at that point in the string.

⑪ `printf("%d %% %d = %d\n", first, second, remainder);`

We show this **printf()** function call to answer the question, "If a percent sign indicates a format, how do we print a percent sign?" The answer is that you use two percent signs together. (Only one is printed.)

Compiling and Running *intarith.c*

Once you have entered the program, save the file and exit the text editor. Compile the program the usual way. Then run the program. The computer will respond with the prompt

Please enter two integers:

Type in 17 and 2, then press RETURN:

Please enter two integers: 17 2 `RET`

This output should appear:

```
17 + 2 = 19
17 - 2 = 15
17 * 2 = 34
17 / 2 = 8
17 % 2 = 1
```

Addition, subtraction, and multiplication work as expected, but shouldn't 17/2 produce 8.5, not 8? We warned you before that integer division might seem a bit peculiar at first. But it is not hard to understand if you remember one important point:

In C, the division of two integers produces another integer.

Because 8.5 is not an integer, the computer simply cuts off the fractional part (.5) to produce the answer 8, which *is* an integer.

You might find it helpful to relate the integer division and remainder operators to long division:

$$
\begin{array}{r}
8 \leftarrow \text{quotient } (17/2) \\
2\overline{)17} \\
-16 \\
\hline
1 \leftarrow \text{remainder } (17\%2)
\end{array}
$$

What happens if you apply the division operator or remainder operator to a negative **int**, such as in **-17/2** or **-17%2**? Unfortunately, the ANSI C standard does not specify how negative numbers are to be treated in such cases. We leave it as an exercise for you to figure out how your system handles division of negative **int** values.

Program Testing

Just because *intarith.c* produces the right results for one case, you should not assume that the program is error-free. Always remember:

A program that compiles and runs may still contain hidden bugs.

A pessimist might say that it *will* contain bugs. Although we are not pessimists, we do urge you to be extremely cautious and test your programs carefully—the more you can test, the better.

It is rarely feasible to test a program with all possible combinations of input values—that would take too long. A more practical approach is to test the program on a set of representative test data. Deciding which values are "representative" can be difficult, but as a start consider the following:

- Positive values (large and small)
- Negative values (large and small)
- Zero
- Erroneous input (e.g., nonnumeric characters)

We will test *intarith.c* using zero and using some large positive values, leaving it to you to try other test values.

Division by Zero

How does *intarith.c* handle division by zero? Run the program and enter 2 and 0 at the prompt:

`Please enter two integers: 2 0``RET`

If you are working on a DOS system, you might discover that your machine has "locked up" and no longer responds to the keyboard. If this happens, you may have to reboot the computer. (Refer to the manual on how to do this.)

On some systems, ~~division by zero causes the program to "crash."~~ In other words, the program terminates abruptly, and the operating system issues an error message like this:

`Arithmetic exception (core dumped)`

A *core dump* creates a **core** file in the current directory. This file can be thought of as a kind of "snapshot" of what was happening when the program crashed; it can be read by means of a special program called a *debugger*. (If a **core** file was created in your directory, you should remove it now: such files take up a lot of disk space.)

Variable Size and Overflow

Next try running the program with two very large positive numbers:

`Please enter two integers: 12345678900 12345678900``RET`

On our system, the program produces output that is obviously wrong:*

```
-539222988 + -539222988 = -1078445976
-539222988 - -539222988 = 0
-539222988 * -539222988 = 343632528
-539222988 / -539222988 = 1
-539222988 % -539222988 = 0
```

Where did the negative numbers come from? The answer is simple: the value 12345678900 is too big to fit in an **int** variable on our machine.

In mathematics, the set of integers is infinite—there is no such thing as a largest or smallest integer. In C, an **int** variable is a storage location of finite size. For example, on some systems, an **int** must be smaller than 32768; on others, an **int** must be smaller than 2147483648. If you try to squeeze in a value that is too large for the box, *integer overflow* occurs. Overflow causes the kind of results you see here—numbers that are completely wrong. (Later in this chapter, we will show you how to determine the minimum and maximum **int** values for your system.)

---

* The output produced by your program may be different.

The #define Preprocessor Directive

Imagine that you had been given the job of editing a program written by another programmer, and that you came across the following statement in that program:

```
size = 4840 * acre;
```

You might guess from the variable names **size** and **acre** that this calculation has something to do with land area, but what is the significance of the number 4840? You can't be sure, unless you happen to do a lot of calculations involving area measured in acres. Constants such as this are sometimes called "magic numbers" because they are so mysterious.

The **#define** directive allows you to eliminate magic numbers from your program. In this case the magic number is a simple conversion factor: There are 4840 square yards in an acre. To improve the readability of the program, you could rewrite the previous statement like this:

```
size = SQ_YD_PER_ACRE * acre;
```

Then you would go back to the top of the program and insert this line:

```
#define SQ_YD_PER_ACRE 4840
```

Note that there is no semicolon at the end of this line because it is a preprocessor directive, not a C statement. This directive tells the preprocessor to search through the source code and replace every occurrence of **SQ_YD_PER_ACRE** with the integer value 4840 before passing the code to the compiler. What the compiler actually sees is this:

```
size = 4840 * acre;
```

SQ_YD_PER_ACRE is an example of a *symbolic constant*. It gives the programmer considerably more information about the program than the bare number 4840, but has the same effect once the preprocessor is finished making the substitution.

By convention, symbolic constants are written entirely in uppercase characters, to distinguish them from variable names (which are usually written in lowercase characters). A **#define** line can appear anywhere in the file, but it only affects the lines below it. Therefore, it is common practice to group all of the **#define** directives near the top of the file, before the start of **main()**. Putting the **#define** lines together at the top of the file also has the advantage of making them easy to find and modify later, if necessary.

Program: *inttime.c*

The Diem Perdidi Track Club plans to sponsor a marathon and needs a program to convert times given in seconds to their equivalents in hours, minutes, and seconds. Let's begin by considering how we would solve this problem by hand. How many hours, minutes, and seconds are in 7761 seconds? First divide by 3600 to find the hours:

$$
\begin{array}{r}
2 \leftarrow \text{hours } (7761/3600) \\
3600 \overline{)7761} \\
-7200 \\
\hline
561 \leftarrow \text{remainder } (7761\%3600)
\end{array}
$$

Divide the remaining seconds by 60 to get the minutes; take the remainder to get the seconds:

$$
\begin{array}{r}
9 \leftarrow \text{minutes } (561/60) \\
60 \overline{)561} \\
-540 \\
\hline
21 \leftarrow \text{seconds } (561\%60)
\end{array}
$$

Thus, 7761 seconds equals 2 hours, 9 minutes, and 21 seconds. (This just happens to be winning time in the men's marathon in the 1984 Olympics.)

The pseudocode outline for this program is

prompt user for total seconds
read total seconds
hours = total seconds / 3600
remaining seconds = total seconds % 3600
minutes = remaining seconds / 60
seconds = remaining seconds % 60
print hours, minutes, and seconds

The C program that implements this is shown in Listing 2–2. Create a file named *inttime.c* and enter the code as shown.

Listing 2–2. *inttime.c*

```c
/* Convert total seconds to hours, minutes, and seconds. */

#include <stdio.h>
#define SEC_PER_HOUR 3600
#define SEC_PER_MIN 60

main()
{
    int total_seconds;
    int hours;
    int remainder;
    int minutes;
    int seconds;

    printf("Enter the total time in seconds: ");
    scanf("%d", &total_seconds);

    hours = total_seconds / SEC_PER_HOUR;
    remainder = total_seconds % SEC_PER_HOUR;
    minutes = remainder / SEC_PER_MIN;
    seconds = remainder % SEC_PER_MIN;

    printf("%d seconds = %d hr, %d min, & %d sec\n",
           total_seconds, hours, minutes, seconds);
}
```

(1) (2) (3)

Dissection of *inttime.c*

(1)
```c
#define SEC_PER_HOUR 3600
#define SEC_PER_MIN 60
```

This is how we create two symbolic constants, the meaning of which should be apparent from their names. Note that there is no semicolon at the end of a **#define** line.

(2)
```c
hours = total_seconds / SEC_PER_HOUR;
remainder = total_seconds % SEC_PER_HOUR;
```

After the preprocessor does its work, these two statements will look like this:

```c
hours = total_seconds / 3600;
remainder = total_seconds % 3600;
```

③ ```
printf("%d seconds = %d hr, %d min, & %d sec\n",
        total_seconds, hours, minutes, seconds);
```

This statement was too long to fit on one line, so we split it over two lines. In general, the C compiler allows this if you do not try to split a string or a variable name. If you have to split a long function call like this, we suggest that you make the break after a comma in the argument list, and that you indent the second line to make it clear that it is a continuation of the preceding line.

### Compiling and Testing *inttime.c*

Compile the program and run it on some test cases:

| Input | Result |
|-------|--------|
| 0 | 0 hr, 0 min, & 0 sec |
| 678 | 0 hr, 11 min, & 18 sec |
| 5437 | 1 hr, 30 min, & 37 sec |
| 25001 | 6 hr, 56 min, & 41 sec |

How does your program handle a negative input? Is the result what you would have expected?

## The *limits.h* Header File

Some symbolic constants are already defined for you in certain header files. For instance, the standard header file *limits.h* contains **#define** lines that look something like this (the actual values may be different on your system):

```
#define INT_MIN -2147483648
#define INT_MAX 2147483647
```

INT_MIN equals the smallest (most negative) value that can be represented as an **int** on your system; **INT_MAX** equals the largest value that can be represented as an **int**. To use these quantities in a program, simply include *limits.h* in your source code:

```
#include <limits.h>
```

The program shown in Listing 2–3 will print out the values of **INT_MAX** and **INT_MIN** for your system. Create a source file named *prlimits.c* and enter the code as shown in the listing.
```

Listing 2–3. *prlimits.c*

```
/* Print int limits */

#include <stdio.h>
#include <limits.h>          (1)

main()
{
    printf("Largest integer (INT_MAX): %d\n", INT_MAX);    (2)
    printf("Smallest integer (INT_MIN): %d\n", INT_MIN);
}
```

Dissection of *prlimits.c*

(1) `#include <limits.h>`

As we said, the *limits.h* file contains the **#define** lines for `INT_MAX` and `INT_MIN`.

(2) `printf("Largest integer (INT_MAX): %d\n", INT_MAX);`

Note that `INT_MAX` appears twice in this line, as part of the control string and as an argument to **printf()**. *The C preprocessor will not recognize a symbolic constant that is part of a string.* In this case, the preprocessor will replace only the second `INT_MAX` with the appropriate value taken from *limits.h*.

Compiling and Testing *prlimits.c*

Compile and run the program as usual. On our computer, *prlimits.c* produces the following output:

```
Largest integer (INT_MAX): 2147483647
Smallest integer (INT_MIN): -2147483648
```

What were the values produced by your program? Although the ANSI C standard does not dictate the exact values for `INT_MIN` and `INT_MAX`, it does set some minimum magnitudes for these quantities:

```
INT_MAX: 32767
INT_MIN: -32767
```

Long Integers

What if the integers available on your system are not large enough for your purposes? C has another integer data type, the **long** integer, that might be useful. If you are interested in **long** integers, refer to the exercises at the end of this chapter.

Order of Operations

You now know about the five arithmetic operators that work on integers (*****, **/**, **+**, **−**, and **%**). To use these operators successfully, you also need to know about the *order of operations*. Consider this expression:

```
5 + 2 * 3
```

Is the addition done before the multiplication, or is the multiplication done before the addition? It does make a difference: If the addition is done first, the expression has the value 21; if the multiplication is done first, the expression has the value 11.

The usual rules of arithmetic apply in this case: multiplication (*****) and division (**/** and **%**) are performed before addition (**+**) or subtraction (**−**). We say that multiplication and division have a *higher precedence* than addition or subtraction.

What about two operators having the same precedence? For example, consider the expression

```
7 / 2 * 4
```

Which is performed first, the division or the multiplication? If the division is done first, the value of the expression is 12; if the multiplication is done first, the result is 0. (Remember, this is *integer* division.)

Whenever there is a choice between two arithmetic operators having the same precedence, the one on the left is done first. We say that the arithmetic operators *associate* left to right, or that they have *left to right associativity*. In this case, the division operator is to the left, so the division is done before the multiplication. But what if you wanted the multiplication to be done before the division? Just as in mathematics, C allows you to use parentheses to alter the normal order of operations. Thus, the parentheses in this expression

```
7 / (2 * 4)
```

cause the multiplication to be done before the division.

A complete table of precedence and associativity for C operators is given in Appendix A. We do not expect you to memorize the table; for now, you can get by with just one rule:

Use parentheses to indicate the proper order of operations.

Program: *upc.c*

A *bar code* is a printed symbol that encodes data as a pattern of parallel bars and spaces that can be read by an optical scanning device. Most products sold in supermarkets are identified by the so-called Universal Product Code (UPC). Here, for example, is the UPC for KELLOGG'S® FROSTED MINI-WHEATS® cereal*:

The first digit (0) indicates the type of product being identified. Next come five digits (38000) that identify the manufacturer. These are followed by five digits (54283) that identify the product. The last digit of the UPC (1) is the *check digit*, which is used to detect errors in scanning the bar code. The check digit is computed as follows:

1. Sum the first, third, fifth, seventh, ninth, and eleventh digits, and multiply by 3;
2. Sum the second, fourth, sixth, eighth, and tenth digits;
3. Add the numbers obtained in steps 1 and 2;
4. Find the smallest number that needs to be added to the total from step 3 to make it equal a multiple of 10. This number is the check digit.

Let's write a program that prompts the user for the first eleven digits of a UPC, then computes and displays the proper check digit. The first step is to try the computation by hand, to be sure we know how it is done. Carrying out this procedure on the UPC 0 38000 54283, we have

Step 1: $(0 + 8 + 0 + 5 + 2 + 3)(3) = 54$
Step 2: $(3 + 0 + 0 + 4 + 8) = 15$
Step 3: $54 + 15 = 69$
Step 4: $69 + 1 = 70 \Rightarrow$ check digit = 1

Although a human can determine the check digit by inspection in Step 4, the computer needs a specific formula. Here is one that seems to work:

---

* KELLOGG'S® and MINI-WHEATS® are registered trademarks of Kellogg Company.

```
(10 - sum % 10) % 10
```

Now that we know how to do the computation by hand, let's design the program:

prompt user for the first 11 digits (separated by spaces)
read the first 11 digits (and print them out again as a check)
carry out the procedure to compute the check digit
print check digit

The C program that implements this is shown in Listing 2–4. Create a source file named *upc.c* and enter the program as shown in the listing.

Listing 2–4. *upc.c*

```c
/* Compute the check digit for a UPC */

#include <stdio.h>

main()
{
    int dig1, dig2, dig3, dig4;      /* UPC digits 1 through 4 */
    int dig5, dig6, dig7, dig8;      /* UPC digits 5 through 8 */
    int dig9, dig10, dig11;          /* UPC digits 9 through 11 */
    int dig12;                       /* The check digit */
    int sum;

    printf("Please enter the first eleven UPC digits, "
           "separated by white space:\n");

    scanf("%d%d%d%d%d%d%d%d%d%d%d", &dig1, &dig2, &dig3, &dig4,
          &dig5, &dig6, &dig7, &dig8, &dig9, &dig10, &dig11);

    printf("%d%d%d%d%d%d%d%d%d%d%d\n", dig1, dig2, dig3, dig4,
           dig5, dig6, dig7, dig8, dig9, dig10, dig11);

    sum = 3 * (dig1 + dig3 + dig5 + dig7 + dig9 + dig11);
    sum = sum + (dig2 + dig4 + dig6 + dig8 + dig10);
    dig12 = (10 - sum % 10) % 10;

    printf("The check digit is %d\n", dig12);
}
```

The circled line markers on the left are: ① ② ③ ④ ⑤ ⑥

Dissection of *upc.c*

①
```
int dig1, dig2, dig3, dig4;      /* UPC digits 1 through 4 */
int dig5, dig6, dig7, dig8;      /* UPC digits 5 through 8 */
int dig9, dig10, dig11;          /* UPC digits 9 through 11 */
int dig12;                       /* The check digit */
```

We want to treat the digits of the UPC separately, so we declare a variable to hold each one. (When we discuss arrays, you will see a much easier way to do this.) The twelfth digit will be the check digit. We might have chosen longer variable names, such as **digit1**, **digit2**, and so on. These would be more descriptive but would also take up more space. We compromised by choosing shorter identifiers and clearly commenting what they mean.

②
```
printf("Please enter the first eleven UPC digits, "
       "separated by white space:\n");
```

The control string was too long to fit on one line, so we split it into two strings. When the C compiler encounters two adjacent string constants, it automatically "fuses" them together to make a single string constant:

```
"Please enter the first eleven UPC digits, separated by white space:\n"
```

③
```
scanf("%d%d%d%d%d%d%d%d%d%d%d", &dig1, &dig2, &dig3, &dig4,
      &dig5, &dig6, &dig7, &dig8, &dig9, &dig10, &dig11);
```

This statement calls **scanf()** to read eleven UPC digits, storing each value in its own variable. Note that there are eleven **%d** formats and eleven variables; also note that the address operator has been applied to each variable.

④
```
printf("%d%d%d%d%d%d%d%d%d%d%d\n", dig1, dig2, dig3, dig4,
       dig5, dig6, dig7, dig8, dig9, dig10, dig11);
```

After reading in the digits, we use **printf()** to print them out immediately as a check that the values were read correctly. This practice is sometimes called *echo-printing*.

⑤
```
sum = 3 * (dig1 + dig3 + dig5 + dig7 + dig9 + dig11);
```

The first step in computing the check digit is to add the first, third, fifth, seventh, ninth, and eleventh digits, then multiply the sum by 3. The parentheses are required here. (Why?)

⑥
```
dig12 = (10 - sum % 10) % 10;
```

The parentheses are necessary here because the remainder operator (**%**) has a higher precedence than the subtraction operator (**-**).

Compiling and Testing *upc.c*

Compile the program and run it on a test case. Be sure to separate the UPC digits by spaces:

0 3 8 0 0 0 5 4 2 8 3 $\boxed{\text{RET}}$

The program should echo the digits you entered, then display the check digit:

```
03800054283
The check digit is 1
```

Even if you get the right answer in this case, do not assume that your program is correct. Recall what we said before about program testing:

A program that compiles and runs may still contain hidden bugs.

We leave it as an exercise for you to try your *upc.c* program on some additional test cases.

Input Field Widths

The *upc.c* program is inconvenient to use because it requires that the UPC digits be separated by spaces, like this:

0 3 8 0 0 0 5 4 2 8 3

It would be better if the user could simply enter the digits, one after the other, like this:

```
03800054283
```

Let's correct this deficiency. First consider the **scanf()** function call as it is currently written:

```
scanf("%d%d%d%d%d%d%d%d%d%d%d", &dig1, &dig2, &dig3, &dig4,
        &dig5, &dig6, &dig7, &dig8, &dig9, &dig10, &dig11);
```

A **%d** in the control string causes **scanf()** to look for an integer in the standard input. Thus, for each of the eleven **%d** formats, **scanf()** will

1. Skip any leading white space
2. Collect digits up to the next white-space character
3. Store the collected digits in the next variable in the list

Now we see the reason the user has to insert a space after each UPC digit. Without the spaces, **scanf()** would attempt to read and store all eleven digits as one integer.

We can improve the program by changing the **scanf()** function call:

```
scanf("%1d%1d%1d%1d%1d%1d%1d%1d%1d%1d%1d", &dig1, &dig2, &dig3,
    &dig4, &dig5, &dig6, &dig7, &dig8, &dig9, &dig10, &dig11);
```

Here we have replaced each **%d** with the format **%1d**. The number **1** between the **%** and the **d** is called a *field width specification*. It instructs the function to read and store just one digit. In other words, for each **%1d** in the control string, **scanf()** will

1. Skip any leading white space
2. Collect one digit
3. Store the digit in the next variable in the list

Note that in this case, it doesn't matter whether the digits are separated by white space or not.

In general, the field width specification sets the *maximum* number of digits that **scanf()** will read. Here are some examples:

Format	Meaning
%d	Read a decimal integer until a white-space character is encountered
%10d	Read a decimal integer until 10 digits have been read or a white-space character is encountered
%4d	Read a decimal integer until 4 digits have been read or a white-space character is encountered
%1d	Read 1 digit of a decimal integer

Revise your *upc.c* program so that it does not require white space between digits.

Output Field Widths

You can also specify a field width when using **printf()**. Suppose the **int** variable **a** contains the value **-4321**. Then the statement

```
printf("%d %3d %-10d %10d", a, a, a, a);
```

causes the value in **a** to be printed four different ways:

```
-4321 -4321 -4321          -4321
```

Let's take a closer look at the output:

$$\underbrace{\text{-4321}}_{\substack{\text{\%d}\\\text{Width: 5}}} \quad \underbrace{\text{-4321}}_{\substack{\text{\%3d}\\\text{Width: 5}}} \quad \underbrace{\text{-4321}\qquad}_{\substack{\text{\%-10d}\\\text{Width: 10}\\\text{(left-justified)}}} \quad \underbrace{\qquad\text{-4321}}_{\substack{\text{\%10d}\\\text{Width: 10}\\\text{(right-justified)}}}$$

In this example, the integer **-4321** fits into a field five spaces wide. If you do not specify a field width—or if you specify one that is too narrow—**printf()** will take as much space as it needs to print the entire number. Thus, both **%d** and **%3d** cause **-4321** to be printed in a field five spaces wide.

On the other hand, if you specify a field that is wider than needed, **printf()** will insert blanks to fill the unused part of the field. In the example above, the format **%10d** causes **-4321** to be printed in a field 10 spaces wide. By default, the number is *right-justified*—it is pushed over to the right limit of the field. A minus sign before the field width (**%-10d**) causes the number to be *left-justified*—pushed to the left limit of the field.

You will learn more about the formatting capabilities of **scanf()** and **printf()** in later chapters.

STYLE

To make our programs in this chapter more readable, we have tried to observe the style guidelines introduced in the previous chapter as well as the following new guidelines:

- Choose descriptive and meaningful variable names. For example, the names **sum**, **diff**, **prod**, **quotient**, and **remainder** clearly describe what the variables are meant to hold.

- Avoid variable names that are too short or too long. Short names may not provide enough information about the intended purpose of the variables. Long names can be tedious to type and hard to read. As a rule of thumb, names of four to ten characters tend to be best.

- Avoid "magic numbers." Instead, use the **#define** directive to create meaningful symbolic constants. Place all **#define** directives at the top of your program so that they will be easy to find and modify, if you should need to. Writing all symbolic constants in capital letters will make them easy to identify within the body of your code.

- Insert a space on either side of an arithmetic or assignment operator. For example, we write **sum = first + second** rather than **sum=first+second**, although the C compiler will accept either one.

- Split very long statements over two or more lines. Be careful, however, never to split a variable name or a string constant. (If you must split a string constant, make it into two separate string constants. The compiler will join two adjacent strings into one string.)

• Use comments to help the reader understand your code.

HELPFUL HINTS

• When designing a computer program to solve a problem, first work through the problem by hand. Often this will help you see patterns that you might not have noticed otherwise, and is especially helpful when you are unsure how to approach the computer solution. Furthermore, the results of your hand calculations can be used to test the completed program.

• Sometimes, the **&** is accidentally omitted from calls to **scanf()**. This may not cause a compiler error but will probably cause the program to crash. Note that **&** is not usually used with **printf()**.

• Be careful not to confuse a 0 (zero) with the letter O. Check your computer screen to see if you can detect the difference. Likewise, do not confuse a 1 (one) with the letter l.

SUMMARY

Preprocessor Directive

`#define OLD 99`   Instructs the preprocessor to search through the source file and replace every occurrence of **OLD** with **99**, except where **OLD** appears as part of a string constant.

Variable Declaration

`int data;`
`int a, b, c;`   Declare **data**, **a**, **b**, and **c** to be integer variables.

Integer Input

`scanf("%d", &data);`   Calls the library function **scanf()** to read a decimal integer (**%d**) from the standard input and store it in the variable **data**. **%d** is a format or conversion specification; **&** is the address operator.

`scanf("%3d", &data);`   As above, except that **%3d** specifies that as many as three digits are to be read.

Assignment

`data = 6;`   Assigns the value 6 to the variable **data**.

Arithmetic Operations

`c = a + b`
`c = a - b`
`c = a * b`
`c = a / b`
`c = a % b`
	Perform arithmetic operations on the values in the integer variables **a** and **b**; assign the results to the variable **c**. (The remainder operator **%** is used only with integers.)

Integer Output

`printf("The answer is %d", c);`	Calls the library function **printf()** to print the contents of **c** as a decimal integer following the phrase **The answer is**.
`printf("The answer is %7d", c);`	As above, but prints the value of **c** in a field at least seven characters wide. If seven characters are not enough, the field width is ignored and sufficient space is taken to print the value.

- Integers are whole numbers, used primarily for counting. Floating-point numbers are used for measuring.

- A variable is a data storage location that has both a name and an address. You select the names for your variables; the computer selects the addresses. Normally, you will not need to know the address of any variable.

- In C, variables must be declared before they can be used. A declaration specifies the type and name of the variable. A variable name can include uppercase and lowercase letters, numerals, and the underscore; the first character cannot be a numeral, and should not be an underscore. Certain keywords that already have a strictly defined meaning in C must not be used as variable names.

- The assignment operator (**=**) is used to put a value into a variable. It does not have the same meaning as the equals sign used in mathematics.

- The standard library function **scanf()** can be used to get a value from the standard input and store it in a variable. This function refers to variables by their addresses, not their names. To get the address of a variable, write the address operator (**&**) before the variable's name.

- The division of two integers produces another integer—any fractional part of the result will be truncated. Integer addition (**+**), subtraction (**−**), and multiplication (*****) behave as expected.

- A variable has a finite size. Overflow occurs when you attempt to store a number that will not fit in a variable. **INT_MAX** is the largest positive value that can be stored in an **int** variable; **INT_MIN** is the smallest (most negative) value that can be stored in an **int** variable. Both symbolic constants are defined in *limits.h*.

- The order of arithmetic operations follows the usual algebraic rules: multiplication and division (`/` and `%`) have higher precedence than addition and subtraction. All of these operations have left-to-right associativity. Use parentheses to insure the correct order of operations.

- A program that compiles and runs successfully may still contain hidden bugs—errors that may cause your program to yield incorrect results. Be sure to test your program with a wide range of test cases. Try zero, small and large positive numbers, and small and large negative numbers.

EXERCISES

1. *Define:* **a.** integer; **b.** variable; **c.** identifier; **d.** address; **e.** declaration; **f.** case-sensitive; **g.** keyword; **h.** reserved word; **i.** assignment; **j.** format; **k.** conversion specification; **l.** decimal; **m.** pseudocode; **n.** precedence; **o.** associativity; **p.** bar code; **q.** check digit; **r.** field width.

2. *Errors.* Create a copy of **inttime.c** called **errors2.c** and introduce into the new file the first error listed below. Run your compiler on the file. If the compiler catches the error, write down both the error and the error message; if not, run the executable file with test data and make a note of any unexpected results.
   Correct the file, then repeat the process with the next error on the list. Continue until you have tried all of the errors.
   a. Omit the variable **hours** from the declaration list.
   b. Omit the address operator (`&`) from the variable **total_seconds** in the **scanf()** call.
   c. Omit the variable **minutes** from the second **printf()** call. (Leave all commas in.)
   d. Remove one variable from the second **printf()** call. (Remove the comma as well.)
   e. Change the spelling of **total_seconds** in the computation for the remainder.
   f. Remove the comma that follows the control string in the second **printf()** call.
   g. Remove the second double quote from one of the **printf()** calls.
   h. Change the line

   ```
   #define SEC_PER_MIN 60   to   #define SEC_PER_MIN = 60
   ```

   i. Change every occurrence of the variable **hours** to the keyword **const**.

3. Repeat Exercise 2, but put all of the errors into the file at the same time.

4. *More errors.* Create a copy of **intarith.c** called **errors22.c**. Follow the instructions given in Exercise 2, but introduce the following errors into the file:
   a. Put a comma between `%d` and `%d` in the **scanf()** call.
   b. Remove the comma between `&first` and `&second` in the **scanf()** call.

5. Indicate which you would use, an integer or a floating-point number, to count or measure each of the following quantities:

   a. Population of your state.

   b. Average height (in meters) of the people in your state.

   c. Average age (in years) of the population of your state.

   d. Number of persons on the U.S. Olympic team.

   e. Winning jump (in meters) in an Olympic long jump.

   f. Winning time in an Olympic 100-meter sprint.

   g. Number of classes taken by a college student.

   h. Average number of hours per day that college students spend studying.

   i. Runs scored in a baseball game.

   j. Batting average of a baseball player.

   k. Density of uranium.

   l. Atomic weight of uranium.

   m. Atomic number of uranium.

   n. The number of coins in your pocket.

   o. Total value of the coins in your pocket, expressed in cents.

   p. Total value of the coins in your pocket, expressed in dollars.

6. For each quantity listed in Exercise 5, write a meaningful and descriptive variable name.

7. Write down the rules for naming C variables. Write down the rules for naming files on your operating system. How do the two compare?

8. Which of the following are valid C variable names? In each case, justify your answer.

`Bozo`	`bozo`	`boZO`
`single`	`double`	`triple`
`long`	`2long`	`too_long`
`23skiddoo`	`jill2`	`intarith.c`
`_underscore`	`this_is_a_big_1`	`far`
`int`	`a9`	`&`

9. Using your program *intarith.c* on the following test cases, determine how your system handles the division of negative integers:

```
17 / (-2)        17 % (-2)
-17 / 2          -17 % 2
-17 / (-2)       -17 % (-2)
```

   a. What rule does your compiler use to handle division of negative integers?

   b. Although different compilers handle the integer division and remaindering operations differently, the C standard requires that the following be true on all systems:

> If **b** is not zero, then **(a/b) * b + a % b** must equal **a**

Does this rule hold on your system?

10. Based on the output from your ***prlimits.c*** program, which of the estimated population figures listed below can be represented as an **int** on your system?

Population	Place
1,703	Cheesequake, NJ
30,772	Inkster, MI
36,163	Purdue University enrollment
130,598	Tippecanoe County, IN
574,283	Boston, MA
3,282,061	British Columbia
27,000,000	Australia and Oceania
248,709,873	United States of America
5,423,000,000	Earth

11. Compute the value of each of the following expressions by hand, assuming that both **a** and **b** have been declared as **int** variables, and that **a** contains the value 10 and **b** the value 7. You may wish to write a C program to check your answers.

   a. `a + 47 / b + a % 2`

   b. `(a + 47) / b + a % 2`

   c. `a + 47 % b + b / 2`

   d. `(a + 47) % b + b / 2`

   e. `a % b + 47`

   f. `a / b + 47`

   g. `a / 5 + b / 5`

   h. `(a + b) / 5`

   i. `a / 5 * b / 5`

   j. `a / (5 + b) / 5`

12. Rewrite the following algebraic expressions into C expressions, assuming that x, a, b, and c are separate variables.

   a. $(x + 1)(x - 3)$ d. $a(b + 4) - 2bc$

   b. $2ab + c$ e. $a^2 - 2bc$

   c. $2(ab + c)$ f. $(x + 6)^2$

13. The following algebraic expressions have been incorrectly translated into C expressions. Correct these C expressions.

   a. $x + y^2$ $\Rightarrow$ `(x + y) * (x + y)`

b. $(x + y^2)^2$ $\Rightarrow$ (x + y * y)(x + y * y)

c. $3xy^2$ $\Rightarrow$ 3x * y * y

d. $\dfrac{x}{y - z}$ $\Rightarrow$ x / y - z

14. Testing **upc.c**. You cannot be sure your **upc.c** program works correctly on the basis of a single computation. You should at least try some additional test cases:

UPC (first eleven digits)	Check Digit
0 8 9 4 0 8 0 1 5 9 2	2
0 1 9 2 0 0 0 2 8 3 6	3
0 7 1 8 1 5 2 6 1 8 9	4
0 4 8 8 9 8 0 9 1 7 5	5
0 7 1 6 4 1 8 2 0 7 4	6
0 1 1 1 1 1 4 0 1 2 9	7
0 7 9 4 0 0 7 6 5 2 0	8
0 8 9 4 0 8 0 3 0 5 2	9
0 3 6 6 0 0 8 1 5 0 1	0

15. **upc.c** *revisited*. This exercise is intended to emphasize a point we made earlier: a program that compiles and runs may still contain hidden bugs. One programmer has proposed a simpler formula to compute the check digit in the **upc.c** program:

```
dig12 = 10 - sum % 10;      /* ? */
```

Does this work? Make a copy of your **upc.c** program and replace the check digit formula with the one shown here. Run it on the test cases listed in the previous exercise. What differences, if any, do you find between the two formulas?

16. *Number of coins*. Write a program that prompts for the number of pennies, nickels, dimes, quarters, and half dollars, and prints the total number of coins.

17. *Value of coins*. Modify the previous program so that it also prints the total value of the change in (a) cents (e.g., 450 cents), and (b) dollars and cents (e.g., 4 dollars and 50 cents).

18. *Pounds to ounces*. Write a program that converts pounds and ounces to total ounces (16 ounces = 1 pound).

19. *Ounces to pounds and ounces*. Write a program that converts total ounces to pounds and ounces (16 ounces = 1 pound).

20. *Inches to feet*. Write a program that converts total inches to feet and inches (12 inches = 1 foot).

21. *Feet to inches.* Write a program that converts feet and inches to total inches (12 inches = 1 foot).

22. *Gross and dozens.* There are 12 items in a *dozen* and 12 dozen (144 items) in a *gross*. Write a program that prompts for the total number of items and converts this total to gross, dozens, and items. (For example, 187 items is equivalent to 1 gross, 3 dozen, and 7 items.) Be sure to use appropriate symbolic constants for the conversion factors.

23. *Pence to pounds, shillings, and pence.* Suppose you are reading your favorite English novel, and you find yourself being confused by the old English monetary system, with its pounds, shillings, and pence. You look in the dictionary and find that there were 20 shillings in a pound and 12 pence in a shilling. Write a computer program that converts pence to pounds, shillings, and pence. (For example, 543 pence is equivalent to 2 pounds, 5 shillings, and 3 pence.) Be sure to use appropriate symbolic constants for the conversion factors.

24. *Guineas to pence.* Formerly, the English monetary system included the *crown* (= 5 shillings) and *guinea* (= 21 shillings) as well as pounds, shillings, and pence. Write a program that prompts for guineas, pounds, crowns, shillings, and pence, and computes the equivalent number of pence. (For example, 2 guineas, 1 pound, 3 crowns, 1 shilling, and 9 pence is equivalent to 945 pence.) Be sure to use appropriate symbolic constants for the conversion factors.

25. *Guineas to pounds, shillings, and pence.* Revise the previous program so that it prompts for guineas, pounds, crowns, shillings, and pence, and computes the equivalent number of pounds, shillings, and pence. (For example, 2 guineas, 1 pound, 3 crowns, 1 shilling, and 9 pence is equivalent to 3 pounds, 18 shillings, and 9 pence.) Be sure to use appropriate symbolic constants for the conversion factors.

26. *ISBN check digit.* Most books carry a 10-digit International Standard Book Number (ISBN), usually on the back cover or the copyright page. For example, 0-697-13172-6 is the ISBN code for *Just Enough UNIX* by Paul K. Andersen. The digits 0-697 identify the publisher (Wm. C. Brown) and the digits 13172 identify the book itself. The last digit (6) is a check digit that helps to detect errors in writing or transmitting the ISBN. The check digit is computed by multiplying each of the first nine digits by its order in the code (the first digit by 1, the second digit by 2, etc.), summing the products, then dividing by 11 and taking the remainder. For the ISBN code 0-697-13172-6, this procedure produces:

$$(0)(1) + (6)(2) + (9)(3) + (7)(4) + (1)(5) + (3)(6) + (1)(7) + (7)(8) + (2)(9) = 171$$

$$171 \% 11 = 6$$

Write a program that prompts the user for the first nine digits of an ISBN, then computes and displays the proper check digit. Test your program on several actual ISBNs. (Note that on many ISBNs, an *X* represents a check digit of 10.)

27. *Rational arithmetic.* An integer variable cannot hold a fraction. However, you can represent a fraction with *two* **int** variables, if you use one variable to hold the numerator and the other to hold the denominator. This is called the *rational representation* of the number. Write a program that prompts the user for the numerators and denominators of two fractions, then computes the sum, product, difference, and quotient of the fractions using the familiar rules for arithmetic on fractions. For example, the sum of the rational numbers n_1/d_1 and n_2/d_2 is given by

$$\frac{n_1}{d_1} + \frac{n_2}{d_2} = \frac{n_1 d_2 + n_2 d_1}{d_1 d_2}$$

To avoid doing integer division, the numerator and denominator must be calculated and stored separately. When printing the result on the standard output, first print the numerator, then a slash (/), then the denominator.

28. *Long integers and **prlimits.c**.* On many systems, the **long int** data type can handle a greater range of integers than the **int** (although this is not required by the ANSI C standard). To see if this is so on your computer, modify your **prlimits.c** program so that it also prints out the values of the symbolic constants **LONG_MAX** and **LONG_MIN**.

29. *Using long integers.* A **long int** variable is declared using the keyword **long**. For example, the declaration

```
long sum;
```

instructs the compiler to create a **long int** variable named **sum**. Make a copy of **intarith.c** named **lngarith.c**, and modify the copy to use **long** variables. Does the new program behave any differently from the original?

30. *Long integer constants.* In a C program, a **long** integer constant is indicated by a suffix letter **L**. Hence, these would all be **long** constants:

```
3600L    36L    -5437L    285001L    0L
```

Create a version of the **inttime.c** program named **lngtime.c** that uses **long** variables and constants throughout.

31. *Rational arithmetic with long integers.* Repeat the *rational arithmetic* exercise using **long** integers.

3.

Floating-Point Data

We have seen how the C programming language uses integers; in this chapter, we consider floating-point data. You may be wondering what the term "floating-point" means. Of course, "point" refers to the decimal point. It is said to "float" because it can appear anywhere in the number. For example, the following are all floating-point quantities:

24371.   2437.1   243.71   24.371   2.4371

See how the decimal point floats? An alternative would be *fixed-point data*, in which the decimal point is always in the same location. A fixed-point scheme might, for example, always represent numbers with two digits to the right of the decimal point:

243.71   0.23   1.51   67690.01   0.00

Although this scheme might be adequate for, say, simple financial computations involving dollars and cents, it would be very limiting. You could not use it to represent numbers such as 0.00005 or 3.141592653589793. That is why C uses floating-point rather than fixed-point numbers.

Precision and Round-Off Error

Unlike integers, floating-point numbers can express fractions as well as whole numbers. Unfortunately, many fractions cannot be represented exactly as floating-point numbers. For instance, 2.0/3.0 has the decimal equivalent 0.666666666 . . . , which would require infinitely many digits to be represented exactly. The computer cannot handle a number that is infinitely long, so 0.666666666 . . . would have to be rounded to a finite number of digits.

The number of digits that are retained by the computer is called the *precision*. Thus, a computer that provides 6 digits of precision might round off 0.666666666 . . . to 0.666667, which is only an approximation to the true value. Although this approximation might be adequate for many computations, there are times when the error introduced by rounding—called *round-off error*—can become unacceptably large.

Floating-Point Variables

We have already said that a variable is a named storage location. Just as with **int** variables, floating-point variables must be declared before they are used. The declaration

```
double area;
```

declares **area** to be a floating-point variable (Figure 3–1). The rules for naming floating-point variables are the same as for **int** variables. The keyword **double** is short for *double-precision floating-point.** Later in this chapter, we will show you how to determine the digits of precision for a **double** variable on your system.

Floating-Point Arithmetic

Four arithmetic operators are used with floating-point quantities:

* *   floating-point multiplication
* /   floating-point division
* +   floating-point addition
* –   floating-point subtraction

There is no such thing as a floating-point remainder operator. The remainder operator (%) is used only with integers. Otherwise, the same symbols are used for floating-point and integer arithmetic.

You may be wondering how the compiler knows when to use integer arithmetic and when to use floating-point arithmetic, since the same operators are used for

---

* Is there such a thing as a *single-precision floating-point* variable? The answer is yes; such variables are declared using the **float** keyword. In this chapter we will focus on **double** rather than **float** variables because (1) the standard mathematical library functions work almost exclusively on **double** values, and (2) on many systems, **double** variables provide more precision than **float** variables.

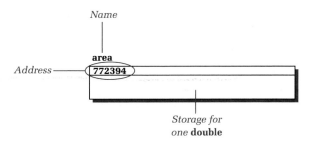

Figure 3–1   A floating-point variable. A **double** variable has a name, an address, and space for one double-precision floating-point number.

both. The answer is simple: whenever you multiply, divide, add, or subtract two integers, the result must be an integer. Hence,

```
1 / 2
```

indicates integer division, and produces the value 0 (not 0.5). Likewise whenever you multiply, divide, add, or subtract two **double** values, the result must be a **double**. Hence,

```
1.0 / 2.0
```

indicates floating-point division and produces the value 0.5. Whenever you multiply, divide, add, or subtract an **int** and a **double**, the result will be a **double**. Consider this expression:

```
1.0 / 2
```

Here we have a **double** divided by an **int**. The result will be a **double**, so 0.5 is the answer. The same result is obtained from the expression

```
1 / 2.0
```

Arithmetic operations involving quantities of different types (an **int** and a **double**) are called *mixed operations* or *mixed arithmetic*.

Mixed arithmetic operations can cause serious trouble for the unwary. For instance, the following statement is intended to convert Celsius temperatures to the Fahrenheit scale (assume **Celsius** and **Fahrenheit** to be **double** variables):

```
Fahrenheit = (9 / 5) * Celsius + 32;      /* Wrong */
```

The compiler will interpret (**9** / **5**) as integer division because both **9** and **5** are integers. Consequently, this statement is equivalent to

```
Fahrenheit = 1 * Celsius + 32;          /* Wrong */
```

which is not correct. Writing all of the constants with decimal points will ensure that floating-point arithmetic is performed:

```
Fahrenheit = (9.0 / 5.0) * Celsius + 32.0;       /* Right */
```

Program: *bubble.c*

The Chimera Bubble Company, a famous manufacturer of spherical domes, space-suit helmets, and goldfish bowls, wants a program to compute the surface areas and volumes of their products. Referring to a standard mathematics handbook, we discover that the Chimera bubbles have the shape that is described as a *spherical segment*:

$$A = 2\pi Rh$$

$$V = \frac{\pi}{3}h^2(3R - h)$$

$$V = \frac{\pi}{6}h(3a^2 + h^2)$$

The president of Chimera says she would like to be able to specify the bubble height h and base radius a, and have the program compute the surface area A and the enclosed volume V. Examining the area formula, we see that it requires R, the radius of the sphere that would just contain the bubble. (Alternatively, you can think of the bubble as being "sliced" from a sphere of radius R.) We do not have a formula for R; however, we have *two* formulas for V, one of which involves R. Solving the second formula for R, we obtain

$$R = \frac{h}{3} + \frac{V}{\pi \cdot h^2}$$

We have three equations and three unknowns. Now let's try a computation by hand. Choose a height of 2 units and a base radius of 1 unit:

$$V = \frac{\pi}{6}(2)(3 \cdot 1^2 + 2^2) = 7.3303828$$

$$R = \frac{2}{3} + \frac{7.3303828}{\pi \cdot 2^2} = 1.25$$

$$A = 2\pi(1.25)(2) = 15.707963$$

Note the order of the computations: first the volume (V), then the radius (R), and last the area (A). A reasonable pseudocode outline for the program would be

prompt user for height
read the height

prompt user for base radius
read the base radius

compute the enclosed volume
compute the sphere radius
compute the surface area

print results

The C code that implements this plan is given in Listing 3–1. Create a file named **bubble.c** and enter the code as shown in the listing.

Listing 3–1. *bubble.c*

```
/*************************************************

    Compute the volume and surface area of a bubble
    having the shape of a spherical segment.
    Reference: "CRC Standard Mathematical Tables"
    27th edition. (p.128)

*************************************************/

#include <stdio.h>
#define PI 3.141592653589793

main()
{
    double height;              /* Height above the base */
    double base_radius;         /* Radius of base */
    double sphere_radius;       /* Radius of sphere */
    double area;                /* Surface area of segment */
    double volume;              /* Volume of segment */

    printf("Enter height of bubble: ");
    scanf("%lf", &height);

    printf("Enter radius of base: ");
    scanf("%lf", &base_radius);

    volume = (PI / 6.0) * height
            * (3.0 * base_radius * base_radius + height * height);

    sphere_radius = (height / 3.0)
                  + (volume / (PI * height * height));

    area = 2.0 * PI * sphere_radius * height;

    printf("Sphere radius: %f\n", sphere_radius);
    printf("Surface area: %f\n", area);
    printf("Volume: %f\n", volume);
}
```

Dissection of *bubble.c*

① `#define PI 3.141592653589793`

Everywhere the symbolic constant **PI** occurs, it will be replaced by the value 3.141592653589793 before the code is sent to the compiler. This is much easier for the programmer than having to write 3.141592653589793 several times.

②
```
double height;          /* Height above the base */
double base_radius;     /* Radius of base */
double sphere_radius;   /* Radius of sphere */
double area;            /* Surface area of segment */
double volume;          /* Volume of segment */
```

This program requires five **double** variables. We have tried to think of meaningful variable names, and we have also included an explanatory comment for each variable.

③ `scanf("%lf", &height);`

The thing to note about this **scanf()** call is the **%lf** (read "percent-el-ef") format. This stands for "long float," another name for **double**. (We don't use **%d** because that means "decimal integer.")

④
```
volume = (PI / 6.0) * height
        * (3.0 * base_radius * base_radius + height * height);
```

Note that we were careful to write the constants 6.0 and 3.0 with decimal points. This makes it clear that we intend this computation to be done with floating-point arithmetic.

⑤
```
printf("Sphere radius: %f\n", sphere_radius);
printf("Surface area: %f\n", area);
printf("Volume: %f\n", volume);
```

Here we have shown how the **%f** format is used to specify the output of a **double** value. However, the **%lf** format must be used with **scanf()** to read a **double** value.

Compiling and Testing *bubble.c*

Compile the program in the usual way. If there are no syntax errors, run the executable code. Enter the value 2 at the prompt and press RETURN:

`Enter height of bubble: 2`[RET]

Enter the value 1 at the next prompt and press RETURN:

`Enter radius of base: 1`[RET]

You should see the following output:

```
Sphere radius: 1.250000
Surface area: 15.707963
Volume: 7.330383
```

These are the same numbers we obtained from our hand computation, which is a good indication that the program is correct. Nevertheless, it is not *proof* that the program is correct. We should at least run it on a few more cases. Try these:

Bubble Height	Base Radius	Sphere Radius	Surface Area	Bubble Volume
0.8	0.3	0.456250	2.293363	0.381180
11.5	45.3	94.971304	6862.306497	37865.605782
1.0	1.0	1.000000	6.283185	2.094395
2.0	0.0	1.000000	12.566371	4.188790

Note the last case. A bubble with a height of 2.0 and a base radius of 0.0 would be a complete sphere. Let's check the surface area and volume computations using the formulas for a sphere:

$$A = 4\pi R^2 = 4\pi\left(\frac{h}{2}\right)^2 = 12.566371$$

$$V = \frac{4}{3}\pi R^3 = \frac{4}{3}\pi\left(\frac{h}{2}\right)^3 = 4.188790$$

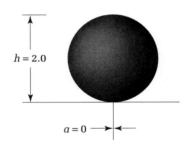

$h = 2.0$

$a = 0$

These agree with the numbers produced by ***bubble.c***—again, not proof that the program is correct, but an indication that it probably is. Apparently, ***bubble.c*** may be used for computing the areas and volumes of spheres, if we set a to 0 and let h equal the diameter of the sphere.

Scientific and Exponential Notation

Variables of type **double** allow you to use very large and very small values. Sometimes it is convenient to use *scientific notation*, in which a number is expressed as a product of a value between 1 and 10 and a suitable power of 10. For example, the number 1000000000000 (a 1 followed by twelve zeros) becomes

$$1.0 \times 10^{12}$$

Unfortunately, ~~scientific notation~~ cannot be displayed on the typical computer terminal screen, which cannot handle superscripts. C therefore allows us to enter floating-point numbers this way:

~~1.0e+12~~

The notation **e+12** stands for $\times 10^{12}$. This is ~~sometimes called~~ *exponential notation*, or *e-notation* for short. Below are some more examples of scientific and exponential notation. Note that there is more than one way to write the e-notation:

Value	Scientific Notation	E-Notation
0.00003761294	3.761294×10^{-5}	3.761294e-05 3.761294e-5
−0.00003761294	-3.761294×10^{-5}	-3.761294e-05 -3.761294e-5
1.5	1.5×10^{0}	1.5e+00 1.5e+0 1.5e0
−1.5	-1.5×10^{0}	-1.5e+00 -1.5e+0 -1.5e0
92979250.0	9.2979250×10^{7}	9.2979250e+07 9.2979250e+7 9.2979250e7

Let's use e-notation with the **bubble.c** program to compute the surface area and volume of the sun. According to the CRC *Handbook of Chemistry and Physics*, the diameter of the sun is 1391000000 meters. Run the program and enter this height in e-notation:

```
Enter height of bubble: 1.391e9 RET
```

Enter a base radius of 0 at the next prompt:

```
Enter radius of base: 0 RET
```

Our computer produces the following output values (yours may differ slightly):

```
Sphere radius: 695500000.000000
Surface area: 6078607935170471936.000000
Volume: 1409223939637021066611654656.000000
```

Long numbers such as these are very inconvenient to work with. Worse, they imply a much higher accuracy than is justified—is it really true that the surface area of the sun is *exactly* 6078607935170471936.000000 square meters? What we need is a way to print the output in e-notation, and to limit the precision of the output. We consider this in the next section.

Input and Output Formats

When reading a **double** value with **scanf()**, you should always use the **%lf** format. In contrast, you have a choice of three different floating-point formats to use with **printf()**:

%f   Print a floating-point value in the regular decimal notation. By default, six digits are printed after the decimal point.

%e   Print in e-notation, with one digit before the decimal point and at least two digits in the exponent. By default, six digits are printed after the decimal point.

%g   Use either **%f** or **%e** notation, whichever requires less space in the output line. Also strip off any trailing zeros after the decimal point.

To get an idea of how these formats work, consider the following examples, which show how three different values (0.000005, 47.3, and 123456789.0) would be printed by the three formats:

Value	%f	%e	%g
0.000005	0.000005	5.000000e−06	5e−06
47.3	47.300000	4.730000e+01	47.3
123456789.0	123456789.000000	1.234568e+08	1.234568e+08

The **%g** format is the most versatile and convenient—it is the one we will prefer for printing floating-point values.

By default, the **%g** format prints no more than six digits, rounding off if necessary. You can change this by specifying a *precision*, which equals the maximum number of digits to be printed (not including the digits in the exponent.) To print four digits, for example, you would use the format

```
%.4g
```

Similarly, you can specify an output precision when working with either the **%e** for the **%f** format. For instance, to print a floating-point value in regular decimal notation with two digits after the decimal point, you would write

```
%.2f
```

To print e-notation with two digits after the decimal point, use

```
%.2e
```

It is important to remember that an output format such as **%.4g** influences only the appearance of a variable as it is printed. *Output formats have no effect on the precision of the values that are stored in variables.*

You can also specify a field width with the output formats **%f**, **%e**, and **%g**. Thus, to print four significant figures left-justified in a field that is twelve spaces wide, you might use the format

```
%-12.4g
```

Now we know how to control the precision of the output. But how many digits of precision should be used? To answer that, you will need to know something about the header file *float.h*.

The *float.h* Header File

The standard header file *float.h* contains various **#define** directives, including those for the symbolic constants **DBL_MIN**, **DBL_MAX**, and **DBL_DIG** (the actual values may be different on your system):

```
#define DBL_MAX 1.79769e+308
#define DBL_MIN 2.22507e-308
#define DBL_DIG 15
```

DBL_MAX equals the largest value that can be represented as a **double** on your system; **DBL_MIN** equals the smallest positive number that can be represented as a **double**. **DBL_DIG** equals the digits of precision for a **double**. The ANSI C standard sets some minimums for these quantities:

```
DBL_MAX: 1.0e+37
DBL_MIN: 1.0e-37
DBL_DIG: 10
```

To use any of these constants in a program, you must include the *float.h* file in your source code:

```
#include <float.h>
```

Modify *prlimits.c* from Chapter 2 so that it also prints the values of **DBL_MIN**, **DBL_MAX**, and **DBL_DIG** that are defined in *float.h* on your system. See Listing 3–2.

Listing 3–2. *prlimits.c* (Modified)

```
/* Print int and double limits */

#include <stdio.h>
#include <limits.h>
#include <float.h>

main()
{
    double diff1, diff2;

    printf("Largest integer (INT_MAX): %d\n", INT_MAX);
    printf("Smallest integer (INT_MIN): %d\n", INT_MIN);

    printf("\nLargest double (DBL_MAX): %g\n", DBL_MAX);
    printf("Smallest positive double (DBL_MIN): %g\n", DBL_MIN);
    printf("Double precision: %d decimal digits \n", DBL_DIG);

    diff1 = (DBL_MAX - DBL_MAX) + 1.0;
    diff2 = DBL_MAX - (DBL_MAX - 1.0);

    printf("\ndiff1 = %g\n", diff1);
    printf("diff2 = %g\n", diff2);
}
```

(1) appears next to `#include <float.h>`

(2) appears next to the `diff1 = (DBL_MAX - DBL_MAX) + 1.0;` lines

Dissection of *prlimits.c*

(1) `#include <float.h>`

Among other things, the *float.h* file contains **#define** lines for **DBL_MAX**, **DBL_MIN**, and **DBL_DIG**.

(2) `diff1 = (DBL_MAX - DBL_MAX) + 1.0;`
`diff2 = DBL_MAX - (DBL_MAX - 1.0);`

By the usual rules of algebra, these statements ought to produce the same result. But as we shall see, they do not.

Compiling and Running *prlimits.c*

Compile and run the program in the usual way. Our computer produces the following output (yours may be different):

```
Largest integer (INT_MAX): 2147483647
Smallest integer (INT_MIN): -2147483648

Largest double (DBL_MAX): 1.79769e+308
Smallest positive double (DBL_MIN): 2.22507e-308
Double precision: 15 decimal digits

diff1 = 1
diff2 = 0
```

As you can see, our system can handle an enormous range of **double** values, from `2.22507e-308` to `1.79769e+308`. Nevertheless, as `diff1` and `diff2` show, this is no guarantee against round-off errors. Let's examine the computation of these two quantities:

```
diff1 = (DBL_MAX - DBL_MAX) + 1.0;
diff2 = DBL_MAX - (DBL_MAX - 1.0);
```

Although you might expect these statements to produce the same result, `diff1` gets the value 1.0 (the correct answer), and `diff2` gets the value 0.0. Why?

A **double** on our system can store no more than about 15 digits of precision. When rounded to 15 digits, the value of

```
1.797693134862316e+308 - 1.0e+00
```

is the same as

```
1.797693134862316e+308
```

In other words, `DBL_MAX` is such a large number that subtracting 1.0 from it makes no apparent difference, just as removing one grain of sand from a beach makes no visible difference in the size of the beach. In fact, you would need a variable with a precision of 308 digits to tell the difference between `DBL_MAX` and (`DBL_MAX` - `1.0`) on our system. This is an extreme example, but it illustrates an important point:

> *Floating-point arithmetic is approximate—beware of errors.*

Mixed Assignments

We warned you about mixing **int** and **double** quantities in arithmetic operations. Now consider a related problem, that of *mixed assignment operations*. As an example, suppose that **k** is an **int**, and that you have the following assignment statement:

```
k = 2.75;    /* k is an int, 2.75 is a double */
```

Here we are trying to assign a **double** constant to an **int** variable. Since **int** variables hold only whole numbers, the fractional part of 2.75 cannot be stored in **k**. The assignment operation cuts off (truncates) the fractional part, and **k** ends up with the value 2, an integer.

Now suppose that **x** is a **double** variable, and that you have the following assignment statement:

```
x = 5;       /* x is a double, 5 is an integer */
```

The integer value 5 must be converted to a **double** before it can be stored in **x**. Thus, **x** ends up with 5.0, a **double** value.

Casts

Fortunately, there is a convenient way to avoid the problems associated with mixed assignment and mixed arithmetic operations. Suppose the Chimera Bubble Company is surveying consumers to find out whether a new line of designer fish helmets will be a hit or a flop. The company wants a computer program to analyze the results of the survey. The program will require these variables:

```
int hits;         /* Number of people answering "hit!" */
int flops;        /* Number of people answering "flop!" */
double ratio;     /* Ratio of hits to flops */
```

A careless programmer might try to compute the hits-to-flops ratio this way:

```
ratio = hits / flops;
```

The problem here is that **hits/flops** will be computed using integer division, which will give the wrong answer in most cases. (What if 50 people answer "hit," and 51 answer "flop"?)

Here is the proper way to compute the ratio:

```
ratio = ((double)hits) / ((double)flops);
```

Note the keyword **double** surrounded by parentheses. This is called a *type conversion operator*, a *typecast operator*, or a *cast*. In essence, the cast operation

```
(double)hits
```

tells the compiler to treat the value of **hits** as if it were a **double** quantity. This does not alter the value as it is stored in the variable; a cast merely changes the way the value is used in computations and assignments. In this case, the cast forces the compiler to use floating-point division.

You can also use casts to make **double** variables behave like **int** variables. For example, suppose that **length** and **width** are declared to be **double** variables and are assigned **double** values:

```
double length;
double width;

length = 10.333333;
width = 7.772635;
```

A cast operation could be used to make the compiler treat **length** and **width** temporarily as **int** variables. In other words, only the integer parts of **length** and **width** would be used in computations. Thus, the expression

```
((int)length) / ((int)width)
```

would be equivalent to

```
(10) / (7)
```

This computation would be carried out using integer division, producing 1 as an answer. The contents of **length** and **width** would not be changed by the cast operation.

Program: *roundpos.c*

We have seen that **double** variables permit us to work with numbers having ten or more digits of precision. However, high precision can be misleading: very few quantities can be measured to ten significant figures. Therefore, it is often a good idea to round off numbers before printing them. Our next program will show how to use cast operators to round positive **double** values to any level selected by the user.

Rounding a positive number to the nearest whole number is easy: simply add 0.5 and truncate the result. For example, we would round 6784.9 like this:

$$(double)((int)(6784.9 + 0.5)) \quad \Rightarrow \quad 6785.0$$

But what if we want to round a number to the nearest multiple of 10, or 100, or 1000? This is a bit more complicated. Suppose, for example, that we wanted to round 6784.9 to the nearest ten. You can verify that the following expression will do the trick:

```
(double)((int)(6784.9/10.0 + 0.5)) * 10.0    ⇒    6780.0
```

The following expression will round 6784.9 to the nearest thousand:

```
(double)((int)(6784.9/1000.0 + 0.5)) * 1000.0    ⇒    7000.0
```

This suggests a general formula for rounding any positive number to a given level:

```
(double)((int)(number/level + 0.5)) * level
```

Now we can write the pseudocode for the program:

prompt for a number
read the number
prompt for the rounding level
read the level
round number using formula above
print rounded number

Listing 3–3 shows the C code for this program.

Listing 3–3. *roundpos.c*

```
/*********************************************

   Round off a positive floating-point number
   to a level specified by the user.

*********************************************/

#include <stdio.h>

main()
{
   double number;
   double level;
   double rounded;

   printf("Please enter number to be rounded: ");
   scanf("%lf", &number);

   printf("Please enter rounding level: ");
   scanf("%lf", &level);

   rounded = (double)((int)(number/level + 0.5)) * level;

   printf("%g rounds to %g\n", number, rounded);
}
```

Compiling and Testing *roundpos.c*

Compile the program in the usual way, and try out some test cases. What does your program do if you specify a rounding level that is less than one? What about a rounding level of zero? Does your program round negative numbers correctly?

HELPFUL HINTS

- Although typecasts are not always necessary in mixed operations, we suggest that you use casts in all such operations to make your intentions clear to anyone who might read your program.
- If your program requires particular units—for example, that all lengths be expressed in meters—be sure to indicate this when prompting the user for input data. In addition, use comments in the code to indicate the proper units.

● ▬▬▬▬▬▬ SUMMARY

Preprocessor Directive

`#include <float.h>`

Instructs the preprocessor to include the file **float.h**, which contains information related to the size and precision of floating-point values.

Variable Declaration

`double data;`
`double a, b, c;`

Declare **data**, **a**, **b**, and **c** to be **double** variables.

Floating-Point Input

`scanf("%lf", &data);`

Calls the library function **scanf( )** to read a floating-point value from the standard input and store it in the **double** variable **data**.

E-Notation

`2.998e+08`
`6.625e-34`

2.998×10^8
6.625×10^{-34}

Casts

`(int)dbl_var`

Treats the value of **dbl_var** as an **int** in assignments and other operations; leaves the actual contents of the variable unchanged.

`(double)int_var`

Treats the value of **int_var** as a **double** in assignments and other operations; leaves the actual contents of the variable unchanged.

Floating-Point Output

`printf("%f", x);`

Calls the library function **printf( )** to print the contents of **x** as a floating-point value.

`printf("%e", x);`

As above, but prints **x** using e-notation.

`printf("%g", x);`

Prints **x** using either %**f** or %**e** format, whichever takes less space in the output line.

`printf("%-10.2g", x);`

As above, but prints **x** left-justified in a field 10 spaces wide, with 2 digits to the right of the decimal point.

- Floating-point data are used for measuring, and may include decimal fractions.
- For values such as **2.0 / 3.0**, the decimal representation is only an approximation. The computer will round these values, possibly introducing error into your results.
- The arithmetic operators **+**, **−**, *****, and **/** work on **double**s; however the integer remainder operator **%** is not used with **double**s.
- You may need to use a **double** variable in an **int** calculation (or vice versa). If this is necessary, use a cast to tell the compiler to treat your **double** value as an **int** (or vice versa). Casts do not affect the value stored in a variable.

EXERCISES

1. *Define:* **a.** floating-point variable; **b.** double variable; **c.** precision; **d.** round-off error; **e.** mixed arithmetic; **f.** scientific notation; **g.** e-notation; **h.** mixed assignment; **i.** typecast; **j.** cast.

2. *Errors.* Create a copy of **bubble.c** called **errors31.c** and introduce into the new file the first error listed below. Run your compiler on the file. If the compiler catches the error, write down both the error and the error message; if not, run the executable file with test data and make a note of any unexpected results. Correct the file, then repeat the process with the next error on the list. Continue until you have tried all of the errors.

   a. Change the line

   ```
   area = 2.0 * PI * sphere_radius * height;
   ```

   to

   ```
   2.0 * PI * sphere_radius * height;
   ```

   b. Change the **%lf** to **%d** in the first **scanf()** call.

   c. Change the **%lf** to **%f** in the first **scanf()** call.

   d. Change the **%lf** to **%g** in the first **scanf()** call.

3. *More errors.* Create a copy of **roundpos.c** called **errors32.c**. Follow the instructions given in Exercise 2, but make the following changes in the file:

   a. Remove the parentheses from the **double** cast (i.e., **(double)** becomes **double**).

   b. Change the line

   ```
   rounded = (double)((int)(number/level + 0.5)) * level;
   ```

   to

   ```
   rounded = (int)(number/level + 0.5) * level;
   ```

   c. Change the line

   ```
   rounded = (double)((int)(number/level + 0.5)) * level;
   ```

to

```
rounded = (double)(number/level + 0.5) * level;
```

d. Change the line

```
rounded = (double)((int)(number/level + 0.5)) * level;
```

to

```
rounded = (int)((double)(number/level + 0.5)) * level;
```

4. Suppose **Fahrenheit** and **Celsius** are both **double** variables. In each of the following cases, what value will **Fahrenheit** receive if **Celsius** contains the value 30.0?

a. **Fahrenheit = 9 / 5 * Celsius + 32;**

b. **Fahrenheit = (9 / 5) * Celsius + 32;**

c. **Fahrenheit = 9 * Celsius / 5 + 32;**

d. **Fahrenheit = (9.0 / 5) * Celsius + 32;**

e. **Fahrenheit = 9 / 5 * Celsius + 32.0;**

5. Rewrite the following algebraic expressions into C expressions; treat x, y, and z as **double** variables.

a. $\dfrac{x + 1.0}{x - 3.0}$

b. $\dfrac{x + 1.0}{x} - 3.0$

c. $\dfrac{y/z + \pi}{\pi - z/y}$

d. $\dfrac{(x + y)(x - y)}{y}$

e. $(x + y) + \dfrac{(x - y)}{y} + \dfrac{z}{xy}$

f. $\dfrac{1}{z}\left[\dfrac{x - (x + z)}{x(x + z)}\right]$

6. The following algebraic expressions have been incorrectly translated into C expressions. Correct these C expressions.

a. $4\pi r$ $\Rightarrow$ **4(PI * r)**

b. $\dfrac{ab}{3x + 1}$ $\Rightarrow$ **a * b / (3x + 1)**

c. $\dfrac{num1 + 4.5}{num2 - 9.0}$ $\Rightarrow$ **num1 + 4.5 / num2 - 9.0**

d. $\dfrac{3(x + y)}{y} + \dfrac{(x - y)}{y^2}$ $\Rightarrow$ **3.0 * ((x + y) / y + (x - y) / y * y)**

e. $\dfrac{a^2 b^2}{2ab}$ $\Rightarrow$ **a * a * b * b / 2.0 * a * b**

7. *Output precision.* Our hand calculation of the surface area of a bubble with a height of 2 units and a base radius of 1 unit yielded 15.707963 square units. Indicate the output formats that would print this number as

a. 15.7

b. 15.71

      c. 15.708

      d. 15.7080

8. *The %g format.* Revise your ***bubble.c*** program so that it uses the %g output format.

9. *More **bubble.c**.* The original ***bubble.c*** assumed that the walls of a bubble had zero thickness. Modify ***bubble.c*** so that, for given outer dimensions (height and base radius), wall thickness, and density of the bubble material, it computes the following:

   - Enclosed volume
   - Inner sphere radius
   - Outer sphere radius
   - Volume of material needed to make the finished bubble
   - Weight of the finished bubble

   Here are some density data that you may find useful in testing your program:

Acrylic polymer	1200 kg/m^3
Glass	2500 kg/m^3
Aluminum	2700 kg/m^3
Steel	7800 kg/m^3

10. *Floats and **prlimits.c**.* On many systems, a variable of type **float** offers less precision than a variable of type **double**, although the ANSI standard does not require this. Investigate the properties of the **float** data type on your system. Modify ***prlimits.c*** so that it also prints the values of FLT_MAX, FLT_MIN, and FLT_DIG, all of which are defined in ***float.h***.

11. *Long doubles and **prlimits.c**.* The ANSI standard introduced a new floating-point data type called **long double**, which on some systems offers more precision than the **double**. Modify ***prlimits.c*** so that it also prints the values of LDBL_MAX, LDBL_MIN, and LDBL_DIG, which are defined in ***float.h***.

12. *Rounding negative numbers.* Write a program named ***roundneg.c*** that rounds any negative **double** number to a level specified by the user.

13. *Celsius to Fahrenheit.* Write an interactive program that converts Celsius temperature to Fahrenheit temperature.

14. *Fahrenheit to Celsius.* Write an interactive program that converts Fahrenheit temperature to Celsius temperature.

15. *Change due.* The Rubric Retail Software Company wants a program that will compute the change due on a cash sale. The program should take as inputs the balance due and the amount tendered, and print out the change due in dollars and cents.

16. *Automated change due.* The Rubric Retail Software Company wants a program that will compute the change due on a cash sale and send a signal to an

automated changer to make change. Modify the program from the previous exercise so that it will also print the number and types of bills and coins that should be returned to the customer. For example, if the change due is $11.88, the program should print this amount, and also print that the customer should be given one $10 bill, one $1 bill, three quarters, one dime, and three pennies. Assume that the changer can give change in the following denominations:

bills—$20, $10, $5, $1

coins—quarters, dimes, nickels, pennies

17. *Seed value.* The owners of the Tenderfoot Turf Company want a program that will help them determine the relative value of grass seed from different suppliers. Because quality and price vary from year to year, they would like the program to be as general as possible. When considering value, they are most interested in four factors:

- *Purity*—percentage of total weight that is pure premium grass seed
- *Germination rate*—percentage of the pure grass seed that will actually germinate
- *Coverage*—weight of pure germinating seed required per unit area
- *Price*—price per unit weight of seed

Write a program that will calculate the weight and price of purchased grass seed that will be required to cover a given area. Then determine which of the following lots of seed is the best value:

Lot	Purity	Germination	Coverage	Price
1	70%	80%	450 lb/ft^2	$1.75 per lb
2	85%	85%	500 lb/ft^2	$2.20 per lb
3	90%	90%	425 lb/ft^2	$2.50 per lb

18. *ACT to SAT.* Colleges and universities in the United States usually require that applicants take either the Scholastic Aptitude Test (SAT) or the American College Test (ACT). Most schools specify which test they prefer, and some will convert an applicant's score from one test to the other. The following two equations have been used in the Department of Freshman Engineering at Purdue University to convert ACT scores to SAT scores:

```
SAT(math) = 12.118 + 22.096(ACT math)
```

```
SAT(verbal) = -22.367 + 20.763(ACT English)
```

When using these equations, the results are to be rounded to the nearest multiple of ten. Write a program to convert ACT scores to SAT scores. When choosing input to test your program, keep in mind that ACT scores are integers that range from 1 to 36. Your results should be integer multiples of 10 that range from 200 to 800.

19. *Thermal expansion of a rod.* The expansion of a homogeneous rod due to a change in temperature is given by

$$\Delta L = \alpha L \, \Delta T$$

where α is a coefficient of thermal expansion, ΔT is the change in temperature, and L is the original length of the rod. Write a program that will calculate ΔL using this equation.

a. For a given ΔT and L, calculate the expansion ΔL of a steel rod and a concrete rod. Assume that $\alpha = 11.7 \times 10^{-6}$ per °C for steel and $\alpha = 9.99 \times 10^{-6}$ per °C for concrete. What is the difference in expansion for the two materials?

b. A steel bridge in West Virginia is 518 m long when the outside temperature is 5°C. Assuming that the equation above describes the thermal expansion of the bridge, how much will its length change from winter to summer (with temperature extremes of -20°C and 35°C)? Assume that $\alpha = 11.3 \times 10^{-6}$ per °C for the bridge.

20. *Stress.* The stress σ on an object is defined by

$$\sigma = \frac{F}{A}$$

where F is the force applied to the object and A is the area over which the force is applied. Write a program that will calculate the stress given the force and the area. To test your program, try the following data:

Situation	Force	Area
High heel of a shoe hitting the pavement	140 lb	1/16 in²
Steel cable supporting a bridge	700,000 lb	28.27 in²
Wrist of person holding a bag by the handle	500 N	3.14 in²
Ice skates gliding on ice	800 N	6 cm²
Sneakers on a sidewalk	800 N	120 cm²
Waterbed on a floor	1.18×10^{4} N	4 m²

21. *Strain.* Strain is a measure of how much a material deforms. The strain ϵ that a thin rod undergoes when it is stretched or compressed along its length is computed by

$$\epsilon = \frac{\Delta x}{x_0}$$

where Δx is the change in length of the rod (final length $-$ original length) and x_0 is the original length of the rod. Write a program that will calculate the strain of an object, given its initial length and final length. Test your program with the following data:

Material	Length Original	Final
Steel rod in a concrete beam	200.0 in.	200.267 in.
Rubber band being stretched	4.0 in.	6.0 in.
Concrete column in a building	120.0 in.	119.9 in.
Nylon rope used in spelunking	20 m	20.01 m
Breadstick being stretched	25 cm	26.4 cm

22. *Young's modulus.* An elastic material is one for which stress is linearly proportional to strain. (See the previous two exercises for discussions of stress and strain.) For such a material, stress and strain are related by

$$E = \frac{\sigma}{\epsilon}$$

where E is Young's modulus, σ is stress, and ϵ is strain for a given material. You can think of E as the material's resistance to deformation.

Write a program that will calculate E for any material, given σ and ϵ. Note that E has the same units as stress. Thus, if σ is measured in MPa, E will be in MPa; if σ is measured in psi, E will be in psi. The following table lists σ and ϵ for four different materials. Note that stress is given in both psi and MPa. For each material, first run your program with values of σ given in MPa, then run it with σ in psi.

Material	σ (MPa)	σ (psi)	ϵ
Aluminum	20.0	3000	2.83×10^{-4}
Concrete	15.5	2250	4.50×10^{-4}
Steel	165.0	2400	8.28×10^{-4}
Wood	15.5	2250	1.28×10^{-3}

23. *Passing efficiency rating.* Quarterbacks in the National Football League (NFL) are rated according to a formula that takes into account passes attempted (Att), passes completed (Cmp), total yards gained passing (Yds), passes caught for touchdowns (TD), and passes intercepted by opponents (Int). The formula is

$$\text{Rating} = \frac{100}{6} \left[\frac{\text{Cmp\%} - 30}{20} + \frac{\text{AvgYds} - 3}{4} + \frac{\text{TD\%}}{5} + \frac{9.5 - \text{Int\%}}{4} \right]$$

Cmp% = Pass-completion percentage = (Cmp / Att) $\times$ 100%
AvgYds = Average yards gained per attempt = Yds / Att
TD% = Percentage of passes caught for touchdowns = (TD / Att) $\times$ 100%
Int% = Percentage of passes intercepted = (Int / Att) $\times$ 100%

For example, here are some results from the 1992–1993 NFL Season:

Player	Att	Cmp	Yds	Td	Int	Rating
Steve Young	402	268	3465	25	7	107.0
Troy Aikman	473	302	3445	23	14	89.5
Dan Marino	554	330	4116	24	16	85.1
Jim Harbaugh	358	202	2486	13	12	76.2
Jeff George	306	167	1963	7	15	61.5
Stan Gelbaugh	255	121	1307	6	11	52.9

Write a program that takes passing data and computes the passer's efficiency rating. Note that Att, Cmp, Yds, TD, and Int are all integer quantities, but that the final rating is a floating-point value.

24. *Home insulation.* The rate at which heat can be transferred by conduction from the inside of a home to the outside (or vice versa) through a wall is described by

$$H = A\left(\frac{T_2 - T_1}{L/k}\right)$$

where H is the heat transfer rate (Btu/hr), A is the surface area (ft²), L is the thickness (ft), and k is the thermal conductivity of the wall (a material-dependent constant that determines how readily the material will conduct heat) and T_1 and T_2 are the temperatures (°F) on either side of the wall.

a. What will be the heat transfer rate if $T_1 = T_2$?

b. The term L/k is the R value. (Most packages of insulation have the R value stamped on them.) Compute, by hand, the R value of the following materials. Note that thickness (in inches) must be converted to feet to make the units consistent:

Material	Thickness (in.)	k (BTU/(hr · ft · °F)
Hardwood siding	1.0	0.092
Concrete block	6.0	0.260
Styrofoam	1.0	0.017
Fiberglass batting	3.5	0.027
Fiberglass batting	6.0	0.027
Drywall	0.5	0.093

c. Write a program that will determine the heat transfer rate across a wall, and print the values of H and L/k (the R value).

d. To insulate a home, we want the heat transfer rate across the outside walls to be low. Which of the materials listed in the table would be the best insulator?

25. *Roadkill.* Imagine that you are driving down a road at a constant speed v when you spot an opossum crossing the road ahead of you. The opossum freezes in its tracks, and you slam on the brakes. Will you be able to stop before hitting the animal?

It takes the average driver about 0.7 seconds to apply the brakes after seeing the need to stop; this is called the driver's *reaction time*. Once the brakes are applied, the car decelerates. Assuming a constant deceleration a, the braking distance x is given by

$$x = \frac{v^2}{2a}$$

The deceleration is given by

$$a = \mu g$$

where g is the acceleration due to gravity (9.8 m/s^2) and μ is the coefficient of friction between the car's tires and the road.

Write a program to calculate the distance that your car will travel from the moment you see the opossum on the road to the moment your car comes to a complete stop. Assume that your reaction time is 0.7 seconds, during which time the car continues moving forward at speed v. To test your program, assume that you spotted the opossum motionless in the road 200 ft (61 m) ahead of you. For each of the test cases listed below, determine whether your car will hit the animal. (*Hint:* Units must be consistent. Have your program convert km/hr to m/s.)

Test Case	Road Conditions	μ	v (km/hr)
1	Wet	0.1	65
2	Wet	0.1	100
3	Dry	0.6	65
4	Dry	0.6	100

26. *Readability formula.* In the early 1940s, Rudolph Flesch (*How to Write Plain English*, Barnes & Noble, 1979) developed a formula for estimating the "readability" of written material based on the average number of words per sentence and the average number of syllables per word:

score = 206.835 − (1.015 (words/sentences) + 84.6 (syllables/words))

The readability score gives an idea of how easy the material is to understand:

Score	Readability	School Level
90 to 100	Very Easy	5th grade
80 to 90	Easy	6th grade
70 to 80	Fairly Easy	7th grade
60 to 70	"Plain English"	8th–9th grade
50 to 60	Fairly Difficult	High school
30 to 50	Difficult	College
less than 30	Very Difficult	College Graduate

For example, the following text from the Internal Revenue Service (Notice 89–67, IRB 1989–24) comprises two sentences, 86 words, and 162 syllables:

> The originality and uniqueness of the item created (or to be created) and the predominance of aesthetic value over utilitarian value of the item created (or to be created) will be considered in determining whether a qualified creative expense is paid or incurred by an artist. Thus, for example, any expense that is paid or incurred in producing jewelry, silverware, pottery, furniture, and other similar household items generally will not be considered as being paid or incurred in the business of an individual being an artist.

Its score would be

$$\text{score} = 206.835 - [1.015 \, (86/2) + 84.6 \, (162/86)] = 3.83$$

which puts this passage in the "Very Difficult" category (along with most other things published by the IRS).

Write a program that prompts for the number of sentences, words, and syllables, then prints the readability score. (*Note:* a contraction or hyphenated word counts as a single word; abbreviations, numbers, symbols, and their combinations count as one-syllable words. Any phrase marked off by a period, colon, semicolon, dash, question mark, or exclamation point counts as a sentence.) **Bonus:** Can you revise the IRS notice so that it qualifies as "Plain English" (readability score 60 to 70)?

27. *Revised readability formula.* Flesch's original readability formula (previous exercise) can be used to estimate the grade level of a particular passage of text. A modified version of Flesch's formula gives the grade level directly:

$$\text{Grade} = 0.39 \, (\text{words/sentences}) + 11.8 \, (\text{syllables/words}) - 15.59$$

(Weiss, *The Writing System for Engineers and Scientists*, Prentice-Hall, 1982). For example, the passage from the IRS given in the previous exercise contains 2 sentences, 86 words, and 162 syllables. Therefore,

$$\text{Grade} = 0.39 \, (86/2) + 11.8 \, (162/86) - 15.59 = 23.4$$

In other words, you would need about 23 years of schooling to readily understand the passage.

Write a program that prompts for the number of sentences, words, and syllables, then prints the grade level. (*Note:* a contraction or hyphenated word counts as a single word; abbreviations, numbers, symbols, and their combinations count as one-syllable words. Any phrase marked off by a period, colon, semicolon, dash, question mark, or exclamation point counts as a sentence.)

4

The Standard Mathematics Library

C has earned a reputation as a fine language for what is called *systems programming*—the writing of operating systems, compilers, text editors, and so on. But C is also well suited for general scientific and engineering applications. It comes equipped with a library of mathematical functions that are useful for such work. Here is a partial listing:

Trigonometric functions: **sin()**, **cos()**, **tan()**

Inverse trig functions: **asin()**, **acos()**, **atan()**

Hyperbolic functions: **sinh()**, **cosh()**, **tanh()**

Logarithmic functions: **log()**, **log10()**

Power functions: **exp()**, **pow()**

Random-number generator: **srand()**, **rand()**

Absolute-value functions: **abs()**, **labs()**, **fabs()**

In this chapter, you will see how to use these functions in your programs.

Function Arguments and Return Values

Let's review for a moment what we know about functions in general. We previously said that a function is a self-contained collection of C statements, grouped

together to perform some task. Every program must include one function named
main(), which can call other functions such as **printf()** and **scanf()**. Here, for example, is a **printf()** function call:

```
printf("%f", x);
```

The items appearing inside the parentheses are called the arguments of the function. Each argument provides information for the function to work on. The first
argument (**"%f"**) is a string that controls the format of the output; the second
argument (**x**) is a variable that provides the value to be printed on the standard
output.

The standard math functions work similarly. For instance, here is how the **log()**
function might be called by **main()**:

```
y = log(x);
```

The argument **x** provides a value for **log()** to work on. However, instead of printing this value on the standard output, **log()** computes its logarithm. The result of
this computation is then sent back to **main()**—in C terminology, we would say that
the function *returns* the logarithm of **x** to **main()**—where it is assigned to the variable **y**. Most of the standard mathematical functions take **double** arguments and
return **double** results; others work on **int** or **long** values.

Program: *trylogs.c*

Let's begin with a program to compute the natural (base-*e*) logarithm and the common (base-10) logarithm of a number entered at the keyboard. Here is the
pseudocode outline for the program:

prompt the user for a positive number
read a number
compute the common log
print the answer
compute and print the natural log

The C code for this program is shown in Listing 4–1.

Listing 4–1. *trylogs.c*

```
/*******************************************
    Compute natural and common logarithms.
*******************************************/

#include <stdio.h>
#include <math.h>

main()
{
    double argument;    /* Argument entered by the user */
    double result;

    printf("Please enter a positive number: ");
    scanf("%lf", &argument);

    result = log10(argument);
    printf("The common log = %.8g\n", result);

    printf("The natural log = %.8g\n", log(argument));
}
```

① ② ③ ④ (margin markers)

Dissection of *trylogs.c*

① `#include <math.h>`

The standard header file *math.h* contains important information about many of the standard mathematical library functions and should be included every time you want to use one of these functions.

② `result = log10(argument);`

The value stored in **argument** is passed to the **log10()** function. The function computes the common logarithm of this value and returns the result to **main()**, where it is assigned to the variable **result**. The value in **argument** is not changed by the function call, so we can use it again later in the program.

③ `printf("The common log = %.8g\n", result);`

This statement prints the value of **result** with a maximum precision of eight digits (**%.8g**).

④ `printf("The natural log = %.8g\n", log(argument));`

We have chosen not to assign the return value from **log()** to a variable. Instead, the answer is passed directly to **printf()**, to be printed with a maximum precision of eight digits.

Compiling and Testing *trylogs.c*

Compile the *trylogs.c* program the usual way. On some systems this will work as expected, creating an executable file. On other systems this will produce an error message like this:

```
ld: Undefined symbol
_log10
_log
```

This message means you need to tell the linker to get the math library code and combine it with your program. On many systems, this is done with the **–lm** option. For instance, if you were using the *gcc* compiler, you would type the command

```
gcc trylogs.c -lm
```

Note the position of the **–lm** option at the end of the command line. This option is a command for the linker, not the compiler. (If this option does not work for you, refer to your system manual.)

Run a number of test cases to check the performance of your program:

Input	Common Log	Natural Log
0.1	−1	−2.3025851
0.5	−0.30103	−0.69314718
1.0	0	0
5.0	0.69897	1.6094379
10.0	1	2.3025851
50.0	1.69897	3.912023
148.41316	2.1714724	5
555.0	2.744293	6.3189681
1000.0	3	6.9077553

Range and Domain Errors

Thus far you have entered only positive numbers in the *trylogs.c* program. Now consider what happens if you enter zero or a negative number. Figure 4–1 shows

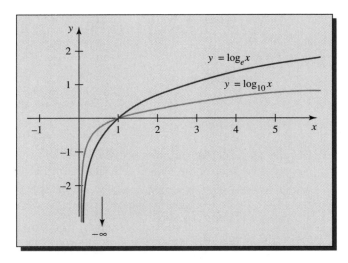

Figure 4–1 The natural and common logarithm functions. Note that both functions approach $-\infty$ as x approaches zero, and are undefined for values of x less than zero.

a graph of the natural and common logarithm functions. Both curves cross the x-axis at $x = 1$ and continue down toward $-\infty$ for values of x approaching zero.

What does this mean for your ***trylogs.c*** program? The computer cannot represent $-\infty$ as a **double** value. Any time you try to compute a number that would not fit in a **double** variable, you get what is called a *range error*.

Find out how your ***trylogs.c*** program handles range errors. Run the program and enter a zero at the prompt:

```
Please enter a positive number: 0 RET
```

With some older versions of C, this would cause the program to "crash." However, the C standard now requires that range errors be handled more gracefully. The function is supposed to return the largest negative **double** it can handle:

```
log10: RANGE ERROR
The common log = -1.79769e+308
Log: RANGE ERROR
The natural log = -1.79769e+308
```

On some systems, you might see something like this:

```
log10: RANGE ERROR
The common log = -infinity
Log: RANGE ERROR
The natural log = -infinity
```

What about negative input values? Referring again to Figure 4–1, you will note that the logarithm is not defined for negative arguments. Thus, for example, `log(-10.0)` is meaningless. A *domain error* results when a function is given an illegal argument.

Let's see how your ***trylogs.c*** program handles domain errors. Run the program and enter −10:

`Please enter a positive number: -10` `RET`

The C standard does not say what value the function should return in the case of a domain error. You might see something like this:

```
log10: DOMAIN error
The common log = 0
log: DOMAIN error
The natural log = 0
```

Or perhaps you will see NaN ("not a number"), another way of saying that the result is undefined:

```
log10: DOMAIN error
The common log = NaN
log: DOMAIN error
The natural log = NaN
```

Function Prototypes

The standard math library includes more than two dozen functions, most of which are listed in Appendix B. If you look in the appendix under the heading "Logarithmic Functions," you will find this table:

Prototype	Description
`double log(double x);`	natural (base-*e*) log of x, $x > 0$
`double log10(double x);`	common (base-10) log of x, $x > 0$

Examine the left column. A *function prototype* (also called a *function declaration*) tells you essential information about the function. Consider, for example, the prototype for the **log()** function:

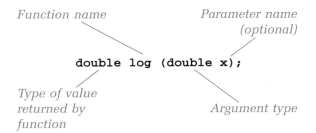

Reading from left to right, the prototype shows (1) the function returns a result of type **double**; (2) the function's name is **log()**; and (3) the function works on one argument of type **double**.

As used here, **x** is a *parameter* (or *formal argument*). This does not mean that you must always use an argument named **x** with this function—the parameter **x** serves only as a placeholder in the prototype. When calling the function, you replace **double x** by the actual argument, which must be a **double** value:

```
result = log(argument);
```

Occasionally a beginning programmer will try to make the function call match the prototype by including the keyword **double** before the function name and argument:

```
result = double log(double argument);          /* Wrong! */
```

This will produce a compiler error.

The *math.h* Header File

You will recall that the standard header file ***math.h*** was included in ***trylogs.c***:

```
#include <math.h>
```

It is important to understand that ***math.h*** *does not contain the math functions themselves*. (The linker still has to get the functions from the standard library when you compile the code.) Nevertheless, you should include ***math.h*** whenever you want to use any of the math functions. Why?

The ***math.h*** file contains the prototypes for all of the standard mathematics functions that take **double** arguments and return **double** results. Without these prototypes, your program will probably not work properly.

The Standard Trigonometric Functions

The C library is equipped with the trigonometric functions **sin()**, **cos()**, and **tan()**. Here are the prototypes and descriptions of these functions, taken from Appendix B:

Prototype	Description
`double sin(double x);`	sine of **x**
`double cos(double x);`	cosine of **x**
`double tan(double x);`	tangent of **x**

Note that the argument **x** *must be expressed in radians.* Thus, if you are working with arguments expressed in degrees, you must convert these to radians using the identity

$$360° = 2\pi \text{ radians}$$

No domain errors are possible with these functions, but a range error occurs if the tangent function is given an argument that is close to an odd multiple of $\pi/2$.

The C library contains four inverse trigonometric functions. Here are their prototypes and descriptions, taken from Appendix B:

Prototype	Description
`double asin(double x);`	arc sine of **x**, $-1 \leq$ **x** ≤ 1
`double acos(double x);`	arc cosine of **x**, $-1 \leq$ **x** ≤ 1
`double atan(double x);`	arc tangent of **x**
`double atan2(double y, double x);`	arc tangent of **y**/**x**

These functions return the principal values of the inverse trigonometric functions, expressed in radians. The ranges of these functions are

$$-\pi/2 \leq \textbf{asin()} \leq \pi/2$$
$$0 \leq \textbf{acos()} \leq \pi$$
$$-\pi/2 \leq \textbf{atan()} \leq \pi/2$$
$$-\pi \leq \textbf{atan2()} \leq \pi$$

A *domain error* occurs with **asin()** or **acos()** if the argument **x** is less than -1 or greater than 1. A *domain error* occurs with **atan2()** if both **x** and **y** are zero.

Program: *asa.c*

Our next program will compute the area of a triangle given two angles β and γ and the length of the side a that lies between those angles (often referred to as the angle-side-angle, or ASA solution). The area is given by

$$A = \frac{a^2 \sin \gamma \sin \beta}{2 \sin \alpha}$$

The unknown angle α can be found from the fact that the angles of a plane triangle must sum to 180 degrees:

$$\alpha = 180° - (\gamma + \beta)$$

Of course, this assumes that the angles are measured in degrees; for angles in radians, we have

$$\alpha = \pi - (\gamma + \beta)$$

Following our usual practice, we will compute an example by hand. What is the area of a triangle for which $\beta = 16.7°$, $\gamma = 47.6°$, and $a = 5.2$ meters? First we convert the known angles to radians:

$$\beta = (16.7°)\left(\frac{2\pi}{360°}\right) = (16.7°)\left(\frac{\pi}{180°}\right) = 0.29147$$

$$\gamma = (47.6°)(\frac{\pi}{180°}) = 0.83078$$

Next we compute the unknown angle α:

$$\alpha = \pi - (\gamma + \beta) = \pi - (0.29147 + 0.83078) = 2.01934$$

Last, we compute the area:

$$A = \frac{(5.2 \text{ m})^2 \sin (0.83078) \sin (0.29147)}{2 \sin (2.01934)} = 3.18 \text{ m}^2$$

Our program will follow the same steps. Here is the pseudocode:

prompt for β, γ, and a
read β, γ, and a
convert β and γ to radian measure
compute third angle α
compute area
print results

The C code that carries out this program is shown in Listing 4–2.

Listing 4–2. *asa.c*

```
/***********************************************************

    Compute area of a triangle given two angles (in degrees)
    and the length of the side that lies between them (ASA).

 ***********************************************************/

#include <stdio.h>
#include <math.h>
#define PI 3.141592653589793

main()
{
    double beta, gamma;        /* Known angles (entered in degrees) */
    double alpha;              /* Computed angle (in radians) */
    double a;                  /* Length of known side */
    double area;               /* Area of the triangle */

    printf("Compute area of a triangle given two angles "
           "and the side between them.\n");

    printf("Please enter the first angle (in degrees): ");
    scanf("%lf", &beta);

    printf("Please enter the second angle (in degrees): ");
    scanf("%lf", &gamma);

    printf("Please enter the length of the known side: ");
    scanf("%lf", &a);

    beta = beta * PI / 180.0;
    gamma = gamma * PI / 180.0;
    alpha = PI - (beta + gamma);
    area = a * a * sin(gamma) * sin(beta) / (2.0 * sin(alpha));

    printf("The area of the triangle is %g\n\n", area);
}
```

Dissection of *asa.c*

① `double beta, gamma;        /* Known angles (entered in degrees) */`

Greek letters are often used in mathematics for variable names. The C compiler does not recognize Greek letters; instead, we spell out the names of the letters.

② `area = a * a * sin(gamma) * sin(beta) / (2.0 * sin(alpha));`

Notice that there are three **sin()** function calls in this statement.

Compiling and Testing *asa.c*

Compile the ***asa.c*** program the usual way. Run the program on the data we used in the hand calculation: $\beta = 16.7°$, $\gamma = 47.6°$, and $a = 5.2$ meters. You should also test it on a few more cases:

β	γ	a	Area
10.0	80.0	45.0	173.148
90.0	0.0	12.4	0
30.0	60.0	22.5	109.606
22.5	44.3	10.0	14.5393

Exponents and Roots

Next we consider three important mathematical functions:

e^x raise e to the x power ($e = 2.718281828\ldots$)
y^x raise y to the x power
$\sqrt{x}$ take the (nonnegative) square root of x

Because the C compiler does not recognize superscripts or the radical symbol ($\sqrt{\ }$), these functions must be written differently in C:

e^x becomes `exp(x)`
y^x becomes `pow(y, x)`
$\sqrt{x}$ becomes `sqrt(x)`

Here are the prototypes and descriptions of **exp()**, **pow()**, and **sqrt()**, taken from Appendix B:

Prototype	Description
`double sqrt(double x);`	square root of x, $x \geq 0$
`double exp(double x);`	exponential function, e^x
`double pow(double x, double y);`	raise x to the yth power, x^y

Refer to the appendix for conditions that cause domain and range errors for these functions.

Program: *stirling.c*

How many different five-card hands can be drawn from a 52-card deck? In general, the number of possible combinations of n objects taken r at a time is given by

$$C(n, r) = \frac{n!}{r!(n - r)!}$$

The notation $n!$ stands for the *factorial of n*, defined as the integer product

$$n! = (1)(2)(3) \ldots (n - 1)(n)$$

The values of the factorial for $n = 0$ to $n = 19$ are shown below. Note that $0! = 1$ by definition:

n	$n!$	n	$n!$
0	1 (by definition)	10	3,628,800
1	1	11	39,916,800
2	2	12	479,001,600
3	6	13	6,227,020,800
4	24	14	87,178,291,200
5	120	15	1,307,674,368,000
6	720	16	20,922,789,888,000
7	5,040	17	355,687,428,096,000
8	40,320	18	6,402,373,705,728,000
9	362,880	19	121,645,100,408,832,000

The standard C library does not have a function that computes the factorial; you will see how to write such a function in a later chapter. For now, let's use the **pow()**, **exp()**, and **sqrt()** functions to *approximate* the factorial as a **double** value. We will use Stirling's formula, which closely approximates the factorial for large values of n:

$$n! \approx n^n e^{-n} \sqrt{2\pi n} \qquad \text{(large } n\text{)}$$

Let's see how well Stirling's approximation works to determine the number of five-card hands. In this case, $n = 52$ and $r = 5$. Hence,

$$C(n,\ r) = C(52,5) = \frac{52!}{5!(52-5)!} = \frac{52!}{5!(47)!}$$

Applying the approximation, we have

$$52! \approx 52^{52}e^{-52}\sqrt{(2\pi)52} = 8.0529 \times 10^{67}$$

$$5! \approx 5^{5}e^{-5}\sqrt{(2\pi)5} = 118.02$$

$$47! \approx 47^{47}e^{-47}\sqrt{(2\pi)47} = 2.5817 \times 10^{59}$$

$$\Rightarrow \frac{52!}{5!(47!)} \approx 2643031.4$$

Note that Stirling's approximation produces a floating-point value, whereas the actual factorial is an integer.

As a check, we can compute the exact value:

$$\frac{52!}{5!(47!)} = \frac{(52)(51)(50)(49)(48)47!}{(5!)47!} = \frac{(52)(51)(50)(49)(48)}{(5)(4)(3)(2)(1)} = 2598960$$

In this example, the use of the approximation results in an answer that is only 1.7% higher than the exact value.

The pseudocode for the ***stirling.c*** program is especially simple:

prompt for a positive integer n
read n from the standard input
compute $n^{n}e^{-n}\sqrt{2\pi n}$
print the result

The C code for this program is given in Listing 4–3.

Listing 4–3. *stirling.c*

```
/**********************************************************

    Approximate the factorial using Stirling's formula

**********************************************************/

#include <stdio.h>
#include <math.h>
#define PI 3.141592653589793

main()
{
    double factorial;
    int n;

    printf("This program approximates the factorial.\n");
    printf("Please enter a positive integer: ");
    scanf("%d", &n);

    factorial = pow((double)n, (double)n) * exp((double)(-n))
                * sqrt(2.0 * PI * (double)n);

    printf("%g\n", factorial);
}
```
(1)

Dissection of *stirling.c*

(1)
```
factorial = pow((double)n, (double)n) * exp((double)(-n))
            * sqrt(2.0 * PI * (double)n);
```

This is how we write Stirling's formula. We use the cast operator **(double)** to emphasize that the library functions **pow()**, **exp()** and **sqrt()** all take **double** arguments. (We leave it as an exercise for you to see what happens—if anything—when the casts are omitted.)

Compiling and Testing *stirling.c*

Compile *stirling.c*, making sure to link the math library to your object code. Then run your program on some test cases. How well does the approximation seem to work? Your program will not compute the factorial of zero. Can you explain why?

Integer Functions and the *stdlib.h* Header File

All of the standard math functions that we have seen thus far take **double** arguments and return **double** results. The standard math library also includes a few functions that work on integers. For instance, C has three absolute-value functions. Here are their prototypes and descriptions, as found in Appendix B:

Prototype	Description
int abs(int n);	absolute value of **n**, |n|
long labs(long n);	absolute value of **n**, |n|
double fabs(double x);	absolute value of **x**, |x|

When computing the absolute value, it is important that you choose the right function: **abs()** works on **int** values, **labs()** works on **long** values, and **fabs()** works on floating-point values (i.e., **doubles**).

The **fabs()** function is declared in *math.h* along with the other **double** functions. In contrast, the prototypes for integer functions such as **abs()** and **labs()** are contained in the *stdlib.h* file:

```
#include <stdlib.h>
```

You should include the proper file whenever you want to use one of these library functions.

Random Numbers

The *stdlib.h* file also contains the prototype for a useful integer function named **rand()**. Although **rand()** is often called a "random-number generator," this terminology is not quite accurate. What **rand()** does is generate sequences of integers that can be made to *appear* random. Such sequences are more properly said to be *pseudo-random* or *quasi-random*. Here are the prototype and description of **rand()**:

Prototype	Description
int rand(void);	pseudo-random **int** in the range 0 to **RAND_MAX**

First note the keyword **void** in the function prototype. This indicates that **rand()**, unlike the other functions we have examined in this chapter, takes no arguments.

Also note that the integers returned by **rand()** can range from zero to **RAND_MAX**. The value of **RAND_MAX** will vary from system to system, but it is required by the C standard to be 32767 or larger. (We leave it as an exercise for you to discover the value of **RAND_MAX** used on your system.)

The number sequence produced by **rand()** is governed by an integer starting value called a *seed*. You should keep in mind that **rand()** does not generate truly random numbers; in fact,

If given the same seed, rand() always generates the same sequence of numbers.

The default value of the seed used by **rand()** is 1, but this can be changed using the **srand()** function. To select a seed value of 4573, for example, you would use the function call

```
srand(4573);
```

In this case, the function **srand()** delivers the seed 4573 to **rand()**. After that is done, each call to **rand()** produces the next number in a pseudo-random sequence of integers.

The trick, of course, is to select a good seed. Our next program will simply ask the user to choose a value. That is not especially elegant, but it will serve to illustrate how the random-number generator works.

Program: *dice.c*

Many popular board games use two or more dice. Let's write a program that simulates the roll of three dice using the **rand()** function. For this we need a method of generating random integers in the range 1 through 6 to simulate the roll of a die. You should verify that the expression

```
1 + rand() % 6
```

will provide a value in the right range. This is the approach we will use. (Be warned, however, because some **rand()** functions are not sufficiently random, this method may not be satisfactory for all applications.)

The pseudocode outline for this program is as follows:

prompt the user for a seed value
read the seed
call **srand(***seed***)**
first die: 1 + **rand()** *% 6*
second die: 1 + **rand()** *% 6*
third die: 1 + **rand()** *% 6*
print results

The C code for this program is given in Listing 4–4.

Listing 4–4. *dice.c*

```
/*********************************************************

   Simulate the roll of three dice

*********************************************************/

#include <stdio.h>
#include <stdlib.h>

main()
{
   int seed;
   int die1, die2, die3;

   printf("This program simulates the roll of three dice.\n");
   printf("Please enter a seed value: ");
   scanf("%d", &seed);

   srand(seed);

   die1 = 1 + rand() % 6;
   die2 = 1 + rand() % 6;
   die3 = 1 + rand() % 6;

   printf("%d %d %d\n", die1, die2, die3);
}
```

Dissection of *dice.c*

① **#include <stdlib.h>**

The prototypes for **rand()** and **srand()** are contained in ***stdlib.h,*** along with the prototypes for other library functions that take and/or return integer values.

② **srand(seed);**

```
die1 = 1 + rand() % 6;
die2 = 1 + rand() % 6;
die3 = 1 + rand() % 6;
```

Note that we call **srand()** just once in this program. Some beginning programmers are tempted to call **srand()** before each call to **rand()**, thinking perhaps that this will produce a "more random" sequence of numbers. Usually, however, it is only necessary to seed the random-number generator once at the start of the program.

Compiling and Testing *dice.c*

Compile *dice.c* the usual way and run the executable file. Enter the value 10 at the prompt:

```
This program simulates the roll of three dice.
Please enter a seed value: 10 RET
```

Your program should print three integer values, each between 1 and 6, something like this:

```
6 5 2
```

(The values produced on your system may be different.) Run the program again with the same seed value. You should see the same output as before:

```
This program simulates the roll of three dice.
Please enter a seed value: 10 RET
6 5 2
```

(Again, the values produced by your system may be different.) Why does the program print the same three values? Recall what we said before:

> *If given the same seed,* rand() *always generates the same sequence of numbers.*

Test your program with a few other seed values.

Rather than ask the user for a seed value, it would better if the program were to choose its own seed. Seeds for **rand()** are often derived from the time kept by the computer's internal clock. We leave it as an exercise for you to do this (Exercise 9).

HELPFUL HINTS

- Whenever you use an unfamiliar math function, be sure that you know the function's name, return type, and the number and types of arguments it takes, as well as the conditions that create range and domain errors. Refer to Appendix B for this information.

- Do not omit *stdio.h* from your programs when including *math.h* or *stdlib.h*. This is a common error made by beginners.
- When squaring or cubing numbers, we suggest that you simply multiply the number by itself the proper number of times, rather than use the **pow()** function. For example, compute a^2 as **a * a**. This is usually more efficient than **pow(a, 2.0)**.

SUMMARY

Preprocessor Directives

#include <math.h>   Instructs the preprocessor to include the file *math.h*, which contains prototypes for many mathematical functions that work on **double**s.

#include <stdlib.h>   As above, but *stdlib.h* contains prototypes for many math functions that work on **int** values.

Function Prototype

double log(double x);   Declares **log()** to be a function that takes a **double** value (**x**) and returns a **double** result.

Function Call

y = log(z);   Calls the library function **log()** to compute the natural logarithm of **z** and store the result in **y**.

- The standard C library contains mathematical functions that are useful to scientists and engineers. Appendix B lists many of these functions, showing the number and type of arguments that each function takes, as well as the type of result that each function returns.
- The standard header files do not contain the functions, but only the function prototypes. To use a standard math function, the linker has to get the appropriate code from the math library.
- A range error occurs when a math function attempts to compute a value that cannot be represented as a **double**. Taking the log of zero, for example, will produce a range error. The function will return the largest **double** value it can handle.
- A domain error occurs when a math function receives an illegal argument. Taking the log of a negative number, for example, produces a domain error. On some systems, the function will return NaN ("Not a number").
- All trigonometric functions work on angles expressed in radians; angles measured in degrees must be converted to radians before those functions are called.

- The pseudo-random-number generator **rand()** is declared in **_stdlib.h_**. The sequence of integers generated by **rand()** depends on a "seed" value; for a given seed, **rand()** always produces the same sequence. The seed can be changed by the **srand()** function.

EXERCISES

1. *Define:* **a.** range error; **b.** domain error; **c.** NaN; **d.** function prototype; **e.** function declaration; **f.** parameter; **g.** formal argument.

2. *Errors.* Create a copy of **_stirling.c_** called **_errors4.c_** and introduce into the new file the first error listed below. Run your compiler on the file. If the compiler catches the error, write down both the error and the error message; if not, run the executable file with test data and make a note of any unexpected results. Correct the file, then repeat the process with the next error on the list. Continue until you have tried all of the errors.

   a. Remove all of the casts from the program.

   b. Remove #include <math.h> from the program.

   c. Remove #include <stdio.h> from the program.

3. Rewrite the following algebraic expressions as C expressions. Use math library functions, when needed.

   a. $\tan[\cos^{-1}(\theta)]$

   b. $w\,|x + y|^{-1} + z$

   c. $\sin^2(\frac{x}{\pi} + y)$

   d. $(e^{\theta + \phi})[\tan(\theta + \phi)] + x^2$

4. The following algebraic expressions have been incorrectly translated into C expressions. Correct these C expressions. Assume that **a, b, c, d, x**, and **phi** are **double** variables.

   a. a^3 $\Rightarrow$ `pow(a, 3)`

   b. $\dfrac{|ab|}{3x + 1}$ $\Rightarrow$ `abs(a * b) / (3 * x + 1)`

   c. $a^b c^d$ $\Rightarrow$ `pow(a * c, b * d)`

   d. $a^{b + 1}$ $\Rightarrow$ `pow(a, b) + 1`

   e. $\sin^{-1}[|\ln(\phi)|]$ $\Rightarrow$ `asin(log10((fabs)phi))`

5. According to Appendix B, which of the following function calls would produce a range error? Which would produce a domain error?

   a. `sin(3.1415926536)`

   b. `cos(3.1415926536)`

   c. `tan(1.5707963268)`

   d. `exp(6.02e23)`

    e. `asin(-1.5)`

    f. `acos(3.1415926536)`

    g. `atan(6.02e23)`

    h. `sqrt(-2.0)`

    i. `sqrt(3.14159)`

    j. `pow(0.0, -2.0)`

    k. `pow(-2.0, 0.0)`

    l. `pow(-2.0, 2.0)`

    m. `pow(2.0, -2.0)`

    n. `pow(6.02e23, 50000.0)`

6. *Tangent functions.* Referring to Appendix B, what is the difference between the **atan()** and **atan2()** functions? Why would you choose one over the other?

7. Modify *prlimits.c* so that it also prints out the value of **RAND_MAX** used on your system.

8. *Improved Stirling's approximation.* The classical form of Stirling's approximation tends to underestimate the factorial. Here is an improved version:

$$n! \approx n^n e^{-n} \sqrt{2\pi n}\left(1 + \frac{1}{12n}\right)$$

Modify *stirling.c* to employ the revised formula. How well does it approximate the factorial? How does it compare with the value produced by the classical formula?

9. *Seed for pseudo–random-number generator.* The program *dice.c* asks the user to choose a seed value for **rand()**. This is adequate for testing and debugging, but normally it is better to have the computer pick the seed. This is often done using the **time()** function, which returns the current time on the system clock:

```
seed = (int)time(NULL);
```

Note the use of a cast to ensure that the seed will be an integer. (The time is typically encoded as a **long**, but the C standard does not require this.) Note too that **time()** requires **NULL** as an argument. To use **time()** in a program, be sure to include the *time.h* header file:

```
#include <time.h>
```

Modify *dice.c* to pick the seed automatically.

10. *Trigonometric functions, radians.* Write a program that prompts for an angle *in radians*, and prints its sine, cosine, and tangent.

11. *Trigonometric functions, degrees.* Write a program that prompts for an angle *in degrees*, and prints its sine, cosine, and tangent.

12. *Inverse trig functions.* Write a program that computes the arcsine, arccosine, and arctangent of a number entered by the user at the keyboard. The program should print the results both in radians and in degrees, properly labeled.

13. *Square root.* Write a program that computes the square root of a number entered by the user.

14. *Cube root.* Write a program that computes the cube root of a number entered by the user. (*Hint:* Use the **pow()** function.)

15. *Raise a number to a power.* Write a program that prompts the user for a number x and a power y, and raises x to the yth power.

16. *Gaussian distribution.* Experimental data are often found to be distributed according to the so-called "bell-shaped curve," known in statistics as the *Gaussian* or *normal curve*:

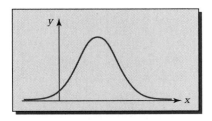

The normal curve has the equation:

$$y = \frac{1}{\sigma \sqrt{2\pi}} \exp\left[-\frac{1}{2}\left(\frac{x - \mu}{\sigma}\right)^2\right]$$

Here, μ is the mean (or average) and σ is the standard deviation of the data. The mean marks the maximum point on the normal curve. (Most of the data cluster around the mean.) The standard deviation is a measure of how much the data scatter about the mean: the larger the standard deviation, the greater the scatter in the data.

Write a program that takes the mean and standard deviation and, for a given x, computes the ordinate y.

17. *Triangle area: three sides known (SSS).* Write a program to compute the area of a triangle given the lengths of the three sides (a, b, and c). The area is given by Heron's formula:

$$A = \sqrt{x(x - a)(x - b)(x - c)} \qquad \text{where } x = \tfrac{1}{2}(a + b + c)$$

18. *Triangle area: two sides and one angle (SAS).* Write a program to compute the area of a triangle given two sides a and b and the included angle γ. (Prompt for the angle in degrees; have the program convert to radians.) The area is given by

$$A = \tfrac{1}{2}ab \sin \gamma$$

19. *Triangle area: two sides and one angle (SSA).* Write a program to compute the area of a triangle given two sides a and b, and the angle β opposite the longer of these two sides. (Assume $b \geq a$.) This requires finding the altitude

h of the triangle. If h is drawn as a perpendicular to side c, thus dividing side c into two parts, c_1 and c_2, then

$$h = a \sin \beta$$

The angle α opposite a (the shorter of the two known sides) can be found from

$$\sin \alpha = \frac{a}{b} \sin \beta$$

The length of the unknown side c is the sum of c_1 and c_2, which are given by

$$c_1 = a \cos \beta \quad \text{and} \quad c_2 = b \cos \alpha$$

Once the lengths of all three sides are known, Heron's formula (Exercise 17) can be used to find the area. Prompt the user to enter the angle in degrees; have the program convert to radians.

20. *Components of force.* Any given force in the x-y plane can be resolved into two components, one parallel to the x-axis (F_x), the other parallel to the y-axis (F_y):

$$F_x = F \cos \alpha \quad \text{and} \quad F_y = F \sin \alpha$$

where α is the angle between F and the x-axis. Write a program that prints F_x and F_y for a given force F and angle α.

21. *Antoine Equation.* Write a program that computes the vapor pressure of water as a function of temperature. The *vapor pressure* of a liquid or solid is the measure of the volatility of that substance: the higher the vapor pressure, the more likely the substance is to vaporize. The dependence of vapor pressure on temperature is often described by the *Antoine Equation:*

$$\ln p = A - \frac{B}{(T + C)}$$

in which p is the vapor pressure (in kPa), T is the absolute temperature (K), and A, B, and C are constants that depend on the substance. For water, $A = 16.5362$, $B = 3985.44$, and $C = -38.9974$. (Use the **#define** directive to set the values of the constants.)

22. *Compound interest, compounded annually.* If the interest earned on a savings account is compounded annually, it can be computed by the following formula:

$$A = P (1 + i)^t$$

where A is the amount of money in the account at the end of the year, P is the principal (i.e., the original amount invested), i is the annual interest rate, and t is the number of years that the money stays in the account at this interest rate.

Write a program that will calculate the amount of money in a savings account at the end of any given year. The program should work for any principal, interest rate, and number of years.

23. *Compound interest, flexible compounding schedule.* Interest rates can be compounded on any schedule (e.g., monthly, quarterly, annually). The following is a general formula for computing compound interest:

$$A = P\left(1 + \frac{i}{n}\right)^{nt}$$

A, P, i, and t are defined in the previous exercise. The parameter n is the number of times in a year that interest is compounded.

a. Write a program that will calculate the amount of money in a savings account at the end of any given year. The program should work for any principal, interest rate, number of years, and compounding schedule.

b. A student is planning to open a savings account at one of the local banks. After calling several banks, the student compiled a list of interest rates available at the banks:

Bank	Interest	Compounding
1	5.0%	quarterly
2	5.0%	annually
3	5.0%	monthly
4	5.0%	daily

After one year, which account would yield the most money for the student?

c. A second student decided to open a savings account in a neighboring city. After calling several banks, the student compiled a list of interest rates available at the banks:

Bank	Interest	Compounding
A	4.75%	quarterly
B	5.00%	annually
C	4.50%	monthly
D	4.25%	daily

After ten years, which account would yield the most money for the student?

24. *Compound interest, compounded continuously.* If D dollars are invested at a continuously compounded annual interest rate r, the total value of the investment after y years will be

$$V = De^{ry}$$

a. Write a program that will calculate the amount of money in a savings account at the end of any given year. The program should work for any principal, interest rate, and number of years.

b. Run the program using the interest rates listed in part **c** of Exercise 23. After ten years, what will be the total value of the investment from Banks A, B, C, and D, assuming continuous compounding?

25. *Foundation excavation.* The Terra Firma Construction Company specializes in foundation excavation. The company owns several different sizes of hauling trucks. Write a program that will determine, for any size excavation, the following:

    - Volume of material to be removed, given the length, width, and depth of the excavation

    - Number of complete round trips that a truck of a given size must make to haul away all of the material

    Make your program as general as possible so that it works for any size excavation site and any size truck. Be sure that the prompts indicate the units of measure required by the program. (*Hint:* Use the **ceil()** function, as described in Appendix B.)

26. *More foundation excavation.* Write a new program for Terra Firma that adds to the previous problem a calculation of the cost of hauling the excavated material, given

    - Cost per mile to operate the truck
    - Time required to fill a truck of a given size
    - Distance from the excavation site to the dumping site
    - Estimated average speed of a truck
    - Hourly wage for a truck driver

27. *Distance on the earth's surface.* Write a program that takes the latitudes and longitudes of two points on the earth's surface and computes the distance between them in nautical miles, miles, and kilometers. The angular distance Δ between two points is given by

    $$\cos \Delta = (\sin \text{lat}_1)(\sin \text{lat}_2) + (\cos \text{lat}_1)(\cos \text{lat}_2)[\cos(\text{long}_1 - \text{long}_2)]$$

    This formula assumes that both longitudes are measured either east of Greenwich or west of Greenwich. Multiplying the angular distance by the radius of the earth gives the surface distance.

28. *Noise levels.* The loudest sounds that the human ear can tolerate (without pain) are about 10^{12} times more intense than the faintest perceptible sounds. However, the sensation of loudness is approximately logarithmic, so the loudest tolerable sounds are not perceived by humans to be that much louder than the softest sounds. The relationship can be described as

    $$\beta = 10 \, \log_{10}\!\left(\frac{I}{I_0}\right)$$

    where β is the relative loudness of a sound (also called the decibel level), I is the intensity of the sound, and I_0 is the softest detectable sound. For humans, $I_0 = 10^{-12}$ W/m^2 (watts per square meter). Thus, the relative loudness of the softest detectable sound is $\beta = 0$ decibels (dB). A sound with an intensity of 1 W/m² will yield $\beta = 120$ dB. Sounds with intensities greater than this will cause pain in the healthy ear.

Write a program to calculate the decibel level of sounds perceived by someone whose threshold of hearing is 10^{-12} W/m². Use the following test data:

Case	Source of Sound	Intensity (W/m²)
1	Rustling leaves	10^{-11}
2	Normal conversation	10^{-7}
3	Busy traffic	10^{-4}
4	Siren or rock concert	10^{0}
5	Jack hammer	10^{1}

29. *Cooling and heating of objects.* Newton's "law" of cooling states that the temperature of an object will change at a rate proportional to the temperature difference between the object and its surroundings. (This is not really a law of nature, but an approximation to what is often observed.) In situations where this law applies, the object's temperature T at any time t can be estimated by

$$T = T_s + (T_1 - T_s)e^{-kt}$$

where k is a constant given by

$$k = \frac{-\ln\left(\dfrac{T_1 - T_s}{T_2 - T_s}\right)}{(t_1 - t_2)}$$

In these equations, T_1 is the temperature of the object at time t_1, T_2 is the temperature at time t_2, and T_s is the temperature of the surroundings. Thus, given the temperature at two different times, you can predict the temperature at a third time. Write a program that will do this, then answer the following questions:

a. A soft drink is moved from the refrigerator to the kitchen table, where it is exposed to 21°C air. At $t = 0$ minutes, the temperature of the drink is 4°C; at $t = 60$ minutes, its temperature is 10°C. What will be the drink's temperature after 90 minutes? After two hours? After four hours?

b. A casserole is taken from the oven and placed in 16°C room air. At $t = 0$ minutes, the temperature of the casserole is 77°C; at $t = 30$ minutes, its temperature is 55°C. What will be the casserole's temperature after 90 minutes? After two hours? After four hours?

c. A hot coal, initially at 302°C, is dropped into 14°C water. After 30 seconds, the temperature of the coal has fallen to 140°C. What will be the temperature of the coal after one minute? After two minutes?

Chapter

5.

Flow of Control: Selection

The term *flow of control* refers to the order in which program statements are executed. Thus far, we have seen what is called *sequential* flow of control, meaning that the program statements are executed in strict order, one after another, from the top of the program to the bottom. This is rather limiting.

The real power of computers depends on the ability to alter the flow of control. In this chapter we will see how to select between alternatives, doing some operations while skipping others, depending on the situation.

The Simple if Statement

We will begin by discussing the simple **if** selection statement, which has the form

```
if (condition) {
    statement(s)
}
```

If the *condition* is true, the statement(s) between the braces will be executed; otherwise, everything between the braces is skipped. In other words, the **if** statement follows the general rule

> *Do if true.*

The condition in an **if** statement typically involves a comparison of two or more values. To make such comparisons, C has a number of special operators:

<	less than
>	greater than
==	equal to
<=	less than or equal to
>=	greater than or equal to
!=	not equal to

These are called *relational operators* because they are used to test the relationship between two numbers or variables. We will see how to use the **if** statement and several of the relational operators in our first sample program.

Program: *pH.c*

In 1909, a Danish chemist named Soren Sorensen defined a quantity called the pH (for "power of the hydrogen ion"), which is commonly used to measure the acidity or basicity of a solution. The pH is given by

$$pH = -\log_{10}[H^+]$$

in which $[H^+]$ is the concentration of hydrogen ions in moles per liter. Table 5–1 lists the pH of some common solutions. Note that the lower the pH, the more acidic the solution. At 25°C

$$pH < 7.0 \Rightarrow \text{acidic solution}$$

$$pH = 7.0 \Rightarrow \text{neutral solution}$$

$$pH > 7.0 \Rightarrow \text{basic solution}$$

Table 5–1   pH of Various Materials

Material	pH	Material	pH
Lemon juice	2.2–2.4	Urine, human	4.8–8.4
Wine	2.8–3.8	Cow's milk	6.3–6.6
Vinegar	3.0	Saliva, human	6.5–7.5
Tomato juice	4.0	Drinking water	5.5–8.0
Beer	4.0–5.0	Blood, human	7.3–7.5
Cheese	4.8–6.4	Seawater	8.3

Source: W. L. Masterton and C. N. Hurley, *Chemistry: Principles and Reactions,* Saunders, 1993.

A related quantity is the pOH, which is defined by

$$pOH = -\log_{10}[OH^-]$$

in which $[OH^-]$ is the concentration of hydroxide ions, also expressed in moles per liter. At 25°C, the pH and pOH are related by

$$pH + pOH = 14$$

Let's write a program that prompts the user for a pH value, determines whether the solution is acidic, neutral, or basic, and computes the hydrogen ion concentration. As usual, we will begin by computing an example by hand. Human blood typically has a pH of about 7.4; hence, blood is slightly basic. Furthermore,

$$[H^+] = 10^{-pH} = 10^{-7.4} = 3.98 \times 10^{-8} \text{ moles/liter}$$

$$pOH = 14.0 - pH = 14.0 - 7.4 = 6.60$$

$$[OH^-] = 10^{-pOH} = 10^{-6.6} = 2.51 \times 10^{-7} \text{ moles/liter}$$

Here is the pseudocode for the program:

prompt for the pH
read the pH
if pH equals 7.0
    print "neutral solution"
if pH < 7.0
    print "acidic solution"
if pH > 7.0
    print "basic solution"
compute [H⁺]
print [H⁺]

The C code that accomplishes this is shown in Listing 5–1.

Listing 5–1 *pH.c*

```
/*************************************************************

   Given the pH, compute the hydrogen ion concentration.

*************************************************************/

#include <stdio.h>
#include <math.h>

main()
{
    double pH;
    double hydrogen_ion;

    printf("\nPlease enter the pH: ");
    scanf("%lf", &pH);

    if (pH == 7.0) {
        printf("\nThe solution is neutral.\n");
    }

    if (pH < 7.0) {
        printf("\nThe solution is acidic.\n");
    }

    if (pH > 7.0) {
        printf("\nThe solution is basic.\n");
    }

    hydrogen_ion = pow(10.0, -pH);
    printf("\nHydrogen ion: %.3g mol/l\n\n", hydrogen_ion);
}
```

Dissection of *pH.c*

① #include <math.h>

The **math.h** file contains the prototype for the **pow()** function.

② if (pH == 7.0) {
      printf("\nThe solution is neutral.\n");
   }

This is the first **if** statement. If the pH exactly equals 7.0, the condition is true, and the statement inside the braces {} is executed. If the pH is not 7.0, the condition is false, and the statement inside the braces is skipped.

③
```
if (pH < 7.0) {
    printf("\nThe solution is acidic.\n");
}
```

If the pH is less than 7.0, the statement inside the braces is executed. Otherwise, nothing is done by this **if** statement.

④
```
hydrogen_ion = pow(10.0, -pH);
```

This statement computes the hydrogen ion concentration. We use the **pow()** function to compute the base-10 antilogarithm.

Compiling and Testing *pH.c*

Compile *pH.c*, making sure to link it to the math library. Then run the program on some test values from Table 5–1. Does your program appear to be working correctly?

Even if your program is correct, it doesn't do as much as it could. We leave it as an exercise for you to modify *pH.c* so that it also computes the hydroxide ion concentration [OH$^-$] (Exercise 7).

A Common Error

One of the most common and insidious errors that a programmer can make is to write the assignment operator (=) instead of the equality operator (==). For example, in *pH.c* we wrote

```
if (pH == 7.0) {
    printf("\nThe solution is neutral.\n");
}
```

Open the *pH.c* file and change the equality operator to the assignment operator:

```
if (pH = 7.0) {
    printf("\nThe solution is neutral.\n");
}
```

Close the file and compile it as you did before. Then run it on some test cases:

Input	Output
14.0	The solution is neutral. Hydrogen ion: 1e-07 mol/l
7.5	The solution is neutral. Hydrogen ion: 1e-07 mol/l
6.0	The solution is neutral. Hydrogen ion: 1e-07 mol/l
1.0	The solution is neutral. Hydrogen ion: 1e-07 mol/l

Regardless of the pH the user entered, the program always reports the solution as being neutral, with a hydrogen ion concentration of **1e-07 mol/l**! To understand why the program behaves this way, you need to know how C decides what is true and what is false.

Expressions and Conditions

We have been using the word "expression" without saying exactly what it means. In C, an *expression* may be defined as a formula for representing or computing some value. The simplest C expression is a constant:

```
90.0
1
-0.04785
MIN_A
```

A C variable name is an expression—it represents the value that the variable contains:

```
score
sum
first
second
```

An arithmetic operation is an expression because it is a formula for computing a value. Thus, the following would all be expressions:

```
first + second
a * b / (c - 47)
3.14159 * radius * radius
```

An assignment operation is an expression, too. Its value is just the value that is put into the variable. For example, the following operation puts 2.54 into the variable **a**, and therefore it is an expression having the value 2.54:

```
a = 2.54
```

A function call is an expression if the function returns a value. Thus, the following function call would be an expression having the value of the logarithm of **x**:

```
log(x)
```

So far so good. Now consider this: A condition or test that uses one of the relational operators is also an expression. For example:

```
pH == 7.0
```

What value does this expression represent? That depends. If the condition is false, the expression has the value zero. If the condition is true, the expression has the integer value one (1). In general,

Zero means false; nonzero means true.

The **if** statement considers any nonzero condition to be true. Therefore, the condition in the following **if** statement is always true:

```
if (1) {
   printf("Always prints this.\n");
}
```

On the other hand, the condition in the following **if** statement is never true:

```
if (0) {
   printf("Never prints this.\n");
}
```

We started this discussion to explain why the altered *pH.c* program reports that every solution is neutral. Perhaps now you can figure it out:

```
if (pH = 7.0) {
   printf("\nThe solution is neutral.\n");
}
```

Regardless of the value entered by the user, the assignment operation (**pH = 7.0**) has the value 7.0. Since 7.0 is nonzero, the condition is considered true.

There are two ways to guard against this kind of error. One is simply to be careful: examine your code very closely. If your text editor has a search capability, you can use it to check all occurrences of the = sign.

The other way to avoid trouble only works when you are comparing a constant and a variable. Just write the constant first:

```
7.0 == pH
```

In this case, if you mistakenly write an assignment operator, the compiler will complain because you cannot assign a value to a constant:

```
7.0 = pH                    /* Error! */
```

Take a moment now and correct your *pH.c* program.

Logical Operators

Relational operators such as `<`, `>`, and `==` are used to compare two values. More elaborate conditions can be written using the *logical operators*. There are three of these:

`&&`   AND
`||`   OR
`!`   NOT

To see how the AND operator (`&&`) works, consider the problem of assigning student grades according to a straight percentage scale. To receive an A, the student must have a score that is greater than or equal to 90%, AND less than or equal to 100%. This condition would be written as

```
(90.0 <= score) && (score <= 100.0)
```

For the AND condition to be true, the expressions on *both* sides of the `&&` operator must be true. Suppose the student enters a score of 101. The condition would then be

```
(90.0 <= 101.0) && (101.0 <= 100.0)
```

The expression to the left of the `&&` is true, but the expression to the right is not, so the entire AND condition is false. Suppose the score were 89. The condition would become

```
(90.0 <= 89.0) && (89.0 <= 100.0)
```

In this case, the right-hand side of the `&&` is true whereas the left-hand side is false, making the entire condition false.

Consider now a score of 95. The condition would be

```
(90.0 <= 95.0) && (95.0 <= 100.0)
```

Both conditions are true, so the entire condition is true. A score of 95.0 would earn an A.

An OR condition (||) is true if either side is true (or if both sides are true). When assigning grades, for example, a score less than 0% OR greater than 100% would be an error. Thus the test for erroneous input might be written as

```
(score < 0.0) || (score > 100.0)
```

A score of −5.0 would make the left-hand condition true, which is enough to make the entire OR condition true. Likewise, a score of 110 makes the right-hand condition true, making the entire OR condition true.

The NOT operator (!) makes a false condition true and a true condition false. This may seem somewhat strange but it does have its uses. We'll show you just one example of how the NOT operator works. Recall that the condition for an A is written with the AND operator like this:

```
(90.0 <= score) && (score <= 100.0)
```

We could also say that to get an A, the score must NOT be less than 90.0 AND it must NOT be greater than 100.0. Therefore, another way to write this condition would be

```
!(90.0 > score) && !(score > 100.0)
```

This is entirely equivalent to the previous condition (if perhaps not as clear).

A Grading Program: *grade1.c*

Our next program informs students of their grades using a straight grading scale. It also handles erroneous input (i.e., scores greater than 100% or less than 0%). The pseudocode outline for this program is:

prompt the user for a score
read the score
if 90.0 ≤ score ≤ 100.0
 print "You have an A!"
if 80.0 ≤ score < 90.0
 print "You have a B."
if 70.0 ≤ score < 80.0
 print "You have a C."

if 60.0 ≤ *score* < 70.0

　　print "You have a D."

if 0.0 ≤ *score* < 60.0

　　print "Unfortunately, you have an F."

　　"See your instructor immediately!"

if *score* < 0.0 <u>OR</u> *score* > 100.0

　　print "Error: your score must be between 0 and 100%."

The C code for this program is shown in Listing 5–2.

Listing 5–2 *grade1.c*

```
/*****************************************
    Determine a student's grade.
*****************************************/

#include <stdio.h>

#define MAX_SCORE 100.0
#define MIN_A 90.0
#define MIN_B 80.0
#define MIN_C 70.0
#define MIN_D 60.0
#define MIN_SCORE 0.0

main()
{
    double score;

    printf("Enter your score: ");
    scanf("%lf", &score);

    if ((MIN_A <= score) && (score <= MAX_SCORE)) {
        printf("You have an A!\n");
    }

    if ((MIN_B <= score) && (score < MIN_A)) {
        printf("You have a B.\n");
    }
```

(continued)

```
    if ((MIN_C <= score) && (score < MIN_B)) {
        printf("You have a C.\n");
    }

    if ((MIN_D <= score) && (score < MIN_C)) {
        printf("You have a D.\n");
    }

    if ((MIN_SCORE <= score) && (score < MIN_D)) {
        printf("Unfortunately, you have an F.\n");
        printf("See your instructor immediately!\n");
    }

    if ((score < MIN_SCORE) || (score > MAX_SCORE)) {
        printf("Error: your score must be between ");
③      printf("%g and %g%%.\n", MIN_SCORE, MAX_SCORE);
    }
}
```

Dissection of *grade1.c*

①
```
#define MAX_SCORE 100.0
#define MIN_A 90.0
#define MIN_B 80.0
#define MIN_C 70.0
#define MIN_D 60.0
#define MIN_SCORE 0.0
```

Setting the grade cutoffs at the top of the file with the **#define** directive makes it easier to change the grading scale later on, if necessary.

②
```
if ((MIN_A <= score) && (score <= MAX_SCORE)) {
    printf("You have an A!\n");
}
```

Remember, the rule with the **if** statement is DO IF TRUE. In this case, the AND operator (&&) requires that both conditions be true: the score must be greater than or equal to **MIN_A** AND it must be less than or equal to **MAX_SCORE** for the grade to be an A.

③
```
printf("%g and %g%%.\n", MIN_SCORE, MAX_SCORE);
```

There are two things to observe about this **printf()** function call. First, we did not write MIN_SCORE and MAX_SCORE as part of the control string. That is to say, we did not write

```
printf("MIN_SCORE and MAX_SCORE%%.\n");
```

The reason for this is that the preprocessor will not make substitutions inside quoted strings. The second point to note is that two percent signs (%%) are used together to print a single percent sign.

Compiling and Testing *grade1.c*

Compile *grade1.c* in the usual way, and try it out on some simple data. It is a good idea to test your program with values that are at the cutoffs, near the cutoffs, and outside the acceptable range:

Cutoffs: 0.0, 60.0, 70.0, 80.0, 90.0, 100.0

Near cutoffs: 59.999, 69.999, 79.999, 89.999, 99.999

Outside range: −10.0, 110.0

Also try nonnumerical input. Run the program, and type the letter A at the prompt:

Enter your score: ARET

What happens is unpredictable—the program is not designed to handle nonnumerical input.

Efficiency of the *grade1.c* Program

There is a subtle problem with the *grade1.c* program. You probably can't tell by running it, but the program is very inefficient. Consider what happens when you enter a score of, say, 95.0%. This score satisfies the first **if** condition, and the program prints the message

You have an A!

At this point, the program's job is finished. But the computer doesn't know that. Instead, it steps through the rest of the program, testing all of the conditions (including the one for erroneous input). This is terribly wasteful of the computer's resources.

A better approach would be for the computer to search through the alternatives until it finds a match, then to skip the remaining choices. This can be accomplished with the **if/else** selection structure, which we will examine next.

The if/else Statement

The **if/else** statement is used whenever you have multiple alternatives, of which *no more than one can be selected.* The simplest form of the **if/else** is used when there are just two alternatives, one of which must be true:

```
if (condition) {
    first set of statements
}
else {
    alternate statements
}
```

If the condition is true, the first set of statements is executed, and the alternate statements controlled by the **else** clause are skipped. If the condition is not true, the first set of statements is skipped, and the alternate statements are executed.

The **if/else** structure can also be used when there are more than two alternatives:

```
if (condition1) {
    first set of statements
}
else if (condition2) {
    second set of statements
}
else if (condition3) {
    third set of statements
}

        ⋮

else {
    default set of statements
}
```

Execution begins at the top with the first **if** clause. If *condition1* is true, the first set of statements is executed, and the rest of the conditions and statements are skipped. Otherwise, *condition2* is checked, then *condition3*, and so on, until a true condition is found. Whenever one of the conditions is found to be true, the computer executes the statement(s) controlled by that condition and skips the remaining conditions and statements.

Note the last **else**: it is not followed by an **if** or a condition. This is called the *default case* and is executed only if none of the previous conditions is true. The default case is not required and may be omitted.

An Even Better Grading Program: *grade2.c*

Our next program uses the **if/else** to check for errors in the student's input and to assign a grade. The pseudocode for this is

prompt the user for a score
scan the standard input for the score
if score > 100.0
    print error message
else if score ≥ 90.0
    print "You have an A!"
else if score ≥ 80.0
    print "You have a B."
else if score ≥ 70.0
    print "You have a C."
else if score ≥ 60.0
    print "You have a D."
else if score ≥ 0
    print "Unfortunately, you have an F."
    "See your instructor immediately!"
else
    print error message

The C program corresponding to this outline is shown in Listing 5–3.

Listing 5–3 *grade2.c*

```c
/*******************************************

    Determine a student's grade.

********************************************/

#include <stdio.h>

#define MAX_SCORE 100.0
#define MIN_A 90.0
#define MIN_B 80.0
#define MIN_C 70.0
#define MIN_D 60.0
#define MIN_SCORE 0.0

main()
{
    double score;

    printf("Enter your score: ");
    scanf("%lf", &score);

    if (MAX_SCORE < score) {
        printf("Error: scores cannot be greater than "
                "%g%%.\n", MAX_SCORE);
    }
    else if (MIN_A <= score) {
        printf("You have an A!\n");
    }
    else if (MIN_B <= score) {
        printf("You have a B.\n");
    }
    else if (MIN_C <= score) {
        printf("You have a C.\n");
    }
    else if (MIN_D <= score) {
        printf("You have a D.\n");
    }
    else if (MIN_SCORE <= score) {
        printf("Unfortunately, you have an F.\n");
        printf("See your instructor immediately.\n");
    }
    else {
        printf("Error: scores cannot be less than "
                "%g%%.\n", MIN_SCORE);
    }
}
```

(1) ← at `if (MAX_SCORE < score) {`

(2) ← at `else if (MIN_A <= score) {`

(3) ← at `else {`

Dissection of *grade2.c*

(1) `if (MAX_SCORE < score) {`

The first thing we test for is a score that is too high. If this occurs, an error message is printed, and the remaining **else** clauses are skipped.

(2) `else if (MIN_A <= score) {`

If the score is not larger than **MAX_SCORE**, this line checks to see if it is large enough for an A. If it is, the appropriate message is printed. Otherwise, the remaining **else if** clauses are checked, one by one, until a true condition is found.

(3) `else {`

This is the last of the **else** clauses. This line is reached only if none of the previous conditions is true. In this case, that would mean that the score is less than **MIN_SCORE**, which is an error.

As we have said, the **if/else** statement is more efficient in this case than several simple **if** statements because the computer does not have to perform all of the tests. You might also have noticed another difference: The conditions in the **if/else** statement tend to be much simpler. For example, to test for an A grade in *grade1.c*, we used the condition

`(MIN_A <= score) && (score <= MAX_SCORE)`

In *grade2.c*, the condition for an A is simply

`MIN_A <= score`

Compiling and Testing *grade2.c*

Compile the program and try the same test cases you applied to *grade1.c*. If you made no mistakes, the new program should handle any numerical input without difficulty. (What happens when you enter nonnumerical data?)

Program: *alcohol.c*

Drunk driving is a major cause of highway deaths in the United States. The management of the Acme Bar and Grill wants a computer program that will help its patrons determine whether they are legally permitted to drive after drinking alcohol. The state of Indiana, where Acme is located, gives the following guidelines for blood alcohol concentrations (BAC):

$0.01\% \leq BAC < 0.05\%$ Seldom illegal (but may complicate other driving infractions)

$0.05\% \leq BAC < 0.10\%$	May be subject to arrest for DWI (at officer's discretion)
$0.10\% \leq BAC$	Automatic DWI (fine and jail sentence)

Various equations have been developed to estimate BAC. One such equation is

$$BAC = \frac{A}{r \cdot w} - \beta \cdot t + K$$

(G. W. Arstein-Kerslake, *Alcohol, Drugs, and Driving*, 2(1): 9–15). Three of the quantities on the right-hand side of this equation will vary from patron to patron:

A = alcohol consumed (in grams)

w = body mass (in hectograms)

t = elapsed time since first drink (in hours)

The remaining three quantities have been estimated from experiments involving a large number of human subjects. We will use average values from the published literature, and we will treat these values as constants:

r = fraction of body mass in which alcohol may be present

  = 0.68 for men, 0.55 for women

β = rate at which alcohol disappears from the blood = 0.015% per hour

K = statistical correction term = 0.0165%

Without the correction term K, the equation underestimates the BAC for about half of the population; with $K = 0.0165\%$, the equation underestimates the BAC for only 5% of the population.

Following our usual practice, let's carry out a calculation by hand before designing the computer program. Compute the BAC for a woman who weighs 125 pounds and has consumed two alcoholic beverages in an hour and a half. First convert body weight in pounds to mass in hectograms (10 hg = 1 kg = 2.2046 lb):

$$w = \left(\frac{10 \text{ hg}}{2.2046 \text{ lb}}\right) 125 \text{ lb} = (4.536 \text{ hg/lb})(125 \text{ lb}) = 567.0 \text{ hg}$$

Estimating alcohol consumption is tricky because the alcohol content of a drink can vary greatly. We will assume that the drinks at Acme contain 11.6 grams of alcohol. Hence, $A = 23.2$ grams, and we have

$$BAC = \frac{23.2 \text{ g}}{(0.55)(567.0 \text{ hg})} - (0.015\%/\text{hr})(1.5 \text{ hr}) + 0.0165\% = 0.068\%$$

It would not be safe for this patron to operate a motor vehicle. In Indiana, she could be arrested, at the discretion of a police officer, for driving under the influence.

Let's try another hand calculation, this time for a 200-lb man who has had eight drinks in four hours. As before, assume each drink contains 11.6 grams of alcohol:

$w = (4.536 \text{ hg/lb})(200 \text{ lb}) = 907.2 \text{ hg}$

$A = (8 \text{ drinks})(11.6 \text{ grams/drink}) = 92.8 \text{ g}$

$$\text{BAC} = \frac{92.8 \text{ g}}{(0.68)(907.2 \text{ hg})} - (0.015\%/\text{hr})(4 \text{ hr}) + 0.0165\% = 0.107\%$$

This man is in no condition to drive. A first conviction for driving while intoxicated (DWI) in the state of Indiana can result in a jail sentence of one year, suspension of driving privileges for 30 days, and a fine of $5000. A drunk driver who causes death or serious injury may be convicted of a felony carrying a maximum sentence of 8 years in prison and a $10,000 fine.

Here is the pseudocode outline for our program:

print a disclaimer

prompt for patron's sex (1 = female, 2 = male)
if female
    set r = 0.55
otherwise
    set r = 0.68

prompt for the patron's body weight
read the weight
convert pounds to hectograms

prompt for alcohol consumption
read alcohol consumption

prompt for elapsed time
read time

compute and print BAC

if BAC < 0.05%
    Seldom illegal
else if BAC < 0.10%
    Possible DWI
else
    DWI

The C code for this program is shown in Listing 5–4.

Listing 5–4 *alcohol.c*

```
/***************************************************

    Estimate Blood Alcohol Concentration (BAC)

    Reference: G. W. Arstein-Kerslake
    Alcohol, Drugs and Driving, 2(1):9-15

****************************************************/

#include <stdio.h>

#define HG_PER_LB 4.5360
#define MALE_MASS_FRACT 0.68
#define FEMALE_MASS_FRACT 0.55
#define ALCOHOL_RATE 0.015
#define CORRECTION 0.0165
#define LIMIT1 0.05
#define LIMIT2 0.10

main()
{
    double blood_alcohol;           /* BAC (percent) */
    double alcohol_ingested;        /* grams */
    double mass_fract;
    double body_mass;               /* hectograms */
    double time;                    /* hours */
    int sex_code;                   /* 1 for female, 2 for male */

    printf("This program estimates blood alcohol concentrations."
        "\nWARNING: The program may underestimate your BAC.\n\n");

    printf("Please enter 1 for female, 2 for male: ");
    scanf("%d", &sex_code);

    if (1 == sex_code) {
        mass_fract = FEMALE_MASS_FRACT;
    }
    else {
        mass_fract = MALE_MASS_FRACT;
    }

    printf("Please enter your weight in pounds:");
    scanf("%lf", &body_mass);
    body_mass = HG_PER_LB * body_mass;
```

(continued)

```
    printf("How much alcohol have you had (in grams)? ");
    scanf("%lf", &alcohol_ingested);

    printf("How many hours since you started drinking? ");
    scanf("%lf", &time);

    blood_alcohol = alcohol_ingested / (mass_fract * body_mass)
                    - (ALCOHOL_RATE * time) + CORRECTION;

    printf("\nYour BAC is approximately %.2f%%\n", blood_alcohol);

    if (blood_alcohol < LIMIT1) {
        printf("\nThis is seldom illegal, but be careful.\n");
    }
    else if (blood_alcohol < LIMIT2) {
        printf("\nCaution: You should not drive.\n"
               "You could be arrested and charged with DWI.\n");
    }
    else {
        printf("\nWARNING: DO NOT ATTEMPT TO DRIVE.\n"
               "A DWI conviction carries a mandatory jail sentence!\n");
    }
}
```

Dissection of *alcohol.c*

① ```
printf("This program estimates blood alcohol concentrations."
    "\nWARNING: The program may underestimate your BAC.\n\n");
```

For situations in which your program's results may have serious consequences, it is a good idea to warn the user that the program is not foolproof.

② ```
printf("Please enter 1 for female, 2 for male:");
scanf("%d", &sex_code);
```

We have chosen to use an integer to distinguish the sex of the user. There is no particular significance to using 1 for female and 2 for male.

```
3   if (1 == sex_code) {
        mass_fract = FEMALE_MASS_FRACT;
    }
    else {
        mass_fract = MALE_MASS_FRACT;
    }
```

The code checks only to see whether the user is female (**1 == sex_code**). If the user enters any integer other than 1, the program assumes that the user is male. Note that we wrote the equality condition as (**1 == sex_code**) rather than (**sex_code == 1**). We did this just in case we were to mistakenly write the assignment operator instead of the equality operator.

Compiling and Testing *alcohol.c*

Compile and run the program the usual way, and try out some test cases. Does it give the expected results? Can you think of any way to improve the program?

Nested if Statements

Just in case you have been wondering, we should mention that it is possible to put an **if** or **if/else** structure inside another. Such an arrangement is called a *nested* **if**. Here is an example:

```
if (age < 12) {
    if (7 == day) {
        ticket_price = SAT_CHILD;
    }
    else {
        ticket_price = CHILD;
    }
}
else {
    if (7 == day) {
        ticket_price = SAT_ADULT;
    }
    else {
        ticket_price = ADULT;
    }
}
```

Nested **if** and **if/else** statements can be useful, even necessary. However, they can make your code hard to read. In most cases, a nested **if** structure can be rearranged to make the code easier to understand. Thus, the previous structure could be rewritten this way:

```
if (age < 12 && 7 == day) {
    ticket_price = SAT_CHILD;
}
else if (age < 12) {
    ticket_price = CHILD;
}
else if (7 == day) {
    ticket_price = SAT_ADULT;
}
else {
    ticket_price = ADULT;
}
```

Most programmers would find this easier to read and understand than the previous arrangement.

STYLE

You may have noticed that we have followed a consistent style in writing **if** statements:

```
                                          Opening brace here
            if (MIN_A < score) {
  Indent ——→ printf("You have an A!/n");
            }
                Closing brace here
```

First note the braces, { and }. These aren't really needed when the **if** controls only one statement. In other words, we could just as well have written

```
if (MIN_A < score)
    printf("You have an A!\n");
```

However, the braces are required whenever the **if** controls more than one statement. In the following case, for example, the braces are necessary because the **if** controls two **printf()** function calls:

```
if ((MIN_SCORE <= score) && (score < MIN_D)) {
    printf("Unfortunately, you have an F.\n");
    printf("See your instructor immediately!\n");
}
```

We follow the convention of always using braces with an **if**, even when they are not strictly required. This ensures that we will not forget to include them when they are required. We put the opening brace on the same line as the **if** and the condition; we put the closing brace on a line all by itself, aligned vertically with the **if**. The idea is to show clearly where the **if** begins and ends.

Also note that the statements inside the braces are indented. This shows which statements are controlled by the **if** or **else if**.

HELPFUL HINTS

We previously warned you against accidentally writing the assignment operator (=) instead of the equality operator (==) in conditions. We offered two suggestions that bear repeating here:

- Examine your code very closely for any occurrence of = where == is expected. If your text editor has a search capability, use it to check all assignment operators.
- When testing for equality of a constant and a variable, write the constant first (7 == pH). If you should then make the mistake of writing an assignment operator, this will produce a compiler error.

As programs become more complicated, testing and debugging become more difficult. The judicious use of **printf()** statements can be helpful:

- Practice echo-printing of input values. That is, immediately print the input values to ensure that they were read and stored correctly.
- Place **printf()** statements at strategic points in the program to print out intermediate values. These **printf()** statements can be removed after you are sure that the program is correct.

SUMMARY

Relational Operators	*Has nonzero value if . . .*
expr1 == expr2	expr1 and expr2 are equal
expr1 != expr2	expr1 and expr2 are not equal
expr1 <= expr2	expr1 is not greater than expr2
expr1 < expr2	expr1 is less than expr2
expr1 >= expr2	expr1 is not less than expr2
expr1 > expr2	expr1 is greater than expr2

Logical Operators	*Has nonzero value if . . .*
expr1 && expr2	both expr1 AND expr2 are nonzero
expr1 || expr2	either expr1 OR expr2 is nonzero
!expression	expression is zero

Simple Selection Structure

```
if (condition){
    statement(s)
}
```

Executes statement(s) in the body of the **if** only if the condition is true.

Double-Alternative Selection

```
if (condition){
    first set of statements
}
else {
    default set of statements
}
```

Tests the condition; if it is true, the first set of statements is executed; otherwise the default set of statements is executed.

Multiple-Alternative Selection

```
if (condition1){
    first set of statements
}
else if (condition2) {
    second set of statements
}
    .
    .
    .
else {
    default set of statements
}
```

Tests the conditions in order until it finds one that is true, then executes the corresponding set of statements. If none of the conditions are true, the default set of statements is executed. (The default alternative is optional.)

- Sequential flow of control means that the program statements are executed in strict order, one after another, from the top of the program to the bottom.
- The real power of computers lies in their ability to depart from sequential flow of control. This often involves selection between alternatives, in which some operations are performed and others are skipped. Selections are made using **if** or **if/else** statements.
- An expression is a formula for representing or computing a value. Constants, variable names, arithmetic operations, assignment operations, and calls to functions that return values are expressions. C conditions are also expressions.
- C allows you to nest **if** statements inside of each other, but two nested **if**s can usually be re-written as a single statement using logical operators.

EXERCISES

1. *Define:* **a.** sequential flow of control; **b.** condition; **c.** relational operator; **d.** expression; **e.** logical operator; **f.** default case; **g.** nested **if**.

2. *Errors.* Create a copy of **pH.c** called **errors51.c** and introduce into the new file the first error listed below. Run your compiler on the file. If the compiler catches the error, write down both the error and the error message; if not, run the executable file with test data and make a note of any unexpected results. Correct the file, then repeat the process with the next error on the list. Continue until you have tried all of the errors.

   a. Put a space between the two halves of the equality operator: `(pH = = 7.0)`.

   b. Remove the opening brace { on the first line of the second **if** statement.

   c. Remove the closing brace } at the end of the first **if** statement.

   d. Remove the closing brace } at the end of the last **if** statement.

3. *More errors.* Create a copy of **grade1.c** called **errors52.c**. Follow the instructions given in Exercise (2), but introduce the following errors into the file:

   a. Substitute the | | operator for the && operator in one of the conditions.

   b. Replace <= with =< in one of the conditions.

   c. Change

   ```
   if ((MIN_A <= score) && (score <= MAX_SCORE)) {
   ```

   to

   ```
   if (MIN_A <= score <= MAX_SCORE) {
   ```

4. Assume that a program includes the following variable declarations:

   ```
   /* Personal information. */

   double height;        /* Height in meters */
   double weight;        /* Weight in kilograms */
   double income;        /* Annual income in dollars. */
   int age;              /* Age in years */
   int children;         /* Number of children */
   ```

   The following C condition would be evaluated as true for a person who is taller than 2 meters and earns more than $200,000:

   ```
   (height > 2.0) && (income > 200000.0)
   ```

   For each of the cases listed below, write an appropriate C condition to describe a person who

   a. is over 21 years of age;

   b. has more than two children;

   c. is 21–35 years old and has an income greater than $100,000;

   d. stands 2 meters tall and is at least 18 years old;

   e. is a teenager weighing less than 45 kg and standing no more than 1.65 m tall;

   f. has at least one child, makes less than $10,000 per year, and is 21 years old;

   g. has six children, has an income of $50,000 to $75,000, and is a senior citizen.

5. Consider the following program:

```
#include <stdio.h>
#define PRICE1 1.5
#define PRICE2 2.0
#define PRICE3 3.5
#define PRICE4 5.0

main()
{
    int age, day;
    double price;
    scanf("%d %d", &age, &day);
    if ((age < 12) && (day == 7))
       price = PRICE1;
    else if (age < 12)
       price = PRICE2;
    else if (day = 7)          /* Careful here! */
       price = PRICE3;
    else
       price = PRICE4;
    printf("Please pay $%.2f\n", price);
}
```

   a. If the values 12 and 7 are entered on the standard input, what will be printed on the standard output?

   b. If the values 10 and 2 are entered, what will be printed?

   c. If the values 2 and 33 are entered, what will be printed?

   d. If the values −1 and 7 are entered, what will be printed?

6. Rewrite *pH.c* to use a simple **if/else** statement instead of three **if** statements.

7. Modify *pH.c* so that it will also compute [OH⁻] and pOH.

8. Modify *stirling.c* (from the previous chapter) so that it defines the factorial of 0 (0!) to be equal to 1.

9. Modify *alcohol.c* so that it prompts for the number of drinks and converts this to grams of pure alcohol consumed. For now, assume that one drink contains 11.6 grams of alcohol. (But use **#define** to allow you to change this if necessary.)

10. The Acme Bar and Grill would like you to add a new feature to *alcohol.c* that will calculate how long a patron who is in the illegal category must wait, without drinking, before driving. Consider the safe driving level to be 0.03% BAC or lower. (*Hint:* make use of the parameter $\beta = 0.015\%$ per hour from the original equation).

11. *Blood alcohol.* Several equations are being used to calculate blood alcohol levels (BAC). Most of these are modifications of the equation we have already used. Watson et al.* propose that BAC can be better represented by

$$\text{BAC} = \frac{A \cdot B_w}{\text{TBW}} - \beta \cdot t$$

The parameters A, β and t are the same as in the example program. The new parameters B_w and TBW, are related to r from the already familiar equation. B_w is the fraction of blood that consists of water, equaling 0.8 for both females and males. TBW stands for "Total Body Water," which is the total volume of water in a person's body (in liters). The TBW depends on the person's sex, height, weight, and age:

TBW (females) $= -2.097 + (0.1069)(\text{height}) + (0.2466)(\text{weight})$

TBW (males) $= 2.447 - (0.09516)(\text{age}) + (0.1074)(\text{height}) + (0.3362)(\text{weight})$

Note that age is important for calculating the TBW only for males. In these equations, height is in centimeters and weight is in kilograms.

Write a program that calculates a person's BAC using the equation by Watson et al. Compare the results of this program to those of *alcohol.c*. Which program would you use to insure that a person is not driving while intoxicated?

12. *Divisors.* Write a program to determine whether an integer x is evenly divisible by another integer y. Both x and y should be entered by the user.

13. *State tax.* Write a program that prompts the user for his or her taxable income, computes the state tax, and displays the result on the screen, properly labeled and formatted. Assume that there are four tax rates:

   a.   0.0% of the first $5,000;

   b.   0.5% of the next $25,000 (i.e., from $5000.01 to $30,000.00);

   c.   1.0% of the next $40,000 (i.e., from $30,000.01 to $70,000.00);

   d.   2.0% of any income over $70,000.

   Use the **#define** directive to set the income limits and tax rates.

14. *Quadratic formula.* Write a program to find the roots of a quadratic equation of the form

$$ax^2 + bx + c = 0$$

---

* P. E. Watson, I. D. Watson, and R. D. Batt. 1981. *Journal of Studies on Alcohol*, 42(7): 547–556.

using the quadratic formula. The program should prompt the user for the three coefficients a, b, and c, and handle the following five cases:

a. $a = b = 0$ [no equation];

b. $a = 0$, b is nonzero [linear equation; root $= -c/b$];

c. The discriminant $b^2 - 4ac$ is negative [no real roots];

d. The discriminant is zero [two real and equal roots];

e. The discriminant is positive [two real and unequal roots].

15. *Employee wages.* Write a program that prompts the user for the total number of hours worked in a given week, and computes the user's wage according to the following rules:

a. print an error message if the user enters less than 0 hours;

b. pay the base rate for the first 40 hours;

c. pay 1.5 times the base rate for the next 20 hours;

d. pay 2.0 times the base rate for hours worked beyond 60 hours;

e. print an error message if the user enters more than 100 hours.

Use symbolic constants to define the base rate (assume $6.75 per hour for now), the overtime rates, and the time limits.

16. *Menu.* The McDowell Restaurant chain has asked you to write a menu program for their new Fast Grub-O-Matic food-service machines. Your program should print a menu like this:

```
************************************************************

               McDowell's Restaurant

************************************************************

    Make your selection from the menu below:

    1. Regular hamburger                        $0.89

    2. Regular cheeseburger                     $0.99

    3. Fish sandwich                            $1.29

    4. Half-pounder with cheese                 $2.49

    5. French fries                             $0.79

    6. Large soft drink                         $0.99

************************************************************

    Select 1, 2, 3, 4, 5, or 6--->
```

Your program should read the customer's selection and compute the price, including 5.5% sales tax. It should print out a message:

```
Please pay [print amount here].
Thank you for eating at McDowell's!
```

To make your program more flexible, use the **#define** preprocessor directives to set the prices and sales tax rate.

17. *Square roots.* Write an interactive square root program that prints an error message if the user attempts to enter a negative argument.

18. *Cube roots.* Write an interactive cube root program that handles both positive and negative inputs. Note that the **pow()** function cannot take the cube root of a negative number. Thus if **x** is negative,

```
root = pow(x, 1./3.);
```

will produce an error message. In that case, you can compute the cube root this way:

```
root = -pow(-x, 1./3.);
```

19. *Area of a triangle.* Write a program to compute the area of a triangle. Have the program print a menu on the screen that allows the user to select the type of problem to be worked:

```
Compute the area of a triangle given:

1. The length of all three sides (SSS);
2. Two angles and the included side (ASA);
3. Two sides and the included angle (SAS);
4. Two sides and the angle opposing the longer side.

Select 1, 2, 3, or 4--->
```

After the user makes a selection, the program should prompt for the necessary input and print the results. (*Hint:* refer to the program *asa.c* and Exercises 17–19 from Chapter 4.)

20. *Boiling point.* The *boiling point* of a liquid is the temperature at which the liquid's vapor pressure equals the pressure of its surroundings. Write a program that prompts the user for the temperature and pressure of the surroundings, and prints out the appropriate message:

```
Liquid will not boil.

Liquid is at its boiling point.

Liquid is above its boiling point.
```

Use the Antoine Equation to calculate the vapor pressure of the liquid (see Exercise 21, Chapter 4).

21. *Fluid drag.* Any object moving through a fluid (a gas or liquid) experiences a retarding force called *drag.* The drag is usually computed from a relationship of the form

$$\text{drag force} = F = \tfrac{1}{2}C_d\,A_f\,\rho\,v^2$$

where

C_d = drag coefficient (dimensionless)

A_f = projected frontal area of the object (m²)

ρ = fluid density (kg m^{-3})

v = speed of the object (m s^{-1})

The drag coefficient is usually measured experimentally. It is often expressed as a function of the *Reynolds Number* Re defined by

$$\text{Re} \equiv \frac{\rho\,L\,v}{\mu}$$

in which ρ is the fluid density, L is some characteristic length of the object (such as its diameter), v is the velocity of the object, and μ is the fluid viscosity.

According to C. Chow (*An Introduction to Computational Fluid Mechanics*, Wiley, 1979), the drag coefficient for a sphere may be approximated by

$C_d = 24\ \text{Re}^{-1}$, for Re ≤ 1

$C_d = 24\ \text{Re}^{-0.646}$, for $1 <$ Re ≤ 400

$C_d = 0.5$, for $400 <$ Re $\leq 3 \times 10^5$

$C_d = 0.000366\ \text{Re}^{0.4275}$, for $3 \times 10^5 <$ Re $\leq 2 \times 10^6$

$C_d = 0.18$, for $2 \times 10^6 <$ Re

Write a program that will compute the drag on a sphere, given the diameter of the sphere, its speed, and the density and viscosity of the fluid.

22. *Wind chill.* The wind chill equivalent temperature T_e is often reported by meteorologists during the winter. T_e is an equivalent temperature that accounts for the increased chilling effects of wind on a human body. T_e is based partly on experiments conducted in Antarctica to determine how wind affects the time required to freeze water, and is given by:

$$T_e = 33 - (10.45 + 10\ \sqrt{v} - v)(33 - T)/22.04$$

where v is the wind velocity (in m/s) and T is the true temperature in degrees Celsius. The equation is not valid at wind speeds below 1.79 m/s.

Write a program that will calculate T_e for any combination of true temperature and wind velocity. If the wind velocity is below 1.79 m/s, your program should not compute T_e but should print out the value of T, along with an appropriate warning message. Since wind chill is not particularly important above temperatures of 20°C, print a warning message if the temperature above this is entered, but proceed with the calculation.

23. *Julian Calendar.* In 46 B.C., Julius Caesar authorized the adoption of a new calendar. It was named the Julian Calendar in his honor, although it was actu-

ally devised by the astronomer Sosigenes of Alexandria. Sosigenes estimated the year to be 365.25 days long. He made his common year 365 days long, adding a day every fourth year to make a "leap year" of 366 days. Write a program that will determine whether a given year is a leap year, according to the Julian Calendar. (Note that years evenly divisible by four are leap years.)

24. *Gregorian Calendar.* The Julian Calendar (see the previous exercise) was used throughout Europe and the Mediterranean for some 1600 years, but it was not perfect. It actually overestimated the length of the year by 11 minutes and 14 seconds, an error of about a day every 128 years. By 1582, the accumulated error was about 10 days.

    Pope Gregory undertook to reform the Julian calendar according to a scheme developed by the astronomer Luigi Lilis Ghiraldi, who estimated the length of the year to be 365.2425 days. (This was within 30 seconds or so of the true value.) Under the new Gregorian calendar, leap years are those years that are evenly divisible by 4 (as with the Julian calendar) except for centesimal years (years ending in 00) that are not evenly divisible by 400. Therefore, 1600 was a leap year, but 1700, 1800, and 1900 were not.

    To account for the 10-day error that had accrued, Pope Gregory decreed that the day following October 4, 1582, should be October 15, 1582. Italy, Spain, France, Portugal, and Luxembourg adopted this new calendar immediately. England waited until 1752. In that year, September 2 was followed immediately by September 14 on the English calendar, making that month only 19 days long.

    Write a program that will determine, for years future or past, whether a given year is a leap year. For dates before the Gregorian adoption year, use the Julian calendar rule for determining the leap year. Thereafter, use the Gregorian leap-year rule. (Take the adoption year to be 1752, but set this with the **#define** directive so that it can be changed later, if necessary.)

25. *Powerlifting competition.* Powerlifting competitions use a handicapping system to determine the winner. They use the following equation to calculate an adjusted total score T for a competitor:

$$T = C(S + B + D)$$

The competitor with the largest T is considered the winner. In this equation, S is the weight lifted in the squat, B is the weight lifted in the bench press, and D is the weight in the deadlift (all weights in kilograms). C is a coefficient based on the lifter's weight. For males between 125 kg and 165 kg, C is calculated as follows:

Body weight (W in kg)	Coefficient (C)
$125.1 \leq W < 135$	$0.5208 - 0.0012(W - 125)$
$135 \leq W < 145$	$0.5088 - 0.0011(W - 135)$
$145 \leq W < 155$	$0.4978 - 0.0010(W - 145)$
$155 \leq W < 165$	$0.4878 - 0.0009(W - 155)$

Write a program that will calculate and print the total score for a competitor. If the competitor's weight is not within the specified range, skip all calculations and print an appropriate error message.

26. *Vision correction.* By changing the shape of its lens, the human eye can focus on objects over a remarkable range of distances. The *near point* is the closest distance for which the lens can produce a sharp image. This distance typically increases with age, from about 18 cm at age ten to 500 cm or more at age 60. (The average for most people with normal vision is about 25 cm.) The *far point* is the greatest distance for which the eye can focus. For a normal eye, this distance is usually taken to be infinite.

    There are two common defects of the eye. In *myopia* (or *nearsightedness*), distant objects cannot be focussed sharply because the far point is closer than normal. In *hyperopia* (or *farsightedness*), nearby objects are blurred because the near point is farther away than normal. Both conditions can be corrected by placing a lens of power P in front of the eye, where P is given by

$$\text{Myopia:} \quad P = -\frac{1}{q}$$

$$\text{Hyperopia:} \quad P = \frac{1}{c} - \frac{1}{p}$$

    Here, q is the uncorrected far point of the eye, p is the uncorrected near point, and c is the desired near point. (By convention, c is usually taken to be 25 cm.) If the distances are measured in meters, P will be in diopters. Note that P will be negative to correct myopia and positive to correct hyperopia. A person can suffer from both myopia and hyperopia, and therefore may require two sets of glasses (or bifocals).

    An optometrist wants a program to help his patients understand their prescriptions. He wants the patient to enter the lens power P (in diopters) and have the program print a message indicating whether the patient is nearsighted or farsighted. If the patient is nearsighted, the program should print the uncorrected far point of the eye, in meters and feet; if farsighted, the program should print the uncorrected near point, also in meters and feet.

27. *Vision correction.* Write a computer program to compute the power of corrective lenses, rounded to the nearest 0.25 diopter, given the uncorrected near and far points of the eye (see previous exercise). The program should also indicate whether the patient suffers from (1) myopia, (2) hyperopia, (3) both, or (4) neither.

6.

Flow of Control: Repetition

One reason computers are so useful is that they are able to do the same things over and over without getting tired or bored. This is called *repetition*, *iteration*, or *looping*. In this chapter we will discuss two types of repetition structures, the **while** loop and the **for** loop.

The while Loop

The most common way to write a loop in C is with the **while** statement, which has the form

```
while (condition) {
    statement(s)
}
```

Did you notice that the **while** has a structure similar to that of the **if**? If the condition in the **while** structure is true, the body of the while is executed once. Next—and this is what distinguishes the **while** from the **if**—the condition is checked again. If it is still true, the body of the loop is executed again. The process continues as long as the condition is true. The first time the condition tests false, the body of the loop is skipped, and flow of control continues on below the **while** structure.

Program: *fact1.c*

You will recall that the *factorial* of n (denoted n!) is defined as the product*

$$n! = (1)(2)(3) \cdots (n-1)(n) = \prod_{i=1}^{n} i$$

By definition, the factorial of 0 is 1; the factorial of a negative number is undefined.

Our first sample program will compute the factorial of an integer entered by the user at the keyboard. We'll use a **while** loop to make this calculation. Here is the pseudocode outline for this program:

prompt the user for n
read n
initialize factorial to 1
initialize counter to 1
while (counter <= n)
    multiply factorial by counter
    add 1 to counter
print factorial

The actual C code for this program is shown in Listing 6–1.

---

* In mathematics, the capital pi is often used to indicate the product of a number of similar terms. Thus,

$$\prod_{i=1}^{5} x_i = x_1 \cdot x_2 \cdot x_3 \cdot x_4 \cdot x_5$$

Listing 6–1 *fact1.c*

```
/*************************************************************

   Compute the factorial of an integer using a while loop.

*************************************************************/

#include <stdio.h>

main()
{
    int n;              /* Value entered by user */
    int i;              /* Counter */
    int fact;           /* Factorial of n */

    printf("Please enter a nonnegative integer: ");
    scanf("%d", &n);

    fact = 1;           /* Initialize fact */
    i = 1;              /* Initialize counter */
    while (i <= n) {
        fact = fact * i;
        i = i + 1;
    }

    printf("The factorial of %d is %d\n", n, fact);
}
```

① ② ③ (markers alongside the code)

Dissection of *fact1.c*

①
```
int n;              /* Value entered by user */
int i;              /* Counter */
int fact;           /* Factorial of n */
```

We need three **int** variables for this program: **n** holds the value that the user enters at the keyboard; **i** takes on the values 1, 2, 3, . . . , $(n - 1)$, n, that are multiplied together; and **fact** holds the value of the factorial as it is being computed.

②
```
fact = 1;           /* Initialize fact */
```

We initialize **fact** to 1. If we didn't, there is no telling what value would be found in this variable when the program begins.

③
```
i = 1;               /* Initialize counter */
while (i <= n) {
   fact = fact * i;
   i = i + 1;
}
```

As long as i does not exceed **n**, this **while** loop does two things: (1) it multiplies **fact** by i; and (2) it increases i by 1.

Compiling and Testing *fact1.c*

Compile *fact1.c* and try out some test values:

n	n!	n	n!
0	1 (by definition)	10	3,628,800
1	1	11	39,916,800
2	2	12	479,001,600
3	6	13	6,227,020,800
4	24	14	87,178,291,200
5	120	15	1,307,674,368,000
6	720	16	20,922,789,888,000
7	5,040	17	355,687,428,096,000
8	40,320	18	6,402,373,705,728,000
9	362,880	19	121,645,100,408,832,000

You will probably notice that your program begins to give erroneous answers after *n* reaches a certain size. For example, on our computer, this program gives correct values until *n* reaches 13. The reason for this is simple: 13! equals 6227020800, a value that is too big for an **int** variable on our system. To handle larger arguments, the program might be rewritten to use **longs** or **doubles** instead of **ints**—we leave this as an exercise (Exercise 14).

The for Loop

The second kind of loop we will examine in this chapter is the **for** loop. Perhaps the best way to see how it works is to compare it to the **while** loop used in the *fact1.c* program;

```
                          ┌─ Initialize counter
i = 1;                    │  ┌─ Test condition
while (i <= n) {
    fact = fact * i;
    i = i + 1;  ──────────── Update counter
}
```

This can be rewritten as an equivalent **for** loop:

```
    Initialize      Test        Update
    counter      condition     counter
        │            │            │
    for (i = 1; i <= n; i = i + 1) {
        fact = fact * i;
    }
```

As before, **i** is the counter. Inside the parentheses of the **for**, the assignment

```
i = 1;
```

sets the starting value of **i**. This is done just once, at the start of the loop. Next comes the condition:

```
i <= n;
```

In this case, the computer checks to see if the current value of **i** is less than or equal to **n**. If this condition is true, the statement between the braces is executed once. Then the counter is updated:

```
i = i + 1;
```

At this point, the condition is checked again. If it is still true, the statement in the body of the loop is executed again, then the counter is updated, and so on. This process—check condition, execute, update counter—continues so long as the condition remains true.

A revised version of the factorial program, in which a **for** loop replaces the **while** loop, is shown in Listing 6–2. (*Hint:* Make a copy of the *fact1.c* program and revise the copy according to Listing 6–2.)

Listing 6-2 *fact2.c*

```
/************************************************************

    Compute the factorial of an integer using a for loop.

************************************************************/

#include <stdio.h>

main()
{
    int n;              /* Value entered by user */
    int i;              /* Counter */
    int fact;           /* Factorial of n */

    printf("Please enter a nonnegative integer: ");
    scanf("%d", &n);

    fact = 1;           /* Initialize fact */

    for (i = 1; i <= n; i = i + 1) {
        fact = fact * i;
    }

    printf("The factorial of %d is %d\n", n, fact);
}
```

Compiling and Testing *fact2.c*

Compile the program as you normally would, then try the same test data that you used with ***fact1.c***. The new program should behave exactly as the previous program.

Choosing a Loop: while vs. for

We have shown you two ways to write a loop; which you use is largely a matter of personal taste. Some C programmers prefer always to use **while** statements; others always use **for** statements. We take a middle ground. Whenever we know how many times the loop is to be executed—in other words, whenever the loop is controlled by the value of a counter—we will use a **for** loop. Otherwise, we will use the **while** loop.

In the factorial program, for example, we know that the loop in the factorial is to be executed n times. This implies that a **for** loop is the proper choice. Nevertheless, as we have seen, you can just as well write a factorial program using the **while** statement.

Counting Up vs. Counting Down

Another question to consider when computing $n!$ is whether to start at 1 and count up to n, or to start at n and count down. The factorial can be computed either way, with the same result:

$$n! = (1)(2)(3) \ldots (n-1)(n)$$

$$n! = (n)(n-1) \ldots (3)(2)(1)$$

In both **fact1.c** and **fact2.c** we chose the first approach—that is, we started at 1 and increased the factors until reaching n. We could just as well have chosen the other method, in which case we would have used the following **while()** loop in **fact1.c**:

```
fact = 1;               /* Initialize fact */

i = n;
while (i >= 1) {
   fact = fact * i;
   i = i - 1;
}
```

Note how we reduce the counter by one each time through the loop. The equivalent **for()** loop would be

```
fact = 1;               /* Initialize fact */

for (i = n; i >= 1; i = i - 1) {
   fact = fact * i;
}
```

We leave it as an exercise for you to modify **fact1.c** and **fact2.c** to compute the factorial by counting down rather than counting up.

Another Look at scanf()

We have seen that the **scanf()** function gets numbers from the keyboard and stores them in variables. Our next program will take advantage of another feature of **scanf()**: It returns a value, just as a mathematical function does. This value is an **int** that indicates how many items (if any) the **scanf()** function was able to read and store.

Let's consider an example. Suppose you have a program containing the following variable declarations:

```
double x, y, z;
int m;
```

Also suppose that your program contains this statement:

```
m = scanf("%lf %lf %lf", &x, &y, &z);
```

This **scanf()** function scans the standard input for three **double** values, which it stores in the variables **x**, **y**, and **z**. It then returns a value, which is assigned to the variable **m**. What value might **m** contain? There are five possibilities:

m	Meaning
3	Three **doubles** scanned and stored
2	Two **doubles** scanned and stored
1	One **double** scanned and stored
0	No value scanned or stored
EOF	"End of File"

If the **scanf()** function is able to read and store three **doubles**, it returns the integer value 3; this value is then assigned to **m**. Suppose, however, that an error occurs while **scanf()** is trying to read the standard input. In that case, **scanf()** returns **2**, **1**, or **0**, depending on how many numbers it was able to store before encountering the error.

There is another possibility: **scanf()** stops reading if it receives an "End of File" signal from the operating system. When that happens, **scanf()** returns a value equal to **EOF**, a symbolic constant defined in the *stdio.h* file. (EOF usually has the value −1, although it may have some other negative value on some systems.)

Program: *ave.c*

The ***ave.c*** program will read in a series of numbers from the standard input until it receives an EOF signal. Then it will compute and print the arithmetic mean of the numbers. Recall that the arithmetic mean of n numbers is defined by*

$$\text{Arithmetic mean} = \frac{x_1 + x_2 + \ldots + x_n}{n} = \frac{1}{n}\sum_{i=1}^{n} x_i$$

For example, the mean of the numbers 1.0, 2.0, 3.0, . . . , 10.0 is

$$\frac{1.0 + 2.0 + 3.0 + 4.0 + 5.0 + 6.0 + 7.0 + 8.0 + 9.0 + 10.0}{10} = \frac{55.0}{10} = 5.50$$

The pseudocode for this program is

initialize counter to 0
initialize sum to 0.0
scan the standard input for next number
while the EOF is not reached
    add next number to sum
    add 1 to count
    scan the standard input for next number
compute average: ave = sum/count
print ave

The pseudocode outline suggests that a **while** loop be used. Why this and not a **for** loop? The answer is simple: We don't know before entering the loop how many numbers will be in the file. The program will continue reading numbers as long as it does not receive an EOF signal. Note that the program counts how many numbers have been read; this is needed to compute the average.

---

* In mathematics, the capital sigma is used to indicate the sum of a number of similar terms. Thus,

$$\sum_{i=1}^{5} x_i = x_1 + x_2 + x_3 + x_4 + x_5$$

Listing 6–3 *ave.c*

```
/*********************************************

   Compute the arithmetic average of double
   values taken from the standard input.

*********************************************/

#include <stdio.h>

main()
{
1     double next_num;
      double sum;
      double ave;
      int count;
      int flag;

2     count = 0;
3     sum = 0.0;

4     flag = scanf("%lf", &next_num);
5     while (flag != EOF ) {
6         sum = sum + next_num;
          count = count + 1;
          flag = scanf("%lf", &next_num);
      }

7     ave = sum/(double)count;
      printf("The average is %g.\n", ave);
}
```

Dissection of *ave.c*

1 `double next_num;`

The variable **next_num** receives each value as it is scanned in from a file or the keyboard. The meanings of the other variables should be obvious from their names.

② `count = 0;`

The variable `count` is initialized to 0 because at this point in the program no numbers have been scanned or stored. If you do not initialize the counter, you cannot be sure what it will contain.

③ `sum = 0.0;`

The variable `sum` is initialized to 0.0; in most cases, this is the proper starting value for a summation.

④ `flag = scanf("%lf", &next_num);`

This **scanf()** attempts to read a **double** value from the standard input; it then returns a value that is assigned to `flag`. When the statement finishes, `flag` can have one of three values:

flag	Meaning
1	One **double** scanned and stored
0	No value stored (error)
EOF	"End of File" (nothing stored)

⑤ `while (flag != EOF) {`

As long as `flag` does not equal **EOF**, the condition remains TRUE, and the body of the loop is executed.

⑥ `sum = sum + next_num;`
`count = count + 1;`
`flag = scanf("%lf", &next_num);`

These statements make up the body of the **while** loop. The first statement keeps a running sum of the numbers entered by the user; the second counts how many numbers have been entered; the third attempts to read another **double** number, then resets the value of `flag`.

⑦ `ave = sum/(double)count;`

This statement, which is executed after the **while** loop finishes, is a good example of the use of a cast operator to avoid mixed arithmetic.

Compiling and Testing *ave.c*

Compile *ave.c* the usual way and run the executable file. Note that this program does not prompt for input. Enter the following numbers, pressing RETURN after each entry:

1 | RET |
2 | RET |
3 | RET |
4 | RET |
5 | RET |
6 | RET |
7 | RET |
8 | RET |
9 | RET |
10 | RET |

The program is waiting for you to enter the next number. It will keep reading and summing numbers until you generate an EOF signal.

Precisely how you generate an EOF is system-dependent. On a UNIX system, type a *d* while holding down the CONTROL key:

| CNTRL | + | d |

On an MS-DOS system, type a *z* while holding down the CONTROL key:

| CNTRL | + | z |

The operating system will send an EOF signal to the program. This causes the program to break out of the **while** loop and compute the average, which is then printed on the standard output:

`The average is 5.5.`

Run the *ave.c* program again, but this time put all of the numbers on the same line, like this:

`1 2 3 4 5 6 7 8 9 10` | RET |

Use the same key combination that you used before to generate an EOF signal:

| CNTRL | + | d | or | CNTRL | + | z |

This should produce the same output as before:

`The average is 5.5.`

Redirection of the Standard Input

The *ave.c* program did not prompt you for input because it is really designed for reading data from a file rather than the keyboard. Operating systems like UNIX and DOS allow you to redirect the standard input so that the program takes its input from a file. If yours is such a system, make up a data file named *data1* containing these numbers:

```
1  2  3  4  5  6  7  8  9  10
```

Save the file and close it. If you are on a UNIX system, run the program this way:

```
a.out < data1 RET
```

On a DOS system, try this:

```
ave < data1 RET
```

On both UNIX and DOS systems, the arrow (<) is the input redirection symbol; it tells the operating system to make *data1* the standard input. The computer will respond with

```
The average is 5.5.
```

This time, it was not necessary for you to generate an EOF signal from the keyboard to mark the end of the data. Why not? When the program reaches the end of the data file, the operating system sends an EOF signal to the **scanf( )** function.

Why would you want to redirect data from a file rather than use the keyboard? If you are testing or running a program that requires a great deal of input data, taking the data from a file will save you time because you only need to enter the data once. If you wish to change the data later, you can modify the file, or set up a new file containing different data.

Infinite Loops

Let's see how well *ave.c* handles erroneous input. Run the program, but this time introduce an error—the letter A—into the input:

```
1  2  3  4  A RET
```

On most systems, you will see nothing—no output, no system prompt—because the program is stuck in an *infinite loop*. It will continue to execute the **while** loop over and over without stopping. We will explain why in a moment, but first you should stop the program with the system *interrupt* or *kill* command. On UNIX and DOS systems this is done with the CONTROL+c combination:

CNTRL + c

This will not work on some DOS systems, and you will have to reboot your machine.

To see why the infinite loop occurs, consider how the program reads numbers:

```
flag = scanf("%lf", &next_num);
while (flag != EOF) {
    sum = sum + next_num;
    count = count + 1;
    flag = scanf("%lf", &next_num);
}
```

The **scanf()** function expects to find a **double** value in the standard input. A non-numeric character such as *A* is definitely not a **double**, so **scanf()** leaves the *A* in the standard input and returns a 0. This value is assigned to **flag**. Next, the condition of the **while** loop is evaluated:

```
while (flag != EOF) {
```

The condition is true—zero is not the same as EOF—so the loop is executed. Inside the loop, **scanf()** tries again to read a **double**, but the character *A* is still sitting in the standard input; **scanf()** leaves it there and returns a zero to **flag**. This makes the **while** condition true, so the loop is executed, with the same result as before. This continues over and over until you stop it with the interrupt command.

The way to prevent this problem is to change the condition in the **while** loop:

```
while (1 == flag) {
```

Now the loop will be executed only so long as the **scanf()** function returns the value 1, which it does each time it reads and stores a **double**. Either a nonnumeric character or an EOF will stop the loop. (Modify your program and try it.)

Note that we write the condition as **(1 == flag)** rather than **(flag == 1)**. This is to guard against an error that we mentioned in Chapter 5, that of writing an assignment operator (=) instead of an equality operator (==). Consider what would happen if you were to modify the loop this way:

```
while (flag = 1) {          /* Wrong! Infinite loop */
```

The assignment expression **flag = 1** always has the value 1, making the **while** condition perpetually true. The program would get stuck in an infinite loop.

An Improved Factorial Program: *fact3.c*

Computer users occasionally make mistakes, especially when entering data at the keyboard. You should anticipate the kinds of errors that users might make and write your programs to handle such errors gracefully. Our next program shows how this can be done. It also shows how a **for** loop can be used as part of an **if/else** structure.

What we want is a factorial program that checks for three possible input errors: nonnumerical input, negative input, and input values that produce factorials too large to fit in an **int** variable. In each of these cases, the program will print an appropriate error message. The pseudocode for this program is shown below.

prompt the user for n
scan the standard input for n
if n is not a number
    print an error message
else if n is negative
    print an error message
else if n is greater than maximum allowable input
    print an error message
else
    [compute and print the factorial as before]

The C code is shown in Listing 6–4. (*Hint:* Make a copy of the *fact2.c* program and alter the copy to match the new listing.)

Listing 6-4. *fact3.c*

```
/*******************************************************

    Compute the factorial of an integer. Check for
    (1) Nonnumeric input;
    (2) Negative arguments;
    (3) Arguments that are too large;

*******************************************************/

#include <stdio.h>
#define MAX_INPUT 12

main()
{
    int n;              /* Value entered by user */
    int i;              /* Counter */
    int fact;           /* Factorial of n */
    int flag;           /* Flag for checking input */

    printf("This program computes the factorial.\n");
    printf("Please enter a nonnegative integer: ");
    flag = scanf("%d", &n);

    if (1 != flag) {
        printf("Input must be an integer.\n");
    }
    else if (n < 0) {
        printf("The factorial is undefined ");
        printf("for negative arguments.\n");
    }
    else if (n > MAX_INPUT) {
        printf("This program cannot handle input values "
                "greater than %d.\n", MAX_INPUT);
    }
    else {
        fact = 1;
        for (i = 1; i <= n; i = i + 1) {
            fact = fact * i;
        }
        printf("The factorial of %d is %d\n", n, fact);
    }
}
```

Dissection of *fact3.c*

(1) `#define MAX_INPUT 12`

The largest input value for which our system can compute the factorial is 12; the largest that your system can handle may be different.

(2)
```
if (1 != flag) {
    printf("Input must be an integer.\n");
}
```

Although we have prompted for a nonnegative integer, the user of the program may accidentally enter a character that is not a digit. If this happens, the error message is printed, all of the **else** clauses are skipped, and the program ends.

(3)
```
else {
    fact = 1;
    for (i = 1; i <= n; i = i + 1) {
        fact = fact * i;
    }
    printf("The factorial of %d is %d\n", n, fact);
}
```

The program computes and prints the factorial only if **n** is a nonnegative integer less than or equal to **MAX_INPUT**.

Compiling and Testing *fact3.c*

Compile *fact3.c* and try some test cases:

Input	Output
abc	Input must be an integer.
−5	The factorial is undefined [etc.]
0	The factorial of 0 is 1
5	The factorial of 5 is 120
50	This program cannot handle [etc.]
4.7	The factorial of 4 is 24
4a7	The factorial of 4 is 24

Pay particular attention to the last two cases. The **scanf()** function expects to find an integer value in the standard input. It reads digits until it encounters either white space or a nonnumeric character. Consequently, it gets only the **4** from **4.7** or **4a7**, leaving the rest of the characters in the standard input.

Square Roots by Iteration

If the C standard mathematics library did not include the **sqrt()** function, would you know how to compute square roots? There is a procedure, called Newton's method, that may be used to approximate square roots. Suppose you wish to compute the square root of x, a positive number. If a is an approximation to the root, then the formula

$$\frac{1}{2}\left(a + \frac{x}{a}\right)$$

will produce a better approximation. The idea is to use this formula over and over again to produce better and better approximations, a process that is known as *iteration*. The iteration ends when a is as close to the true value of the root as desired, at which point we say that the program has *converged* to an answer.

Let's try this procedure to compute the square root of 5.0 to nine decimal digits. To begin, we need an initial guess for the root. It does not matter what value we choose for our initial guess, as long as it is positive. Let's try 3:

$$\frac{1}{2}\left(3 + \frac{5}{3}\right) = 2.333333333$$

If 2.333333333 is indeed the root we seek, then squaring it should produce the result 5.0:

$$(2.333333333)^2 = 5.444444445$$

That is not close enough, so we reapply the formula until we are satisfied with the result:

$$\frac{1}{2}\left(2.333333333 + \frac{5}{2.333333333}\right) = 2.238095238$$

Check: $(2.238095238)^2 = 5.009070295$

$$\frac{1}{2}\left(2.238095238 + \frac{5}{2.238095238}\right) = 2.236068896$$

Check: $(2.236068896)^2 = 5.000004106$

$$\frac{1}{2}\left(2.236068896 + \frac{5}{2.236068896}\right) = 2.236067977$$

Check: $(2.236067977)^2 = 5.000000000$

We conclude that the square root of 5.0, to nine decimal digits, is 2.236067977.

Program: *sqroot.c*

Let's write a computer program that computes square roots by iteration. Here is the pseudocode:

prompt user for x
read x
make initial approximation: a = 1
while (a² is not close enough to x)
     a = 0.5 * (a + x/a)
print a

This looks simple enough, but how do we decide when a^2 is "close enough" to x? At first, you might be tempted to write something like this:

```
while (a * a != x) {
```

This is not a good idea, as you can see from the case of $x = 2$. The square root of 2 is an irrational number, a nonterminating decimal:

$$\sqrt{2} = 1.4142135624\ldots$$

No matter how good our approximation, it can never equal the root exactly. Consequently, the program would get caught in an infinite loop.

When dealing with problems such as this, it is helpful to define a quantity called the *relative error*. In general,

$$\text{Relative error} \equiv \left| \frac{\text{true value} - \text{approximation}}{\text{true value}} \right|$$

where the vertical bars denote absolute value. In the square root problem, the relative error might be written as

$$\text{Relative error} = \left| \frac{x - a^2}{x} \right|$$

We do not expect to reduce the relative error to zero because, as we have seen, that may be impossible. The best we can hope for is to reduce the error to some very small amount. In other words, we want the program to continue iterating as long as

$$\left| \frac{x - a^2}{x} \right| \geq \epsilon$$

where ϵ is a small positive number called the *tolerance*. Rearranging this, we obtain an equivalent condition that avoids the possibility of division by zero:

$$|x - a^2| \leq \epsilon \cdot |x|$$

How do we choose ϵ to get a small error without the risk of an infinite loop? The answer is provided by the C standard library. We cannot safely choose a tolerance smaller than **DBL_EPSILON**, which is a symbolic constant defined in the standard header file *float.h*. Even that might be too small a tolerance, so we will use 4.0 times **DBL_EPSILON** for ϵ:

$$\left| x - a^2 \right| \geq 4.0 \cdot \textbf{DBL\_EPSILON} \cdot \left| x \right|$$

Hence, the condition of the **while** loop becomes

```
while (fabs(x - a * a) >= 4.0 * DBL_EPSILON * fabs(x)) {
```

Listing 6–5 sets out the C code for computing square roots by Newton's method.

Listing 6–5. *sqroot.c*

```
/*****************************************************
    Compute the square root of a positive number
    using Newton's method.

*****************************************************/
#include <stdio.h>
#include <float.h>
#include <math.h>

main()
{
    double x;          /* Value entered by user */
    double a;          /* Approximation to the root */

    printf("This program computes square roots.\n");
    printf("Please enter a positive number: ");
    scanf("%lf", &x);

    a = 1.0;           /* Make initial guess of root. */

    while (fabs(x - a * a) >= 4.0 * DBL_EPSILON * fabs(x)) {
        a = 0.5 * (a + x/a);
    }

    printf("The square root of %g is %g\n", x, a);
}
```

Dissection of *sqroot.c*

1 ```
   #include <stdio.h>
   #include <float.h>
   #include <math.h>
   ```

This program uses three standard header files: *stdio.h* contains the prototypes for **printf()** and **scanf()**; *float.h* contains the definition of DBL_EPSILON; and *math.h* contains the prototype for the floating-point absolute value function, **fabs()**.

2  ```
   double x;        /* Value entered by user */
   double a;        /* Approximation to the root */
   ```

We chose **x** and **a** as variable names to match the variables in the original mathematical formula. However, these aren't very descriptive, so we also provide explanatory comments.

3 ```
   a = 1.0;   /* Make initial guess of root. */
   ```

Someone unfamiliar with computing square roots by iteration might not understand why the variable **a** is initialized to 1.0. The comment tells the reader that this value is just a starting guess.

---

Compiling and Testing *sqroot.c*

Compile *sqroot.c* and try the program on some test cases. You will notice that it gets stuck in an infinite loop for nonpositive input values. We leave it as an exercise for you to correct this deficiency (Exercise 12).

## Round-off Error and Infinite Loops

In our discussion of the *sqroot.c* program, we warned you not to write the condition of the **while** loop the obvious way, like this:

```
while (a * a != x) {              /* Warning! */
```

The explanation we gave at the time was that nonterminating decimals (such as the square root of 2) cannot be represented exactly as **double** values. Therefore, **a** * **a** would never equal **x** exactly, and the loop would never stop.

But that tells only part of the story—nonterminating decimals are not the only numbers that would cause an infinite loop. For instance, the square root of 13.69 is 3.7. Surprising as it may seem, neither 13.69 or 3.7 can be represented exactly as a **double** value, although neither number is a nonterminating decimal. The rea-
```

son becomes clear when we recall that the computer stores everything in binary form:

$$(13.69)_{\text{decimal}} = (1101.10110000101 \dots)_{\text{binary}}$$

$$(3.7)_{\text{decimal}} = (11.101100110011 \dots)_{\text{binary}}$$

Although 13.69 and 3.7 have finite decimal representations, their binary representations are infinite. Consequently, the computer must round off these numbers to store them as **double**s. The resulting round-off error makes it impossible to compute the root exactly.

For another example, consider the following loop:

```
sum = 0.0
while (sum != 1.0) {              /* Infinite loop? */
    sum = sum + 0.1;
}
```

You might expect this loop to compute the sum $0.1 + 0.1 + 0.1 + 0.1 + 0.1 + 0.1 + 0.1 + 0.1 + 0.1 + 0.1 = 1.0$, stopping after ten iterations. But on many systems, this loop would never stop—the sum would never be exactly 1.0 because of rounding. The moral of the story is this:

> *Do not use* $==$ *or* $!=$ *to compare two floating-point values in a loop condition.*

Instead, always use the operators $<$, $<=$, $>=$, or $>$. Thus the previous loop could be more safely written as

```
sum = 0.0
while (sum < 1.0) {
    sum = sum + 0.1;
}
```

This will prevent an infinite loop but still does not guarantee that the loop will be executed the proper number of times. (On some systems, this loop will be repeated eleven times.) To ensure that the loop is executed exactly ten times, you could use a **for** loop with an integer counter:

```
sum = 0.0
for (i = 1; i < 10; i = i + 1) {
    sum = sum + 0.1;
}
```

Because integers are not subject to round-off error, there is less danger of an infinite loop occurring when an integer-valued condition is used to control a loop.

When Are Loops Useful?

In this chapter we have shown you a number of examples of **while** and **for** loops. Even so, if you are like many beginning programmers, you may still have trouble deciding when to use a loop in a program. We have some suggestions that might help.

First, recognize that many everyday situations involve repetition. For instance, consider the problem of sharpening a pencil. Here is one way to summarize the process:

check the pencil point
while (point is not sharp)
    insert point into sharpener
    operate the sharpener
    remove pencil from sharpener
    check the point

This outline is not as detailed as it might be. In particular, if the sharpener is a hand-cranked model, then the instruction "operate the sharpener" would itself involve repetition:

check the pencil point
while (point is not sharp)
    insert point into sharpener

    for (10 revolutions)
      turn the crank

    remove pencil from sharpener
    check the point

No doubt you can think of other familiar situations that involve repetition. We suggest you try writing pseudocode outlines for some of these situations. (See Exercise 6.)

STYLE

When writing either a **while** or a **for** loop, we always indent the statement(s) forming the body of the loop, and we always enclose the body of the loop in braces. The idea here, as always, is to improve readability:

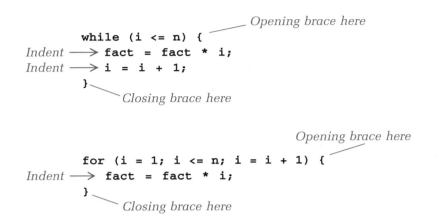

```
                                                              Opening brace here
                 while (i <= n) {
   Indent  ----> fact = fact * i;
   Indent  ----> i = i + 1;
                 }
                     Closing brace here
```

```
                                               Opening brace here
                 for (i = 1; i <= n; i = i + 1) {
   Indent  ----> fact = fact * i;
                 }
                     Closing brace here
```

Another convention that we frequently follow is to use **i**, **j**, **k**, **m**, and **n** as counters. (This is a holdover from Fortran, which by default assumes that variable names beginning in **i**, **j**, **k**, **m**, or **n** hold integer values.)

HELPFUL HINTS

To avoid infinite loops, we recommend the following:

- Make sure that the condition controlling a **while** or **for** loop will eventually test false—i.e., that it will eventually reach zero.
- Do not change the value of the loop counter inside the body of a **for** loop.
- When attempting an iterative solution, be careful not to select an error tolerance that is too small. If your program becomes stuck in an infinite loop, try a larger tolerance.

You may have noticed that sometimes we initialize variables—give them explicit starting values—sometimes we don't. We offer three rules of thumb regarding initialization of variables:

- Any variable that appears on the right side of an assignment operator (=) requires initialization.
- A variable that is part of a condition controlling a **while** loop must be initialized before the start of the loop.
- When computing the sum of a set of data (as in the *ave.c* program), the variable holding the sum is usually initialized to zero. When computing the product of a data set (as in the *fact.c* program), the product is usually initialized to one, not zero.

● ▓▓▓▓▓▓▓▓ **Summary**

while Loop

```
while (condition) {
    statement(s);
}
```

Tests the condition; if it is true, the statements in the body of the loop are executed. Repeats this as long as the condition tests true.

for Loop

```
for (initialize; test; update) {
    statement(s);
}
```

Performs initialization before the start of the first repetition only. If the test condition is true, the statements in the body of the loop are executed, then the update is performed. Repeats this process—test, execute, update—as long as the condition tests true.

End-of-File Condition

```
flag = scanf("%lf", &x);
while (flag != EOF) {
    sum = sum + x;
    count = count + 1;
    flag = scanf("%lf", &x);
}
```

Reads **double** values from the standard input, then sums and counts them, until **scanf( )** returns EOF.

End-of-File Signals

CNTRL + d

CNTRL + z

Signals End of File on UNIX machines.

Signals End of File on DOS machines.

System-Interrupt Signal

CNTRL + c

Interrupts a program (UNIX and DOS).

- Much of the power of computers lies in their ability to perform a task over and over, without getting tired or bored. This is called *repetition, iteration,* or *looping.*

- The two most common repetition structures in C are the **while** loop and the **for** loop. If the loop is to be controlled by a counter—that is, if it is to be executed a certain number of times—we prefer the **for** loop. Otherwise, we use the **while** loop.

- The **scanf( )** function returns an integer value that indicates the number of items that were read and stored. If an end-of-file signal is received, it returns a negative value equal to EOF. (EOF is defined in **stdio.h.**) If **scanf( )** encounters a nonnumeric character while trying to read an **int** or **double** value, that character is left in the standard input.

- Operating systems like UNIX and DOS allow the standard input to be redirected so that **scanf()** will read data from a file rather than the keyboard.
- An infinite loop occurs when the condition controlling the loop is always true. An infinite loop can be stopped by a system interrupt or by rebooting.
- Many mathematical problems can be solved by iteration. An iterative solution begins with an initial guess or approximation to the answer. This approximation is repeatedly improved until it satisfies some convergence criterion. Because of the finite size of computer variables, some problems cannot be solved exactly.

EXERCISES

1. Define: **a.** repetition; **b. while** loop; **c.** counter; **d. for** loop; **e.** EOF; **f.** arithmetic mean; **g.** input error; **h.** iteration; **i.** convergence; **j.** relative error; **k.** tolerance.

2. *Errors.* Create a copy of *ave.c* called *errors61.c* and introduce into the new file the first error listed below. Run your compiler on the file. If the compiler catches the error, write down both the error and the error message; if not, run the executable file with test data and make a note of any unexpected results. Correct the file, then repeat the process with the next error on the list. Continue until you have tried all of the errors.

   a. Remove the ! from the condition of the **while** loop.
   b. Remove the line `flag = scanf("%lf", &next_num);` from the **while** loop.
   c. Remove the closing brace } from the **while** loop.
   d. Insert a semicolon between the closing parenthesis of the **while** condition and the opening brace of the loop body.

3. *More errors.* Create a copy of *fact3.c* called *errors62.c*. Follow the instructions given in Exercise 2, but introduce the following errors into the file:

   a. Remove the semicolon from the condition in the **for** loop.
   b. Remove the < from the condition in the **for** loop.
   c. Replace the first `i` with a `1` in the `i = i + 1` statement of the **for** loop.
   d. Replace the `i = i + 1` expression of the **for** loop with `i + 1`.
   e. Remove the closing brace } from the body of the **for** loop.
   f. Insert a semicolon between the closing parenthesis of the **for** loop condition and the opening brace of the loop body.

4. How many times is the **for** loop in the following program executed? What is printed on the screen?

```
main()
{
    int a;
```

```
        double prod;
        prod = 1.0;
        for (a = 10; a > 0; a = a - 3) {
           prod = prod * a;
           printf("%d %g\n", a, prod);
        }
     }
```

5. What is wrong with the following loop? How would you correct the problem?

```
first = -10;
second = 15;
while (!(first == second)) {
   printf("first = %d, second = %d \n", first, second);
   first = first + 3;
}
```

6. Write pseudocode outlines to describe how you would perform the following tasks:

   a. Washing a window;

   b. Walking up a flight of stairs (assume n steps);

   c. Climbing stairs to the top of a building (assume the number of steps is not known);

   d. Sharpening a box of pencils using a manual sharpener;

   e. Eating an apple.

7. Convert the following pseudocode into a working program.

   initialize counters

   prompt for first number

   read first number

   while the number is read correctly

      increase numbers_read by 1

      if number is even

       increase even_numbers by 1

      else

       increase odd_numbers by 1

      prompt for the next number

      read the next number

   print out the results

   Consider *numbers_read, even_numbers,* and *odd_numbers* to be variable names.

8. Modify *prlimits.c* so that it also prints the value of DBL_EPSILON (which is defined in *float.h*) and the value of EOF (which is defined in *stdio.h*).

9. We previously noted that the factorial may be computed by starting at *n* and decreasing the factors until reaching 1; we called this "counting down."

    a. Make a copy of *fact1.c* called *fact1dwn.c* and modify the program so that it computes the factorial by counting down rather than counting up.

    b. Make a copy of *fact2.c* called *fact2dwn.c* and modify the program so that it computes the factorial by counting down rather than counting up.

10. Modify the *ave.c* program so that it also prints out the number of items read from the standard input.

11. There is one problem with the *ave.c* program: If a user should fail to enter any data—or redirects the standard input to take data from an empty file—a division by zero will result. Modify your *ave.c* program so that it does not attempt to compute the average when no data are read, but instead prints No data read.

12. Correct the program *sqroot.c* so that it handles negative inputs. (Hint: Negative numbers have imaginary roots.)

13. Make a copy of *sqroot.c* called *sqroot2.c* and modify it so that it prints out the approximation of the square root (**a**) each time through the loop. Run the program and note the results. Next, for each case listed below, modify the error tolerance, compile and run the code, and note the results.

    a. Decrease the error tolerance from 4.0 * DBL_EPSILON to DBL_EPSILON.

    b. Decrease the error tolerance to zero.

    c. Increase the error tolerance to 10.0 * DBL_EPSILON.

    d. Increase the error tolerance to 100.0 * DBL_EPSILON.

    e. Increase the error tolerance to 1.0.

14. As we pointed out earlier, the factorial quickly becomes too large to fit in an **int** variable. There are two ways around this problem:

    a. Use **long** integers. On many systems, **long**s can hold larger values than **int**s. Make a copy of *fact3.c* named *fact4.c* and modify it to compute the factorial using **long**s. What is the largest input value the new program can handle?

    b. Use **double**s. In general, **double**s can represent larger values than **int**s. Make a copy of *fact3.c* named *fact5.c* and modify it to compute the factorial using **double** variables throughout. What is the largest input value the new program can handle?

15. Write a program that reads **double** numbers from the standard input, and prints the number of positive, negative, and zero values. For example, given the input data

```
12.3  -7.6  0.00  -99.9  0.667  0.00  14.7  -0.75  -47.0
```

the program would print

```
You entered:
   3 positive values
   2 zero values
   4 negative values
```

16. *Geometric mean.* Write a program called **geomean.c** that reads positive **double** numbers from the standard input, and computes the *geometric mean*, defined by

$$\text{Geometric mean} = \overline{G} \equiv \sqrt[n]{x_1 x_2 \ldots x_n} = \sqrt[n]{\prod_{i=1}^{n} x_i}$$

Your program should test the data as they are read; if any value is negative or zero, the program should print an appropriate error message and quit.

The geometric mean is used for averaging ratios or percentage rates of increase. For example, suppose the ratio of the price of gold to the price of silver is 71.7288 the first day, 68.4155 the second day, and 64.5890 the third day. The average ratio of the prices for the three days would be

$$\text{Average price ratio} = \sqrt[3]{(71.7288)(68.4155)(64.5890)} = 68.1819$$

Note that the average ratio of silver to gold prices would be just the reciprocal of this value: $1/68.1819 = 0.01467$. (This would not be true if we had used the arithmetic mean.)

17. *Harmonic mean.* Write a program called **harmean.c** that reads **double** numbers from the standard input, and computes the *harmonic mean*, defined by

$$\text{Harmonic mean} = \overline{H} \equiv \frac{n}{\left(\dfrac{1}{x_1} + \dfrac{1}{x_2} + \cdots + \dfrac{1}{x_n}\right)} = \frac{n}{\displaystyle\sum_{i=1}^{n} \dfrac{1}{x_i}}$$

What conditions, if any, will cause an error in this program? (If such an error occurs, the program should print an appropriate message, then quit.)

One use of the harmonic mean is the computation of the average speeds for repeated trips over the same distance. For example, suppose that a car, during practice for the Indianapolis 500 race, completes one lap at 150.3 mph, a second lap at 188.9 mph, and a third lap at 230.4 mph. The average speed for all three laps would be

$$\text{Average speed} = \frac{3}{\left(\dfrac{1}{150.3} + \dfrac{1}{188.9} + \dfrac{1}{230.4}\right)} = 184.2 \text{ mph}$$

18. *Quadratic mean.* The *quadratic mean*, also known as the *root mean square*, is used in certain physical situations instead of the more familiar arithmetic mean. For example, the total kinetic energy of n identical gas molecules moving with speeds $v_1, v_2, \ldots, v_n$ is given by

$$E = n\left(\frac{1}{2}mv_{\mathrm{rms}}^2\right)$$

where E is the total energy, m is the mass of one molecule, and v_{rms} is the quadratic mean of the individual molecular speeds:

$$\text{Quadratic mean speed} = v_{\mathrm{rms}} = \sqrt{\frac{v_1^2 + v_2^2 + \cdots + v_n^2}{n}}$$

$$= \sqrt{\frac{1}{n}\sum_{i=1}^{n} v_i^2}$$

Write a program called **quadmean.c** that reads **double** numbers from a file or the standard input, and computes the quadratic mean. What conditions, if any, will cause an error in this program? (If such an error occurs, the program should print an appropriate message, then quit.)

19. *McDowell's Restaurant.* Just as a loop can be put inside an **if/else** statement, so too can an **if/else** structure be put inside a loop. Write a program for McDowell's Grub-O-Matic food service machine that prints the following menu on the screen:

```
*************************************************************
                    McDowell's Restaurant
*************************************************************

Make your selection from the menu below:

1. Regular hamburger                                  $0.99

2. Regular cheeseburger                               $1.09

3. Fish sandwich                                      $1.49

4. Half-pounder with cheese                           $2.79

5. French fries                                       $0.99

6. Large soft drink                                   $0.99

Type Q when you are finished with your selections.


*************************************************************

Select 1, 2, 3, 4, 5, or 6 ---->
```

Your program should read the customer's selection and print a prompt asking how many orders of that item the customer wants:

How many orders of item number [*print item number here*] **would you like?**

After reading the number, the program should print the menu again, and continue until the customer types the letter Q. Then the program should compute the price (assume 5.5% sales tax for now) and print out a message:

Please pay [*print total bill here*]**.**
Thank you for eating at McDowell's!

To make your program more flexible, use **#define** preprocessor directives to set the prices and sales tax rate.

20. *Cube roots by iteration.* If *a* is an approximation to the cube root of *x*, then the formula

$$\frac{1}{3}\left(2a + \frac{x}{a^2}\right)$$

will produce an even better approximation. Write your own cube root program that uses nothing from the C mathematical library except the absolute value function.

21. *Fibonacci numbers.* In 1202, Leonardo Fibonacci of Pisa published the following problem:

A pair of newborn rabbits begins mating at age 1 month and thereafter produces one pair of offspring per month. If we start with a newly born pair of rabbits, how many rabbits will there be at the beginning of each month?

Fibonacci offered a solution:

Month	0	1	2	3	4	5	6	7	...	*m*
Pairs	1	1	2	3	5	8	13	21	...	$P_m = P_{m-1} + P_{m-2}$

The sequence of integers 1, 1, 2, 3, 5, 8, 13, ... has been named the *Fibonacci sequence* in honor of the mathematician. The first two Fibonacci numbers are both 1; thereafter, each number in the sequence is the sum of the two preceding numbers. Write a program that prompts the user for an integer *m*, then prints the *m*th Fibonacci number. Your program should print an appropriate error message if the user enters a negative integer.

22. *Greatest common divisor.* The *greatest common divisor* (gcd) of two nonzero integers *p* and *q* (*p* > *q*) is the largest positive integer that will evenly divide both *p* and *q*. The "brute force" method of finding the gcd involves checking each of the divisors *q*, *q* − 1, *q* − 2, ..., 4, 3, 2, 1 until you find one that will divide both *p* and *q*. Write a program that carries out this procedure. (*Hint:* if an integer *d* evenly divides *p*, then the remainder *p* % *d* is zero.)

23. *Euclid's algorithm* is an ancient method for finding the gcd (see previous exercise) of two nonnegative integers *p* and *q*, *p* ≥ *q*. If *q* = 0, the gcd is just *p*. Otherwise, we carry out the following three steps:

$r = p \% q$ (take the remainder)

$p = q$ (replace p by q)

$q = r$ (replace q by the remainder)

Repeat these three steps until $q = 0$, at which point the gcd is p. Write a program that employs Euclid's algorithm to compute the gcd of two integers entered by the user.

24. *Prime numbers.* An integer is said to be *prime* if it is divisible evenly only by 1 and itself. The "brute force" method for determining whether an integer n is prime involves checking to see if any of the divisors 2, 3, 4, 5, $\ldots$, n divides n evenly. (Actually, it is not necessary to try divisors larger than the square root of n.) Write a program to determine whether an integer entered by the user is prime.

25. *Day of the year.* A financial planning firm wants a program that will determine the day of the year for a given date. For example, 12-18-1953 (December 18, 1953) was the 352nd day of the year. Write a program that determines the day of the year for a given date. (*Hint:* You will need to account for leap years; see Exercises 23 and 24, Chapter 5. For years before and including 1752, use the Julian calendar; for years after 1752, use the Gregorian Calendar.)

26. *Depreciation: straight-line method.* Companies that own high-ticket items, such as buildings and machines, often find it to their advantage (e.g., to reduce their taxes) to calculate the depreciation of these items over time. The simplest method of calculating depreciation is the straight-line method:

$$D = V_0 / L_e$$

where D is the amount that the item depreciates in one year, V_0 is the original value of the item, and L_e is the expected life (in years) of the item. Thus, the item decreases in value by the same amount (D) each year for the expected lifetime (L_e) of the item.

Write a program that prompts for the original value of an item and its expected life, then prints a table listing the following information for each year of the expected life: (1) the year; (2) D for that year; and (3) the depreciated value of the item at the end of the year.

27. *Depreciation: 15-year accelerated method.* As an alternative to the straight-line depreciation method described in the previous problem, some companies use the 15-year accelerated method of depreciation. Under this plan, property is depreciated 12 percent of the original value in the first year; 10 percent of the original value in the second year; 9, 8, and 7 percent of the original value in the third, fourth, and fifth years, respectively; then 6 percent for four years, and 5 percent for the remaining six years.

Write a program that reads in the original value of a piece of property, and prints a depreciation table. For example, for an initial property value of $30,000, the table should look similar to the following:

Year	Depreciation (%)	Depreciation ($)	Balance ($)
0	– –	– –	30000.00
1	12.0	3600.00	26400.00
2	10.0	3000.00	23400.00
3	9.0	2700.00	20700.00
4	8.0	2400.00	18300.00
5	7.0	2100.00	16200.00
6	6.0	1800.00	14400.00
7	6.0	1800.00	12600.00
8	6.0	1800.00	10800.00
9	6.0	1800.00	9000.00
10	5.0	1500.00	7500.00
11	5.0	1500.00	6000.00
12	5.0	1500.00	4500.00
13	5.0	1500.00	3000.00
14	5.0	1500.00	1500.00
15	5.0	1500.00	0.00

28. *Safe training heart rate.* The Acme Fitness Corporation is designing computerized exercise systems that they plan to install in their gyms. One feature that they want is software that will help patrons exercise at safe training heart rates. They have adopted the following standard (Covert Bailey, *Fit or Fat*, Boston: Houghton Mifflin Co., 1978):

$$TR = (MR - RR) \times 0.65 + RR$$

in which TR is the proper training heart rate (in beats per minute), MR is the maximum safe heart rate (equal to the person's age subtracted from 220), and RR is the resting heart rate. To train properly, a person should maintain a heart rate that is within ± 10 beats per minute of the calculated TR for at least 20 minutes.

Write an interactive program that will first take as input the patron's age and average RR, then compute and print MR and TR. After that, the program will continue to prompt for the client's actual exercising heart rate (ER) until the patron signals a desire to stop. (If this program were actually used by a fitness club, the client would probably be hooked up to a monitor that would continuously measure the heart rate. Lacking such equipment, assume that the patron will stop exercising periodically, measure his/her ER manually, and enter the data into the computer.) For each entry, the program will print a warning if the ER is not within ± 10 beats of the TR, or a message of encouragement if it is in the proper range.

29. *Designing wall insulation.* Hacienda Construction plans to design and build energy-efficient homes. The company has hired you to write a program to compute heat-transfer rates through a wall consisting of one or more layers of material. The rate at which heat can be transferred by conduction across these multiple layers is described by

$$H = A\left(\frac{T_2 - T_1}{\sum R_i}\right)$$

where H is the rate of heat transfer (in BTU/hr), A is the outside surface area of the wall (ft^2), T_1 and T_2 are the interior and exterior temperatures (°F), and $\sum R_i$ is the sum of the R values for the individual layers of the wall. The R value for the ith wall layer is given by

$$R_i = \frac{L_i}{k_i}$$

where L_i is the thickness of the layer (ft) and k_i is its thermal conductivity in BTU/(hr · ft · °F).

Your program should allow the user to enter the surface area A, the temperatures T_1 and T_2, and the L and k values for as many layers as desired. It should then compute and print the value of $\sum R_i$ and H across the layered wall. Suppose you wanted to insulate a wall made of concrete blocks, 6 inches thick. Which would provide better insulation, a 3.5-inch layer of fiberglass batting, or a 1-inch layer of polystyrene foam? How would each of these insulating materials affect the heat transfer rate? (Use the data given in Exercise 25 of Chapter 3.)

30. *Trapezoidal rule.* The trapezoidal rule is a method of numerical integration in which the area under a curve is approximated by dividing the area into small trapezoids and summing the areas of these trapezoids:

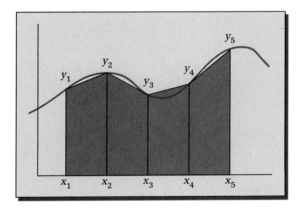

The sum of the trapezoidal areas can be computed as

$$\sum_{i=2}^{n} \frac{(y_i + y_{i-1})}{2}(x_i - x_{i-1})$$

Where n is the number of trapezoids. Write a program that computes the area under a curve, given n and the x and y values for each trapezoid.

Chapter 7.

User-Defined Functions

A C program consists of one or more units called *functions*—self-contained subprograms that perform various tasks. You already know about quite a few functions, including

Input and output functions: **scanf()**, **printf()**

Trigonometric functions: **sin()**, **cos()**, **tan()**

Logarithmic functions: **log()**, **log10()**

Power functions: **exp()**, **pow()**

These functions are all supplied for you as part of the C system. In this chapter, you will see how to write your own functions.

Why Functions?

Beginning programmers frequently ask why they should bother breaking their programs up into functions—why not put everything into **main()** and be done with it? There are at least three very good reasons to use functions.

First, it is often easier to design a large, difficult program by breaking it down into smaller, more manageable functions.

Second, functions allow us to develop a program in stages, writing and testing one part of the program before moving on to the next part. This can be extremely important when developing a large, complicated program, especially when more than one programmer is working on it.

Third, a function written for one program can often be reused in other programs. Consider the functions in the mathematical library. Because someone else took the trouble to write them, you do not have to. (How would you like to have to write your own **log()** function?) Over time, you can build up your own personal library of useful functions.

A Rounding Function

Our first program will round a **double** value to any specified level. It will consist of two functions, **main()** and **round()**. Here is the pseudocode for **main()**:

prompt user for a number
scan the standard input for number
prompt user for a rounding level
scan the standard input for level
*call **round()** to round off the number*
print the result on the standard output

You may recall that in Chapter 3, we developed a formula for rounding a positive **double**:

```
rounded = (double)(int)(number/level + 0.5) * level;
```

This works for positive values, but what about negative ones? Let's try rounding −36.9 to the nearest ten. Applying the formula, we obtain

```
(double)(int)(-36.9/10.0 + 0.5) * 10.0    ⇒    -30.0 (?)
```

which is the wrong result. Obviously, the formula has to be modified for negative numbers:

```
rounded = (double)(int)(number/level - 0.5) * level;
```

Check this for the case of −36.9:

```
(double)(int)(-36.9/10.0 - 0.5) * 10.0    ⇒    -40.0
```

This is the right result, but you should try a few more cases to make sure that the formula does indeed round negative numbers correctly.

Here is the pseudocode for the **round()** function:

receive number and rounding level from **main()**
if number is nonnegative
    use first formula to round number
otherwise
    use second formula to round number
return rounded value to main program.

Create a file named ***round.c*** and enter the C code as shown in Listing 7–1.

Listing 7–1. *round.c*

```
/**********************************************************

    Test a function that rounds double values.

**********************************************************/

#include <stdio.h>
```

(1) `double round(double number, double level);       /* Prototype */`

```
main()
{
    double input;
    double level;
    double result;

    printf("Round a number to a specified level.\n");

    printf("Please enter the number: ");
    scanf("%lf", &input);

    printf("Please enter the rounding level: ");
    scanf("%lf", &level);
```

(2)   `result = round(input, level);`

```
    printf("%f rounds to %f\n", input, result);
}

/**********************************************************

    round(): Round a number to a specified level.

    For example, if the number is 6784.9, and the level
    is 10.0, the function will return the result 6780.0.

**********************************************************/
```

(3) `double round(double number, double level)       /* Header */`
(4) `{`
(5)   `double rounded;`

```
    if (number >= 0.0) {
        rounded = (double)(int)(number/level + 0.5) * level;
    }
    else {
        rounded = (double)(int)(number/level - 0.5) * level;
    }
```
(6)   `return (rounded);`
(7) `}`

Dissection of **main()**

(1) `double round(double number, double level);`   `/* Prototype */`

This is a function declaration, usually called a *function prototype*. Reading left to right, the prototype tells the compiler three things about **round()**:

1. The function produces a **double** value;
2. Its name is **round()**;
3. The arguments that go inside the parentheses are both **double**s.

The parameter names **number** and **level** are optional, but are included here for clarity. This declaration is not the same as the function *definition*, which is the actual C code that performs the function's task; that is described below.

(2) `result = round(input, level);`

You can call **round()** by writing its name with appropriate arguments inside the parentheses. Here, the value returned by the function is assigned to the variable **result** using the assignment operator.

Dissection of **round()**

(3) `double round(double number, double level)`   `/* Header */`

The first line of the function definition is called the *function header*. It resembles the function prototype we discussed earlier, in that it shows us three things about **round()**:

1. The function produces a **double** value;
2. Its name is **round()**;
3. The arguments that go inside the parentheses are both **double**s.

The parameter names **number** and **level** are required, and may not be omitted from the function header. This is in contrast with the function prototype, in which the parameter names are optional. (Also note that there is no semicolon following the function header.)

(4) `{`

The body of the function definition begins with an open brace.

(5) `double rounded;`

The function **round()** uses a **double** variable named **rounded** to hold the rounded value. Because **rounded** is declared inside **round()**, this variable is invisible to the **main()** function.

⑥ `return (rounded);`

This return statement does two important things. First, it immediately returns control back to the **main()** function. Second, it sends the value in **rounded** back to **main()**, where it can be assigned to the variable **result**. If the **return** were omitted, the value of **result** would not be sent back, although control would eventually be returned to **main()**. The parentheses are optional; the same effect would be achieved by the statement

`return rounded;`

⑦ `}`

The function definition ends with a closing brace.

Compiling and Testing *round.c*

Compile the program the usual way. (Since neither **main()** nor **round()** uses any library math functions, it is not necessary to link the math library to the executable code.) Then try some test cases:

Number	Level	Result
1953.7	1.0	1954.000000
1953.7	10.0	1950.000000
1953.7	1000.0	2000.000000
−1953.7	1.0	−1954.000000
−1953.7	10.0	−1950.000000
−1953.7	1000.0	−2000.000000
1953.7	0.0	?
1953.7	−10.0	?

For the last two test cases in the table, we have put a question mark (?) in the result column. We leave it as an exercise for you to modify **round()** to handle nonpositive rounding levels correctly (Exercise 6).

How a Function Works

Let's examine in greater detail how the *round.c* program works. Figure 7–1 is a diagram representing the functions **main()** and **round()** just before program execution begins. Note that each function occupies its own space in memory, with its own definition and variables. Note too that the variables in the two functions are entirely separate. Thus, although there is a variable named **level** in the

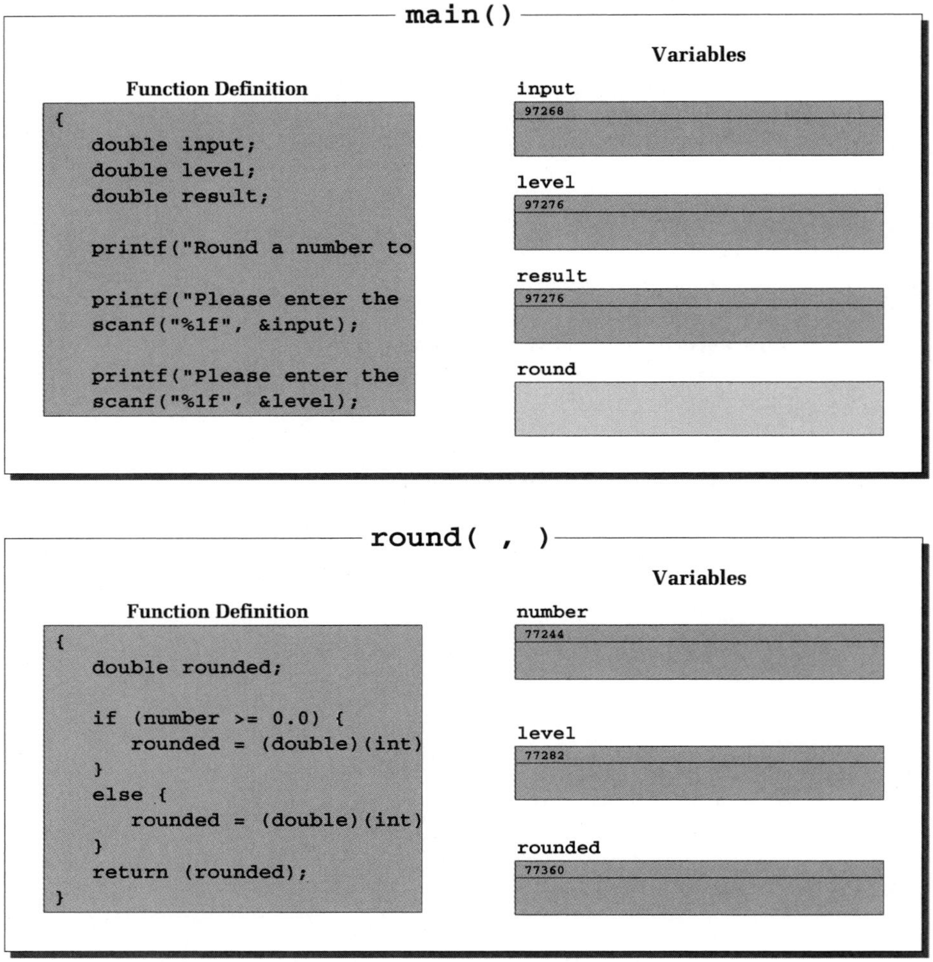

Figure 7–1 The functions **main()** and **round()**. Each function has its own variables and definition. Although there are two variables named **level**, one belongs to **main()**, the other to **round()**; these represent separate and distinct storage locations.

main() function and another named **level** in **round()**, *these are two different variables*. Neither function has direct access to the variables in the other function. In fact,

> *No function knows the name of any variable belonging to another function.*

Each function jealously guards the names of its variables, and it never allows any other function to know those names. Consequently, whenever you see the variable name **level** in the function **main()**, that name refers to the storage location in

main(), and not to a storage location in any other function. Likewise, whenever you see the variable name `level` in the function **round()**, that name refers to the storage location in **round()**, and not to the storage location of the same name in the function **main()**.

Before the program begins, nothing is stored in the variables (except perhaps some "garbage" values left over from previous programs). We have shown this in Figure 7–1 by shading the variable boxes.

Execution Begins

Program execution always begins with the function **main()**. The first executable statement in **main()** prints out a message:

```
Round a number to a specified level.
```

The next statement prompts the user for input. Suppose the user enters 1609.34721869 and presses RETURN:

```
Please enter the number: 1609.34721869 RET
```

This step is illustrated in Figure 7–2. The **scanf()** function obtains 1609.34721869 from the standard input and places this value in the variable `input`.

The next statement in **main()** calls the **printf()** function again to prompt for the rounding level. This time, suppose the user enters 10 and presses RETURN:

```
Please enter the rounding level: 10 RET
```

As shown in Figure 7–3, **scanf()** obtains the value 10.0 from the standard input and stores it in the variable `level`. Be careful to note that this is the variable named `level` that belongs to **main()**; it has no effect on the variable named `level` that belongs to **round()**. Always bear in mind that these two variable names refer to different storage locations.

Calling the Function

After **scanf()** does its job, the program steps down to the very next statement in **main()**:

```
result = round(input, level);
```

Whenever we encounter an assignment statement such as this, we first perform any operation that appears on the right hand side of the = operator. In this case, that would be the function call

```
round(input, level);
```

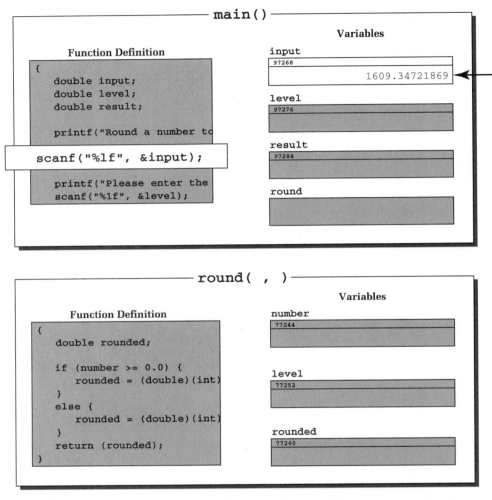

Figure 7–2 Filling the variable **input** in **main()**. The **scanf()** function gets the value 1609.34721869 from the standard input and puts it into **input**.

Figure 7–4 shows what this call does:

1. The values 1609.34721869 and 10.0 are copied from the variables **input** and **level** in **main()** and are sent to **round()**.
2. The function **round()** takes the values 1609.34721869 and 10.0 and stores them in **number** and **level**, respectively.
3. The function **round()** begins to work. (We would say that control of the program passes to the **round()** function.)

The **main()** function waits while **round()** does its work.

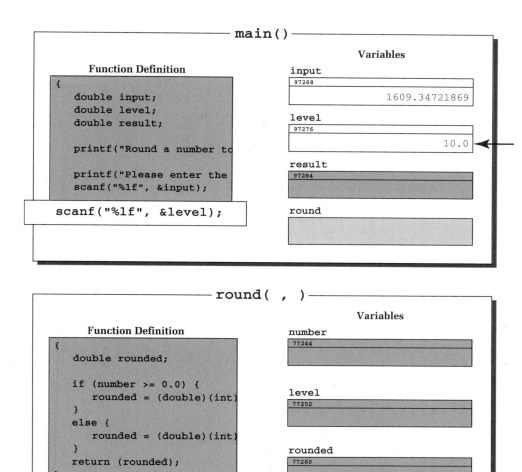

Figure 7–3 Filling the variable **level** in **main()**. The **scanf()** function gets the value 10.0 from the standard input and puts it into **level**.

round() Takes Over

The **round()** function tests to see if the value of **number** is nonnegative. If it is, the function rounds the value using the formula

```
rounded = (double)(int)(number/level + 0.5) * level;
```

Otherwise, the function uses the formula

```
rounded = (double)(int)(number/level - 0.5) * level;
```

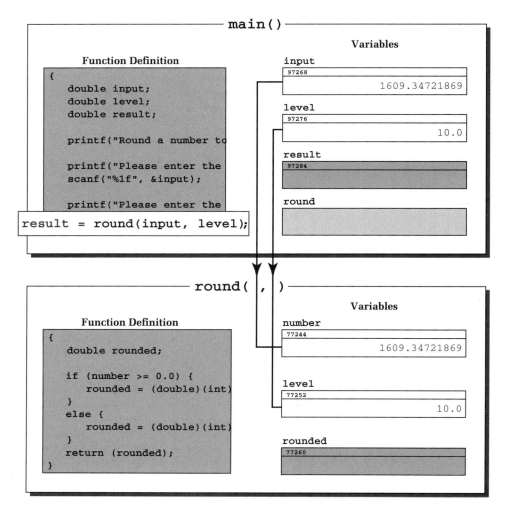

Figure 7–4   Calling the **round()** function. A copy of the values 1609.34721869 and 10.0 is sent to the function, which stores them in the variables **number** and **level**.

In this case, 1609.34721869 is positive, so the first formula is selected. It assigns the result 1610.0 to the variable **rounded**.

The last statement in **round()** is the **return** statement:

```
return (rounded);
```

This takes a copy of the number 1610.0 from **rounded** and sends it back to the **main()** function, where it is placed in a temporary storage space (Figure 7–5). The **return** statement also transfers control back to **main()**. With its work done, **round()** is shut down.

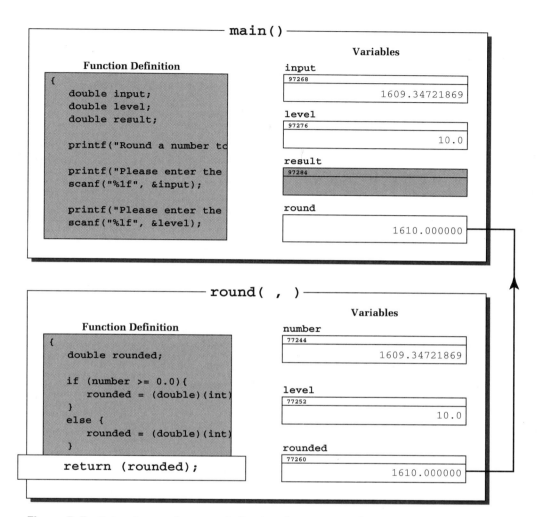

Figure 7–5   Returning a value to **main()** using the **return** mechanism. Note that the value is placed in a temporary storage location—not a regular variable—named **round**.

Saving the Returned Value

What happens to the returned value 1610.0 once it arrives in **main()**? We have shown it being placed in a storage location named **round**—the same name as the function. The important thing to keep in mind is that this is not a regular variable, but only a temporary storage location that lasts until the next statement is executed. If you want to save this value for later use, you must assign it immediately to a regular variable (see Figure 7–6).

It is extremely important that you understand the difference between

```
round(input, level);
```

and

```
result = round(input, level);
```

The first statement calls up the function **round()** and sends it the values of **input** and **level** to work on. It does not "catch" the value returned by the function. The

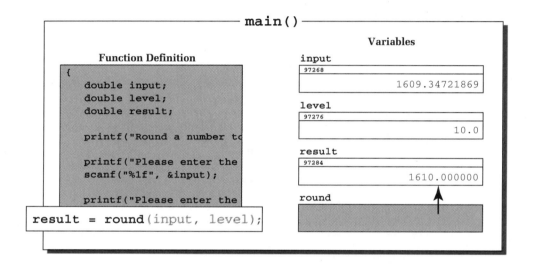

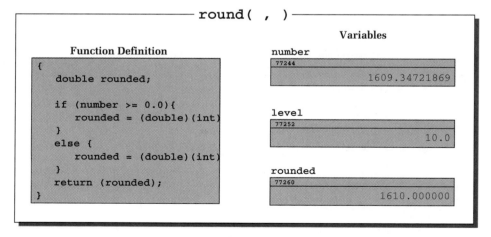

Figure 7–6   Assigning a returned value to a variable. If this assignment were not done right away, the value returned by the function would be lost.

second statement calls **round()** with the values of `input` and `level`, and it assigns the returned value to the variable `result`, which can then be used later in the **main()** function.

Once 1610.0 is assigned to `result`, the next statement in **main()** is executed:

```
printf("%f rounds to %f\n", input, result);
```

This prints out the answer on the standard output, like this:

```
1609.347219 rounds to 1610.000000
```

There are no more executable statements in **main()**, so the program terminates and control is sent back to the operating system.

Function Prototypes

Let's examine the prototype for the **round()** function in greater detail:

```
double round(double number, double level);       /* Prototype */
```

Reading from left to right, the prototype tells us (1) the type of value the function returns; (2) the function's name; and (3) the number and type(s) of arguments the function expects. The parameter names **number** and **level** serve only as placeholders here; they are ignored by the compiler. Therefore, you may omit them:

```
double round(double, double)       /* Prototype */
```

However, because parameter names can help a human reader understand how the function is supposed to work, we recommend that you always use them.

As we have said, the function prototype must match the function header:

```
double round(double number, double level)       /* Header */
```

As used here, the identifiers **number** and **level** are *not* merely placeholders, and *must* be included. Why? When you write

```
double number, double level
```

in the function header's parameter list, you are really declaring two **double** variables to hold the values passed to the function. For the compiler to create these variables, you must give them names.

A function prototype allows the compiler to check that you are calling the function with the proper number and types of arguments. It also tells the compiler the type of value that the function is supposed to return. *If you omit the function prototype, the compiler will simply assume that your function returns an* **int**. As you can imagine, this can cause serious errors in your program.

Program: *cbrt.c*

Our next program will compute the cube root of a number entered at the keyboard. The pseudocode for the **main()** function is:

prompt user for a number x
scan the stdin for x
call **cbrt()** *to compute the cube root of x*
print the answer to the stdout

The C code for this function is shown in Listing 7–2. Create a file named *cbrt.c* and enter this code into the file.

Listing 7–2. **main()** *Function for cbrt.c*

```
/**************************************************

    Compute cube roots.

**************************************************/

#include <stdio.h>

double cbrt(double x);          /* Prototype */

main()
{
    double input, root;

    printf("This program computes cube roots.\n");
    printf("Please enter a number: ");
    scanf("%lf", &input);

    root = cbrt(input);

    printf("The cube root is %g.\n", root);
}
```

Dissection of main()

(1) `double cbrt(double x);          /* Prototype */`

This is the prototype for the function **cbrt()**. Reading from left to right, the prototype tells us (1) the function returns a **double** value; (2) the function's name is **cbrt()**; and (3) the function takes one argument of type **double**. The parameter name **x** is optional and is ignored by the compiler.

(2) `double input, root;`

We need two **double** values: **input** will hold the number that the user enters at the *stdin*; **root** will receive the value returned by the **cbrt()** function.

(3) `root = cbrt(input);`

This statement does three things: (1) it calls the **cbrt()** function; (2) it passes the value of **input** to **cbrt()**; and (3) it assigns the returned value to **root**.

● ▭▭▭▭ Function Stubs

Before writing **cbrt()**, we would like to make sure that **main()** works correctly. Let's see what happens if you try to compile the program as it is. Run the compiler on the *cbrt.c* file in the usual way. For example, if you are using the *gcc* compiler, type

```
gcc cbrt.c RET
```

You should get no error messages from the compiler (assuming, of course, that the file contains no syntax errors). However, you will see an error message from the linker, something like

```
ld: Undefined symbol
_cbrt
```

You might see a slightly different message, such as

```
Link failed
Undefined: cbrt
```

Regardless of the exact wording of the message, its meaning is the same: The linker complained because it could not find **cbrt()** in the file.

The problem is that **main()**, by itself, is not a complete program—it requires the **cbrt()** function, which you have not yet written. What we need is a way to compile and test **main()** without having to write **cbrt()** first. (Remember, we said that one of the advantages of functions is that they allow you to develop your program in stages.) For this we make use of a dummy function called a *stub*.

Listing 7–3 shows a stub for the **cbrt()** function. Note that the function body consists of a single **return** statement that always returns the same value:

```
return (1.0);
```

Although the stub will not compute anything, it is a complete function as far as the compiler and linker are concerned.

Listing 7–3. cbrt() *Function for cbrt.c*

```
/***************************************************
    Stub for cbrt() function.
***************************************************/

double cbrt(double x)
{
    return (1.0);        /* Change this later. */

}
```

Reopen the file *cbrt.c* and append the code for the stub, then compile the file in the usual way. If there are no syntax errors in your program, the compiler will produce an executable file. Run the program and enter a number at the prompt:

```
This program computes cube roots.
Please enter a number: 1492.10 RET
```

Since **cbrt()** is not yet finished, the program will always print 1 as the cube root:

```
The cube root is 1.
```

Obviously, this is not the correct answer, but it does suggest that the **main()** function is working correctly. (Just to be sure, it is a good idea to test a few other input values before going on.)

The cbrt() Function

Once you are satisfied that **main()** works as it ought to, you are ready to complete **cbrt()**. Recall that the cube root of x can be written as a fractional power of x:

$$\sqrt[3]{x} = x^{1/3}$$

Thus, to compute the cube root of x, **cbrt()** will use **pow()** to raise x to the 1/3 power:

```
root = pow(x, 1.0/3.0);
```

Open *cbrt.c* and replace the function stub with the code shown in Listing 7–4.

Listing 7–4. cbrt() *Function for cbrt.c* (Revised)

```
/*****************************************************

    cbrt(): Compute the cube root of a double.

*****************************************************/
```

① `#include <math.h>`

②
```
double cbrt(double x)
{
    double root;
```

③
```
    root = pow(x, 1.0/3.0);

    return (root);
}
```

Dissection of cbrt()

① `#include <math.h>`

The prototype for the standard math function **pow()** is contained in the standard header file *math.h*. If this file were not included, the value returned by **pow()** would be treated as an **int** rather than a **double**.

② `double cbrt(double x)`

The header for **cbrt()** shows that the function takes a **double** argument and returns a **double** result. It also declares **x** to be a local variable belonging to **cbrt()**.

③ `root = pow(x, 1.0/3.0);`

Note that the second argument to **pow()** is written as `1.0/3.0`—what do you suppose would happen if it were written as `1/3` instead?

Compiling and Testing *cbrt.c*

Save the file and compile it, making sure that the linker gets the code for the **pow()** function from the math library. (Don't forget the **–lm** flag if your system requires it.) Once you have obtained an executable file, try a few test cases:

Input	Root
27	3
54.3	3.78675
101	4.65701
1000.0	10
−27	−3

Negative inputs will cause a domain error because the **pow()** function cannot compute the power of a negative number. Thus

```
pow(-27.0, 1.0/3.0)
```

produces a domain error. We leave it as an exercise for you to remedy this problem (Exercise 5).

Multiple Source Files

The *cbrt.c* file contains source code for the two functions **main()** and **cbrt()**. Often it is more convenient to put each function in its own source file. (For one thing, it is easier to reuse functions if they are kept in separate files.) Your system can compile and link multiple source files into a single program. For example, suppose you have a program consisting of the source files *main.c*, *first.c*, *second.c*, and *third.c*. To compile and link these files using the *gcc* compiler, you could type

```
gcc main.c first.c second.c third.c RET
```

If there are no syntax errors in any of the files, this will produce a single executable file.* The actual order in which the files are listed on the command line does not matter. Thus, the same effect would be produced by the command line

```
gcc third.c main.c second.c first.c RET
```

Program: Convert Time

For our next program we will write a function that takes the number of hours, minutes, and seconds, and returns the total number of seconds. We will begin by writing the **main()** function. Here is its pseudocode:

---

* You may have to refer to your manual for details of how your system deals with multiple source files.

prompt user for hours, minutes, seconds
scan the stdin for the hours, minutes, seconds
call **hms_to_sec()** *to compute total_seconds*
print result to stdout

As shown in Listing 7–5, **main()** calls **printf()** and **scanf()** to handle data input and output; it calls the **double** function **hms_to_sec()** to do the actual computation. Create a file named ***hmssmain.c***, and enter the code as shown in the listing.

We would like to test **main()** before writing **hms_to_sec()**. For this we will need to use the stub function shown in Listing 7–6. Enter this code into a separate source file named ***hmss.c***.

Listing 7–5. ***hmssmain.c***

```
/****************************************************

    Convert time expressed in hours, minutes, and
    seconds to time expressed in total seconds.

****************************************************/

#include <stdio.h>

double hms_to_sec(int hrs, int min, double sec);

main()
{
    int hours, minutes;
    double seconds, total_seconds;

    printf("Enter the number of hours: ");
    scanf("%d", &hours);

    printf("Enter the number of minutes: ");
    scanf("%d", &minutes);

    printf("Enter the seconds: ");
    scanf("%lf", &seconds);

    total_seconds = hms_to_sec(hours, minutes, seconds);

    printf("Total seconds: %g\n", total_seconds);
}
```

Listing 7–6. *hmss.c*

```
/**************************************************

    Stub for hms_to_sec() function.

**************************************************/

double hms_to_sec(int hrs, int min, double sec)
{

    return (1.0000);        /* Change this later. */

}
```

Compiling and Testing *hmssmain.c*

You are now ready to test the **main()** function. Compile and link *hmssmain.c* and *hmss.c*. If you are using the *gcc* compiler, for example, type

```
gcc hmssmain.c hmss.c RET
```

If there are no syntax errors in either file, the compiler will compile both functions and send them to the linker, which will produce an executable file. Run the executable file and enter some appropriate numbers at the prompts:

```
Enter the number of hours: 7 RET
Enter the number of minutes: 34 RET
Enter the seconds: 22.6 RET
```

You should see the output line

```
Total seconds: 1
```

Although the answer isn't correct, it indicates that the **main()** function works properly. If you see different output, your program contains an error that you should fix before going on.

The hms_to_sec() Function

The formula for computing the total seconds is very simple:

```
total_seconds = 3600 * hr + 60 * min + sec
```

Let's use this formula to do a computation by hand. How many seconds are in 7 hours, 34 minutes, and 22.6 seconds?

(7 hr)(3600 sec/hr) + (34 min)(60 sec/min) + 22.6 sec = 27262.6 seconds

Open the **hmss.c** file and replace the function stub with the C code shown in Listing 7–7.

Listing 7–7. *hmss.c (Revised)*

```
/*****************************************************

   hms_to_sec(): Convert time in hours, minutes, and
   seconds to time in seconds.

*****************************************************/
```

① ```
#define SEC_PER_HR 3600.0
#define SEC_PER_MIN 60.0
```

② ```
double hms_to_sec(int hrs, int min, double sec)
{
    double total_sec;

    total_sec = (double)hrs * SEC_PER_HR + (double)min *
            SEC_PER_MIN + sec;

    return (total_sec);
}
```

Dissection of *hmss.c*

① ```
#define SEC_PER_HR 3600.0
#define SEC_PER_MIN 60.0
```

The symbolic constants are defined in the file ***hmss.c***, because they are needed by the **hms_to_sec()** function. If they were defined in ***hmssmain.c*** instead, they would be usable in that file only.

② ```
double hms_to_sec(int hrs, int min, double sec)
```

Note the variable names declared in the **hms_to_sec()** function header: **hrs**, **min**, **sec**. These are not the same names used in the **main()** function: **hours**, **minutes**, **seconds**. That's all right—

the names refer to different storage locations. On the other hand, we *could* have chosen the same variable names in both functions—it doesn't matter because

No function knows the name of any variable belonging to another function.

Compiling and Testing the Complete Program

Compile the source files and link them into an executable program. Then run a few test cases to check the program:

Hours	Minutes	Seconds	Total Seconds
7	34	22.6	27262.6
0	17	0	1020
3	0	0	10800
0	0	47.8	47.8
23	23	59.9	84239.9

How does your program handle negative inputs? Suppose you were to enter -7 hours, 34 minutes, and 22.6 seconds—what do you get? What would you expect? (What does it mean to say -7 hours, anyway?)

Call by Value

Remember what we told you about variable names:

> *No function knows the name of any variable belonging to another function.*

Each function closely guards the names of its variables. (We would say that the variable names are *local* to the function.)

At this point you may be wondering how a function can guard its variable names and still use the names as arguments when calling another function. Consider, for example, the function call to **round()** in Listing 7–1:

```
result = round(input, level);
```

Doesn't this give away the secret that **main()** has a variable named **input** and another named **level**? The answer is no. In the function call, it is not the variable name that gets sent to the function, but rather the *contents* of the variable. Thus, if **input** contains 2339.7 and **level** contains 1.0, the function call acts this way:

```
result = round(2339.7, 1.0);
```

All that **round()** ever sees are the values 2339.7 and 1.0; it has no way of knowing the name of the variable (if any) from which the values came. And **main()** does not know what happens to the values once they are inside **round()**.

This method of passing numbers to functions is referred to as *call by value*. Although it may seem somewhat restrictive at first, call by value is really a safety feature. It prevents a function from accidentally altering the contents of another function's variables. This is especially important when the same variable names have been used in both functions.

We should point out that the **return** statement also hides variable names. Consider this line from **round()**:

```
return (rounded);
```

When this statement is executed, the value contained in **rounded** is sent back to **main()**, which has no way of telling the name of the variable the value came from. Nor does **round()** know what happens to this value once it reaches **main()**.

void Functions

A function that does not return a value is called a **void** function. Consider, for example, the following prototype for the (hypothetical) function **do_something()**:

```
void do_something(double x);     /* Prototype */
```

The keyword **void** tells us that **do_something()** returns no value. The function does take one **double** value as an argument; here is how this function might be called in a program:

```
do_something(x);                       /* Function call */
```

It is also possible to create functions that take no arguments and return no values. Suppose **do_something_else()** is to be such a function; its prototype would look like this:

```
void do_something_else(void);    /* Prototype */
```

This function would be called this way:

```
do_something_else();                   /* Function call */
```

The parentheses are left empty because the function does not take any arguments—nevertheless, the parentheses are required and may not be omitted.

A Coin-Flipping Function

To illustrate the use of **void** functions, let's write a function that simulates the toss of a coin. The idea behind this program is simple: use the library function **rand()** to generate a pseudorandom integer; if the integer is even, print "Heads"; if the integer is odd, print "Tails." We will repeat this *n* times. The pseudocode for this program is shown below.

receive n from the calling program
call **time()** *to get a seed value*
call **srand()** *with seed value*

repeat n times:
    if random number is even
        print "Heads"
    otherwise
        print "Tails"

The C code for this function is shown in Listing 7–8.

Listing 7–8. *flipcoin.c*

```
/*******************************************************

    flip_coins(): Simulate the flip of a coin n times;
    write the result to the screen.

*******************************************************/

   #include <stdio.h>
①  #include <stdlib.h>
   #include <time.h>

②  void flip_coins(int n)
   {
       int seed;
       int i;          /* Counter */

③      seed = (int)time(NULL);
        srand(seed);

        for (i = 0; i < n; i = i + 1) {

④          if ((rand() % 2) == 0) {
               printf("Heads\n");
            }
            else {
               printf("Tails\n");
            }

        }        /* End loop body */

   }
```

Dissection of flip_coins()

① #include <stdlib.h>
   #include <time.h>

The *stdlib.h* file contains the prototypes for **rand()** and **srand()**; the *time.h* file contains the prototype for the **time()** function.

② `void flip_coins(int n)`

Reading left to right, this tells us several things about the function:

1. The function returns no value;
2. Its name is **flip_coins()**;
3. The argument that goes inside the parentheses is an **int**.

③ `seed = (int)time(NULL);`
`srand(seed);`

We use **time()** to generate a seed for the random-number generator. The **time()** function returns a numerical value representing the current time on the system clock. On many systems, this return value is a **long**; the cast converts this to an integer. Note that **time()** requires **NULL** as an argument.

④ `if ((rand() % 2) == 0) {`

This is how we check to see whether the value returned by **rand()** is even.

Compiling and Testing *flipcoin.c*

We leave it for you to write a **main()** function that will test **flip_coins()**.

● ▬▬▬▬▬▬▬ **HELPFUL HINTS**

- Although it is not strictly required, we prefer always to include the parameter names in the function prototype—this helps to make the purpose of the function clear.

- Many beginning programmers confuse the function prototype and the function header, and have difficulty remembering which requires the semicolon. A prototype is a declaration; like a variable declaration, it ends in a semicolon. In contrast, the function header is part of the function definition and must be followed by a brace {.

- There is a quick and easy way to ensure that a prototype agrees with the function's header. With your text editor, make a copy of the header and use it as the function prototype. Be sure to add a semicolon to the prototype after doing this.

- It is an error to declare a local variable having the same name as the function or one of its parameters. For example, the following program fragment contains two errors:

```
int ifact(int n)
{
    int ifact;    /* Wrong! ifact is the function's name */
    int n;        /* Wrong! n is the parameter's name */
```

● ▬▬▬▬   SUMMARY

Function Prototype

`int ifact(int sum);`   Shows the function's return type (**int**), name (**ifact**), and argument type (**int**). The parameter name **sum** is optional.

Function Definition

```
int ifact(int n)
{
   [function body]
}
```

Defines the function. The first line is a function header that shows the function's return type and name, and declares the parameter **n**. Braces surround the function body.

Function Call

`fact = ifact(input);`   Calls the function **ifact()** and sends it the contents of the variable **input**; assigns the value returned by the function to the variable **fact**.

Return Mechanism

`return (prod);`   Transfers control back to the calling function and sends it the value of **prod**.

- A C program consists of one or more functions, which are self-contained subprograms that perform various tasks. Some functions are supplied as part of the C library, others you write yourself.
- Functions simplify the design and writing of programs in at least three ways: (1) using functions, large programs can be broken into smaller, more tractable parts; (2) programs can be developed and tested in stages; and (3) functions developed for one program can often be reused in other programs.
- A function prototype or function declaration tells the compiler the name of a function, the number and types of arguments it takes, and the type of value it returns. This information must agree with the first line of the function definition, which is called the function header. If the prototype is omitted, the compiler assumes that the function returns a value of type **int**.
- A function is called by writing its name followed by parentheses enclosing the appropriate arguments. The parentheses are required even if the function takes no arguments.
- Each function occupies its own space in memory and has its own definition and local variables. No function knows the name of any variable belonging to any other function. Thus, even if two functions use the same variable names, these names refer to separate and distinct memory locations.

- Call by value is a method of passing numbers between functions. In call by value, the contents of a variable—but not its name or location—are sent to a function through the argument list. Call by value prevents one function from accidentally altering the contents of a variable belonging to another function.

- The **return** statement transfers control from a function back to the function that called it and may be used to transfer a value as well. Any value returned by a function is placed in a temporary storage location in the calling function. To use this value later in the program, you must immediately assign it to a variable.

- When developing a large program, you can save time by writing and debugging **main()** before working on any other functions. This may require the use of dummy functions called stubs, which are later replaced by working functions.

- It may be more convenient to keep each function in its own source file, especially if the function is to be reused. Multiple source files can be compiled and linked together to make a working program.

- A function that is not designed to return a value is called a **void** function.

EXERCISES

1. *Define:* **a.** function; **b.** function prototype; **c.** function definition; **d.** function header; **e.** function body; **f.** parameter; **g.** function stub; **h.** function call; **i.** local variables; **j.** call by value; **k. void** function.

2. *Errors.* Create a copy of **round.c** called **errors7.c** and introduce into the new file the first error listed below. Run your compiler on the file. If the compiler catches the error, write down both the error and the error message; if not, run the executable file with test data and make a note of any unexpected results. Correct the file, then repeat the process with the next error on the list. Continue until you have tried all of the errors.

   a. Remove the semicolon from the function prototype at the top of the program.

   b. Remove the return type from the function prototype. That is, change

   ```
   double round(double number, double level); to
   round(double number, double level);
   ```

   c. Change

   ```
   result = round(input, level); to
   result = round(double input, double level);
   ```

   d. Append a semicolon to the function header of **round()**.

   e. Remove the keyword **return** from the bottom of the function **round()**.

   f. Remove the closing brace from the bottom of the function **main()**.

   g. Remove a parameter from the function call.

   h. Remove the function prototype from the top of the program.

3. For each of the prototypes listed below, determine whether the prototype is correct or not. (Explain your answers.)

```
(int) area(double a, int size);
double area(double side1, side2);
area = circle_area(radius, pi);
int selection(int low_range, int high_range);
double force( , , double x);
int positive((int)x, (int)y);
int read(int how_many);
```

4. Given the program fragment

```
int count(int a, int b);
double volume(double side1, double side2, double side3);

main()
{
    double a, b, c, d;
    int p, q, r, s;
```

determine which of the following statements would be valid if written inside the **main()** function:

```
a = volume(b, c, d, p);
p = count(s, (int)volume(a, c, d));
count(a);
r = (int)volume();
count = q + r;
printf("%d", count(r,s));
d = volume(double a, double b, double c);
count(p,q) = volume(a, b, c);
```

5. *Improved cube-root function.* The cube root program presented in this chapter does not handle negative numbers. Modify **cbrt()** so that it takes either positive or negative arguments. Note that the function call

```
root = pow(x, 1.0/3.0);
```

will result in a domain error if **x** is negative. In that case, you should use the statement

```
root = -pow(-x, 1.0/3.0);
```

6. *Improved rounding function.* The **round()** function presented in this chapter works correctly only if the value of **level** is positive. Modify the function so that it also handles non-positive values. If **level** is zero, no rounding should occur. If **level** is negative, the function should ignore the minus sign and treat **level** as if it were positive. Thus, for example, a rounding level of −10.0 should have the same effect as a rounding level of 10.0.

7. *Volume functions.* For each of the shapes listed below, write a separate function that will compute the volume. If any of the dimensions passed to the function is less than zero, the function should return a volume of zero. Write a **main()** function to test your volume functions.

    a. Right circular cylinder: $f(r, h) = \pi r^2 h$, where r = radius and h = height.

    b. Right circular cone: $g(r, h) = (1/3)\pi r^2 h$, where r = radius and h = height.

    c. Rectangular pyramid: $h(l, w, h) = 1/3(l \cdot w \cdot h)$, where l = length of base, w = width of base, and h = height of pyramid.

8. *Time conversion.* Write a function **wdhms_to_sec()** that takes the number of weeks, days, etc., and returns the total number of seconds. For testing, write a **main()** function that calls this function. (There are 604,800 seconds in one week; based on the size of this number, of what type should your function **wdhms_to_sec()** be?)

9. *Integer powers.* Write a function **ipow(m, n)** that returns m^n where n is a nonnegative integer. Do not use the **pow()** library function. (*Hint:* Use a **for** loop to carry out n multiplications.) For testing, write a **main()** function that calls this function.

10. *Squaring numbers.* Write a **double** function **sq()** that will compute the square of **x** as **x * x**.

11. *Cubing numbers.* Write a **double** function **cube()** that will compute the cube of **x** as **x * x * x**.

12. *Factorials.* Write an **int** function **ifact()** that computes the factorial $n!$, where n is a positive integer. If the function receives a negative argument, it should return the value 0 and print an error message (**Domain error**). If the function receives an argument that would produce too large a result, it should return the value of **INT_MAX** and print an error message (**Range error**).

13. *Sign function.* Write an **int** function named **sign()** that takes a **double** argument and returns −1 if the argument is negative, 0 if the argument is zero, and 1 if the argument is positive. Write an appropriate **main()** function to test **sign()**.

14. *Alternating-sign function.* Write an **int** function named **alt_sign()** that takes an **int** argument and returns −1 if the argument is odd, 1 if the argument is even. Write an appropriate **main()** function to test **alt_sign()**.

15. *Stirling's approximation.* Write a **double** function **stirling()** that approximates the factorial $n!$, where n is a positive integer, using the improved Stirling's formula:

$$n! \approx n^n e^{-n} \sqrt{2\pi n}\left(1 + \frac{1}{12n}\right)$$

If the function receives a negative argument, it should return the value 0 and print an error message (**Domain error**). If the function receives an argument that would produce too large a result, it should return the value of **DBL_MAX** and print an error message (**Range error**).

16. *Series approximation—sine.* Many important mathematical functions can be expressed as infinite series. For example, the sine function has the following Taylor-series expansion:

$$\sin{(x)} = \frac{x^1}{1!} - \frac{x^3}{3!} + \frac{x^5}{5!} - \frac{x^7}{7!} + \cdots = \sum_{i=0}^{\infty} (-1)^i \frac{x^{2i+1}}{(2i+1)!}$$

Often a good approximation can be obtained by summing the first few terms of the function's infinite series expansion. Write a program named ***series.c*** to investigate this. The program should prompt for x and n, then compute and print an approximation to $\sin(x)$ using the first n terms of the series. (*Hint:* You may find it convenient to use the functions **alt_sign()** and **stirling()**, described in Exercises 14 and 15.) As a check, have the program also print $\sin(x)$ as computed by the appropriate library function. In general, how many terms of the expansions must be used to provide the same accuracy as the library function?

17. *Series approximation—cosine.* Repeat the previous exercise using the Taylor-series expansion for cosine:

$$\cos{(x)} = 1 - \frac{x^2}{2!} + \frac{x^4}{4!} - \frac{x^6}{6!} + \cdots = \sum_{i=0}^{\infty} (-1)^i \frac{x^{2i}}{(2i)!}$$

18. *Series approximation—exponential.* Repeat Exercise 16 using the Taylor-series expansion for e^x:

$$e^x = 1 + x + \frac{x^2}{2!} + \frac{x^3}{3!} + \frac{x^4}{4!} + \cdots = \sum_{i=0}^{\infty} \frac{x^i}{i!}$$

19. *Fibonacci numbers.* The sequence of integers 1, 1, 2, 3, 5, 8, 13, . . . is called the Fibonacci sequence. (See Exercise 21, Chapter 6.) The first two Fibonacci numbers are both 1; thereafter, each number is the sum of the two numbers that precede it in the sequence. Write a function **fibonacci()** that returns the mth Fibonacci number. For testing, write a **main()** function that calls **fibonacci()**.

20. *Radians to degrees.* Write a **double** function **radians_to_degrees()** that takes an angle measured in radians and returns the equivalent in degrees.

21. *Degrees to radians.* Write a **double** function **degrees_to_radians()** that takes an angle measured in degrees and returns the equivalent in radians.

22. *Trigonometric functions—degree measure.* Write alternative trigonometric functions **sine()**, **cosine()**, and **tangent()** that take their arguments as angles expressed in degrees. (*Hint:* Use the function **degrees_to_radians()** you wrote for the previous exercise along with the appropriate library functions.)

23.   *Compound interest.* Write a function **compound_interest()** that computes the value of a principal sum of money left on deposit for a given length of time at a given interest rate. The function will take as arguments the principal, interest rate, and number of compounding periods; it will return the total value. (See Exercises 22–24 in Chapter 4 for information about compound interest.) For testing, write a **main()** function that calls this function.

24.   *Square roots by iteration.* Write a function **square_root()** that computes square roots by iteration. It should not use any C library math function, except perhaps the absolute value function. As described in Chapter 6, if *a* is an approximation to the root, then the following formula will produce a better approximation:

$$\frac{1}{2}\left(a + \frac{x}{a}\right)$$

If the function receives a negative argument, it should return the value 0.0 and print an error message (**Domain error**). Write an appropriate **main()** function to test **square_root()**. (Hint: Refer to Listing 6–5.)

25.   *Cube roots by iteration.* Write a function **cube_root()** that computes cube roots by iteration. It should not use any C library math function, except perhaps the absolute value function. As described in Exercise 20, Chapter 6, if *a* is an approximation to the root, then the following formula will produce a better approximation:

$$\frac{1}{3}\left(2a + \frac{x}{a^2}\right)$$

Write an appropriate **main()** function to test **cube_root()**.

26.   *Gaussian distribution.* As discussed in Exercise 16, Chapter 4, the Gaussian or normal curve used in statistics is described by the equation

$$y = \frac{1}{\sigma\sqrt{2\pi}}\ \exp\left[-\frac{1}{2}\left(\frac{(x - \mu)}{\sigma}\right)^2\right]$$

Write a function named **normal_curve()** that takes *x*, μ, and σ, and returns *y*. Write an appropriate **main()** function to test **normal_curve()**. Use the function **sq()** that you wrote for Exercise 10.

27.   *Greatest common divisor.* Write a function **gcd()** that computes the greatest common divisor (gcd) of two integers *p* and *q* using Euclid's method. (See Exercise 23, Chapter 6, for a description of Euclid's method.)

28.   *Prime numbers.* Write a function **is_prime()** that takes a single integer argument and returns 1 if the argument is prime, 0 otherwise. (See Exercise 24, Chapter 6, for a description of one method for finding prime numbers.)

29.   *Day of the year.* Write a function **day_of_year()** that determines the day of the year for a given date. (See Exercise 25, Chapter 6.)

30. *Distance formula.* Write a function **distance_3d()** that computes the distance
    d between two points (x_1, y_1, z_1) and (x_2, y_2, z_2) as

    $$d = \sqrt{(x_1 - x_2)^2 + (y_1 - y_2)^2 + (z_1 - z_2)^2}$$

    Write a **main()** that takes the coordinates of two points as input, passes these
    to **distance_3d()**, and prints the results to the standard output.

31. *Random integers in a given range.* Write a function **rand_int()** to randomly
    select an integer that lies within a specified range. The upper and lower limits
    of that range should be passed to **rand_int()**. For example, if the limits of the
    range are 5 and 11, then the function should return one of the following
    numbers: 5, 6, 7, 8, 9, 10, or 11.

32. *Automated multiplication tester.* Multiplex Math Software, Inc. wants a
    program that will help elementary school students learn their multiplication
    tables. The **main()** function will call **rand_int()** (see previous exercise) to
    select two positive one-digit integers. Next, **main()** will call **printf()** to dis-
    play the two integers and prompt for their product: **What is** [*number1*]
    times [*number2*]**?** After getting the student's reply, **main()** will compute
    the correct answer and check it against the student's answer. If the answer
    is correct, the program should print **You are correct! Let's try
    another:** and prompt for the product of two new integers. If the answer is
    incorrect, the program should print **That is not correct. Try again:**
    and prompt for the product of the same two numbers, until the correct answer
    is entered.

33. *Fitness test.* Healthy's Spa has hired you to design a program that determines
    the fitness level for a client according to the following classification scheme
    (Kenneth H. Cooper. *The Aerobics Way,* New York: M. Evans and Co., Inc.,
    1977):

Level	Description	Level	Description
1	Very poor condition	4	Good condition
2	Poor condition	5	Excellent condition
3	Fair condition	6	Superior condition

The fitness level may be determined from the time (in seconds) it takes a
person to run 1.5 miles. The equation used to compute the fitness level
for a male depends on his age:

Age	Fitness Equation	Age	Fitness Equation
13–19	−4.21 + 5308.51 / time	40–49	−3.63 + 6019.73 / time
20–29	−3.31 + 4782.36 / time	50–59	−3.12 + 6079.92 / time
30–39	−3.80 + 5856.84 / time	60+	−2.55 + 6348.67 / time

Write a function **fitness_run()** that calculates the fitness level, given the individual's age and time in the 1.5-mile run. Note that the fitness level is an integer; if the equation produces a fitness level of, say, 5.6, this should be truncated to 5 using a cast. If the function computes a fitness level less than 1, it should return 1; if it computes a fitness level greater than 6, it should return 6.

Also write a function **describe_fitness_level()** that takes the fitness level and prints the level and the corresponding description on the standard output.

Write a program that uses **fitness_run()** and **describe_fitness_level()** to inform clients of their fitness levels. The program should allow as many clients to be tested as the user wishes until an **EOF** is generated. In addition, for the following situations, the program should print an appropriate message, skip all computations, and terminate:

a. The client has not been cleared by a doctor to take the test.

b. The client is under the age of 13.

c. The client has not exercised regularly (at least 15 minutes of exercise, three times per week) for the past 6 months. In this case, he or she should not take the fitness test, but should be assigned a fitness code of 0 (classified as a beginner).

34. *Trapezoidal rule, equal trapezoid widths.* The area under a curve can be approximated by using the trapezoidal rule of numerical integration:

$$\int_{x_0}^{x_n} f(x)\ dx \approx \sum_{i=1}^{n} \frac{f(x_{i-1}) + f(x_i)}{2}\ \Delta x, \qquad \Delta x = \frac{x_n - x_0}{n}$$

where x_0 and x_n are the lower and upper limits of integration, respectively (i.e., x_0 is the minimum value of x, and x_n is the maximum value), Δx is the width of each trapezoid, n is the number of trapezoids, and $f(x_i)$ is the value of $f(x)$ at $x = x_0 + i \cdot \Delta x$.

Write a program that computes the area under a curve, given x_0, x_n, and n. Test your program on the following functions:

a. $f(x) = \sin x$

b. $f(x) = \cos x$

c. $f(x) = \dfrac{1 + \sin x}{x}$

For convenience, keep each function $f(x)$ in its own file. Note that every time you change the function, you must recompile the program.

35. *Number of days between two dates.* We frequently need to know the number of days that have elapsed between two dates. For example, 366 days elapsed between Jan 30, 1963 and Jan 31, 1964. Write a program to calculate the number of days between any two dates. You may wish to write functions such

as **leap_year()** and **between_dates()**, and make use of **day_of_year()**, described in Exercise 29.

This program should allow the dates to be entered in either order (either the earlier date first, or the later date first). It should work for dates within the same year, as well as dates from two different years. To simplify the program, assume that all dates entered will be after 1752, the English Gregorian adoption year.

Chapter

8.

Functions and Call by Reference

In the previous chapter, we wrote a function **hms_to_sec()** that takes several arguments (hours, minutes, and seconds) and returns a single result (total seconds):

```
total_seconds = hms_to_sec(hours, minutes, seconds);
```

In this chapter we will write a function named **sec_to_hms()** that reverses the effect of **hms_to_sec()**. That is, the new function will take the total number of seconds and convert this to hours, minutes, and seconds. In writing such a function, we run into a problem: The **return** statement can only return one value at a time. Therefore, we cannot write

```
return (hours, minutes, seconds);     /* Not allowed.*/
```

Nor is it possible to use three separate **return** statements:

```
return (hours);     /* This will be executed. */
return (minutes);   /* This will never be executed. */
return (seconds);   /* This will never be executed. */
```

The first **return** statement would send control back to the calling function. Consequently, the other two **return** statements would never be executed.

What we need is a way to bypass the limitations of the **return** statement to send multiple values to the calling function. For this we will employ *call by* *reference*, in which a function is allowed to use a variable belonging to another function. In essence, the two functions share the same variable, thereby eliminating the need to use the **return** statement.

● ━━━━━ **Pointers**

In our discussion of call by value, we stressed that functions pass to each other the *contents* of their variables but never the *names* of their variables. How can one function share another's variables without knowing their names?

You will recall that a variable has an address as well as a name. Although names cannot be passed between functions, addresses can be. Once given the address of a variable, a function is able to locate and use that variable without knowing its name.

Referring to a variable by its address is not really a new idea. You already do this each time you call the **scanf()** function:

```
scanf("%d %d %lf", &a, &b, &x);
```

Addresses such as **&a**, **&b**, and **&x** are often called *pointers*. (You might think of the address as "pointing the way" to the variable.) Given the pointers **&a**, **&b**, and **&x**, **scanf()** is able to get the values from the standard input and store them in the appropriate locations. Because it takes the addresses of the variables, **scanf()** can fill more than one variable at a time.

● ━━━━━ **Aliases**

A pointer tells a function where to find a variable but not what to call it. The function does not know the variable's original name, so it uses its own name for the variable. This alternative name is called an *alias*.

You can easily distinguish an alias from other identifiers because the alias begins with an asterisk (*****). Thus, the following would all be aliases:

```
*first  *second  *upside_down  *somewhere_else
```

As used here, the asterisk is the *indirection* or *dereferencing operator*.

Program: **Swapping Variables**

As our first example of call by reference, let's write a program that exchanges the contents of two **double** variables. This program will consist of two functions, **main()** and **swap_doubles()**. Here is the pseudocode for **main()**:

prompt user for two numbers

read and store the numbers

call **swap_doubles()** *to interchange the numbers*

print the numbers

The C code for **main()** is shown in Listing 8–1. Enter this code into a file named ***swapmain.c***.

Swapping the contents of two variables is a three-step process that requires a third variable to hold one of the values temporarily during the swap. The process is so simple that we will forgo the pseudocode—refer to the C code shown Listing 8–2.

Listing 8–1. ***swapmain.c***

```
   /* Test the swap_doubles() function. */

   #include <stdio.h>

1  void swap_doubles(double *first, double *second);

   main()
   {
      double in1, in2;

      printf("Please enter two numbers: ");
      scanf("%lf %lf", &in1, &in2);

2     swap_doubles(&in1, &in2);

      printf("The values swapped: %g %g\n", in1, in2);
   }
```

Dissection of ***swapmain.c***

```
1  void swap_doubles(double *first, double *second);
```

This is the prototype for **swap_doubles()**. As used here, the keyword **void** indicates that **swap_doubles()** does not use the **return** statement to return a value. Inside the parentheses, the entries

```
double *first, double *second
```

indicate that the function uses two aliases for **double** variables.

② `swap_doubles(&in1, &in2);`

This is how **main()** calls **swap_doubles()** to interchange the contents of **in1** and **in2**. The pointers `&in1` and `&in2` will enable **swap_doubles()** to find **in1** and **in2**, even though these variables belong to **main()**.

Listing 8–2. *swapdbl.c*

```
/* Swap the contents of two double variables. */

void swap_doubles(double *first, double *second)
{
    double temp_save;

    temp_save = *first;
    *first = *second;
    *second = temp_save;
}
```

Dissection of *swap_doubles()*

① `void swap_doubles(double *first, double *second)`

This is the first line of the function definition. As in the prototype, the keyword **void** indicates that **swap_doubles()** does not use the **return** statement to return a value. Inside the parentheses, `*first` and `*second` are declared to be aliases for **double** variables.

② `double temp_save;`

Besides the two aliases, **swap_doubles()** also uses a **double** variable named `temp_save`.

③ `temp_save = *first;`
  `*first = *second;`
  `*second = temp_save;`

This is how we swap the contents of two variables using `temp_save` to save one of the values during the swap.

Compiling and Testing the Complete Program

Once you have finished entering *swapmain.c* and *swapdbl.c*, compile and link the files. For example, if you are using the *gcc* compiler, type the command line

```
gcc swapmain.c swapdbl.c RET
```

If the compiler finds no errors, it will produce an executable file. Run this file and enter two **double** values at the prompt:

```
Please enter two numbers: 63 7.2 RET
```

The program will respond with the output

```
The values swapped: 7.2 63
```

If your program behaves differently, it contains an error (which you should correct before continuing).

How the Swapping Program Works

Let's take a closer look at the operation of the **swap_doubles()** function. Figure 8–1 shows **main()** and **swap_doubles()** just before program execution begins. Note the two arrow-shaped variables belonging to the **swap_doubles()** function. These variables will hold the pointers from **main()**, and are called, appropriately enough, *pointer variables*.

Reading a Value from the Standard Input

Program execution always begins with the **main()** function; **main()** calls **printf()** to prompt the user for input:

```
printf("Please enter two numbers: ");
```

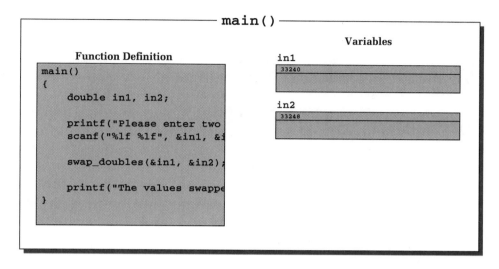

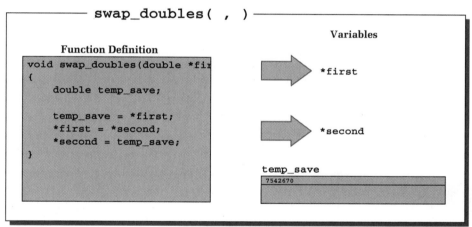

Figure 8–1 The functions **main()** and **swap_doubles()** just before program execution begins.

We will assume that the user enters the values 57.3987645 and −17.889. The next statement in **main()** calls **scanf()** to read these numbers and store them in the variables **in1** and **in2**:

```
scanf("%lf %lf", &in1, &in2);
```

Figure 8–2 shows the effect of this statement on the contents of **in1** and **in2**.

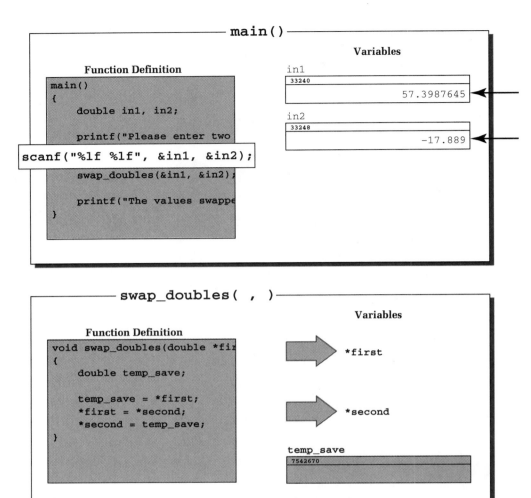

Figure 8–2 Calling **scanf()**. We are assuming that the user entered 57.3987645 and −17.889 on the standard input; these values are put into the variables **in1** and **in2**, respectively.

Calling swap_doubles()

Next, **main()** calls **swap_doubles()**. As shown in Figure 8–3, **swap_doubles()** receives pointers to **in1** and **in2**. Once it has these pointers, **swap_doubles()** can refer to **in1** and **in2** by the aliases ***first** and ***second**. In other words,

*first *is another name for* **in1**.

*second *is another name for* **in2**.

In Figure 8–4, on page 214, we show the connection between the variables and their aliases by solid black lines.

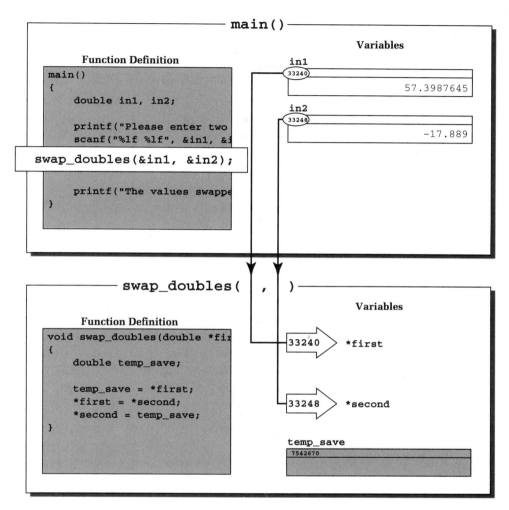

Figure 8–3 Calling **swap_doubles()**. Pointers to **in1** and **in2** are passed to **swap_doubles()**.

Swapping the Values

Once the connection has been made between a variable and its alias, **swap_doubles()** treats the aliases just as it would any other variable name. Thus, the statement

```
temp_save = *first;
```

assigns the value of ***first** to the variable **temp_save**. But ***first** is just an alias for the variable **in1**, which belongs to the **main()** function. Therefore, the contents of **in1** are copied into **temp_save**.

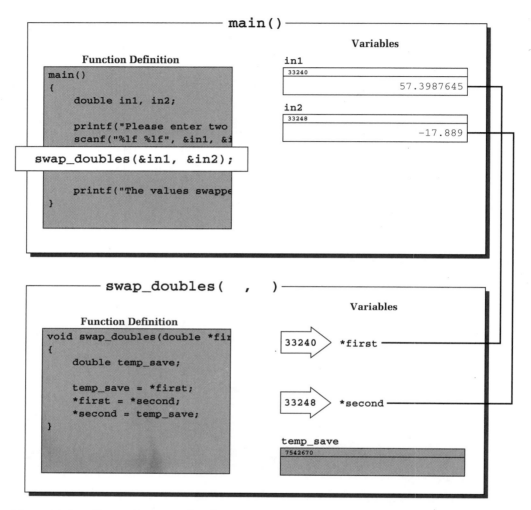

Figure 8–4 Aliases. The **swap_doubles()** function uses the aliases ***first** and ***second** to refer to the variables **in1** and **in2** that belong to **main()**.

Likewise, the statement

```
*first = *second;
```

copies the value of ***second** into the variable ***first** (which is the same as copying **in1** into **in2**). Then the statement

```
*second = temp_save;
```

copies the value of **temp_save** into the variable ***second**. The net result of these operations is shown in Figure 8–5.

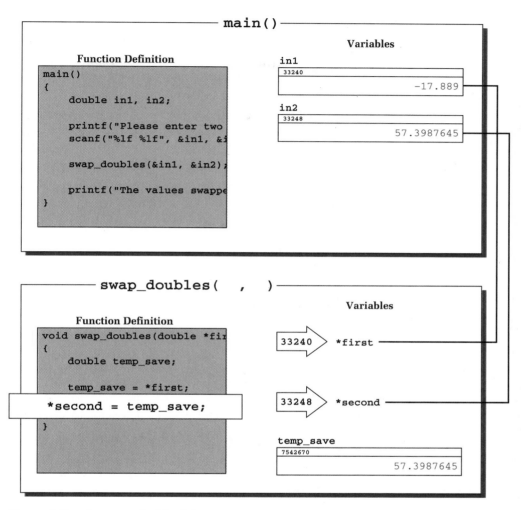

Figure 8–5 The **swap_doubles()** function finishes its work. The contents of **in1** and **in2** have been exchanged.

Prototypes and Call by Reference

Let's examine the prototype for **swap_doubles()** once again:

```
void swap_doubles(double *first, double *second);
```

The indirection operators (*****) are required to indicate that the function uses two aliases. If you prefer, you can omit the parameter names, like this:

```
void swap_doubles(double *, double *);
```

Although it makes no difference to the compiler whether you name the parameters in a function prototype, it helps any human reader figure out what your code does. Therefore, we prefer always to name the parameters.

A common error committed by beginners is to write the address operator (**&**) in place of the indirection operator (__*__) in the function prototype:

```
void swap_doubles(double &first, double &second); /* Wrong */
```

Although this resembles the way the function is called, it is not correct and will cause a compilation error.

Call by Reference and the return Statement

Although we presented call by reference as an alternative to using the **return** statement, we should mention that a function can use both. A good example of this is our old friend, the **scanf()** function. Consider an example from Chapter 6:

```
m = scanf("%lf %lf %lf", &x, &y, &z);
```

Here, **scanf()** uses call by reference to put values into the variables **x**, **y**, and **z**. It also returns an integer that indicates how many values were successfully read and stored:

m	Meaning
3	Three **double**s scanned and stored
2	Two **double**s scanned and stored
1	One **double** scanned and stored
0	No value scanned or stored
EOF	"End of File"

For our next program we will write a function that uses call by reference and the **return** statement to communicate values to the **main()** function. The **split()** function will take a **double** argument and compute its whole part and its fractional part. Here is the prototype for the function:

```
double split(double original, int *whole_part);
```

Reading from left to right, we see first that the function returns a **double** value; this will be the fractional part of the original number. The first parameter is a **double** variable named **original**; as you might guess, this variable will receive the number that is to be split. The second parameter, __*whole_part__, is an alias for the **int** variable into which the whole part of **original** will be put. Thus we see that **split()** uses call by value, call by reference, and the **return** statement.

At this point, you may be wondering why we chose to make ***whole_part** an alias and **original** a call-by-value parameter. Our choice was determined by the direction the data will travel. Because it will be used to communicate a result to **main()**, ***whole_part** must be an alias. In contrast, **original** will receive a value from **main()**, but will not be needed to send anything back to **main()**. Therefore, **original** is declared to be an ordinary **double** parameter.

The body of the **split()** function is very simple. To obtain the whole part of **original**, we use a cast:

```
*whole_part = (int)original;
```

Next, we take the difference between **original** and ***whole_part** to get the fractional part:

```
fract_part = original - (double)*whole_part;
```

The C code for **main()** is shown in Listing 8–3. The code for *split.c* is shown in Listing 8–4. Create two files, *spltmain.c* and *split.c* and enter the code as shown in the listings.

Listing 8–3. *spltmain.c*

```c
/*********************************************************

    Split a double into its whole and fractional parts.

*********************************************************/

#include <stdio.h>

double split(double original, int *whole_part);

main()
{
    double input, fraction;
    int whole;

    printf("Enter a number: ");
    scanf("%lf", &input);

    fraction = split(input, &whole);

    printf("Whole part: %d\n", whole);
    printf("Fractional part: %g\n", fraction);
}
```

Listing 8–4. *split.c*

```
/**************************************************************

    Split a double value into whole and fractional parts.

**************************************************************/

double split(double original, int *whole_part)
{
    double fract_part;

    *whole_part = (int)original;
    fract_part = original - (double)*whole_part;
    return (fract_part);
}
```

Compiling and Testing the Complete Program

Compile and link *spltmain.c* and *split.c*, and try a few test cases:

```
Enter a number: 57.3987 RET
Whole part: 57
Fractional part: 0.3987
```

Try a negative input:

```
Enter a number: -123.4567 RET
Whole part: -123
Fractional part: -0.4567
```

Note that both output values are negative. (Is this correct?) Consider what happens if the input has no fractional part:

```
Enter a number: 999 RET
Whole part: 999
Fractional part: 0
```

Try two more examples:

```
Enter a number: 0.000000 RET
Whole part: 0
Fractional part: 0
```

```
Enter a number: 0.0000000001 RET
Whole part: 0
Fractional part: 1e-10
```

Program: Convert Seconds to Hours, Minutes, and Seconds

This is the program we promised you at the beginning of the chapter. What we want is a program that will first prompt the user for the total number of seconds:

```
How many seconds? 19682.74 RET
```

It will then respond with output like this:

```
19682.74 sec = 5 hr, 28 min, & 2.74 sec
```

Note that the program should handle fractions of a second.

Let's write this program in stages, starting with the **main()** function. The pseudocode outline for **main()** is quite simple:

prompt the user for total seconds

scan the standard input for total seconds

call **sec_to_hms()** *to compute hours, minutes, seconds*

print results to the standard output

According to this plan, **main()** calls another function, **sec_to_hms()**, to carry out the computation.

We're not quite ready to write **sec_to_hms()**, but we should at least design its prototype. This function receives the total time in seconds and computes hours, minutes, and seconds. Since it computes three values, **sec_to_hms()** must use call by reference to communicate its results back to **main()**. An appropriate prototype for **sec_to_hms()** would be

```
void sec_to_hms(double, int *, int *, double *);
```

The keyword **void** indicates that the function does not use the **return** mechanism to return a value. Inside the parentheses, we see that the function is designed to receive a **double** value and that it uses two **int** aliases and a **double** alias. Although this will suffice, we prefer to name the parameters in the parameter list:

```
void sec_to_hms(double total, int *hr, int *min, double *sec);
```

We are now ready to write the C code for the **main()** function, as well as a stub for **sec_to_hms()**. Create two files, *timemain.c* and *shms.c*. Enter the code shown in Listings 8–5 and 8–6.

Listing 8–5. *timemain.c*

```
/************************************************************

    Convert time in seconds to hours, minutes, seconds

************************************************************/

#include <stdio.h>

void sec_to_hms(double total, int *hr, int *min, double *sec);

main()
{
    double total_seconds, seconds;
    int hours, minutes;

    printf("How many seconds? ");
    scanf("%lf", &total_seconds);

    sec_to_hms(total_seconds, &hours, &minutes, &seconds);

    printf("%g sec = %d hr, %d min, & %g sec\n",
            total_seconds, hours, minutes, seconds);
}
```

①

②

Listing 8–6. *shms.c*

```
/************************************************************

    Stub for sec_to_hms()

************************************************************/

void sec_to_hms(double total_sec, int *hr, int *min, double *sec)
{
    *hr = 111;          /* Modify later. */
    *min = 222;         /* Modify later. */
    *sec = 33.3;        /* Modify later. */
}
```

③

Dissection of *timemain.c* and *shms.c*

① `double total_seconds, seconds;`
   `int hours, minutes;`

Since we are going to allow fractions of a second, **total_seconds** and **seconds** should be **double** variables. However, because we will deal only in whole hours and minutes, these should be **int** variables.

② `sec_to_hms(total_seconds, &hours, &minutes, &seconds);`

In this function call, **sec_to_hms()** receives a copy of the value contained in **total_seconds**. It also receives the pointers to **hours**, **minutes**, and **seconds**, so it can create aliases for these variables.

③ `*hr = 111;          /* Modify later. */`
   `*min = 222;         /* Modify later. */`
   `*sec = 33.3;        /* Modify later. */`

These three lines form the body of the function stub. Regardless of the values entered by the user, the stub function will produce 111 hours, 222 minutes, and 33.3 seconds. We have labeled these statements to remind ourselves that they are to be replaced with the proper code later.

Compiling and Testing the Program

Compile, link, and run *timemain.c* and *shms.c*. Enter a number at the prompt:

`How many seconds? 1492.7` `RET`

Since **sec_to_hms()** is not finished, you'll always get the same output:

`1492.7 sec = 111 hr, 222 min, & 33.3 sec`

If you see this, you can be fairly sure that **main()** is correct. On the other hand, if there is some problem with **main()**, you should correct it before proceeding further.

The Function sec_to_hms()

If your **main()** function is working properly, you are ready to write **sec_to_hms()**. It is helpful to begin by computing an example by hand. How many hours, minutes, and seconds are there in 15732.89 seconds? First we convert 15732.89 seconds to hours:

$$\frac{15732.89 \text{ sec}}{3600 \text{ sec/hr}} = 4.370247222 \text{ hours}$$

Next we split this result into its whole part (4 hours) and its fractional part (0.37024722 hours). The whole part is the number of complete hours. We compute the number of minutes from the fractional part:

$$(0.370247222 \text{ hr}) \left(60\frac{\text{min}}{\text{hr}}\right) = 22.21483332 \text{ minutes}$$

Splitting this result, we get the number of whole minutes (22) and the fraction of a minute left over (0.214833). From the fraction we compute the seconds:

$$(0.21483332 \text{ min}) \left(60\frac{\text{sec}}{\text{min}}\right) = 12.8899992 \text{ seconds}$$

As you might expect, the **split()** function we wrote earlier in the chapter can be used to advantage in this computation. The trick is knowing how to call **split()**. This is how we did it before:

```
fraction = split(input, &whole);
```

split() takes two arguments: the original value (a **double**) and a pointer to the **int** variable that is to receive the whole part. The function returns the fractional part, which can then be assigned to a variable.

In the **sec_to_hms()** function, we want to split total hours (**total_hours**) into whole hours (***hr**) and fractional hours (**frac_hour**). Hence, we might write

```
frac_hour = split(total_hours, &*hr);
```

Although this will work, most experienced C programmers would write it differently. Note that the second argument is **&*hr**, a pointer to an alias. C offers a shorthand notation for such pointers:

hr *has the same value as* **&*hr**

Therefore, we can write the function call as

```
frac_hour = split(total_hours, hr);
```

The C code for **split()** is shown in Listing 8–7. Open **shms.c** and replace the stub with the code from this listing.

Listing 8–7. *shms.c*

```
/**********************************************************

    Convert time in seconds to hours, minutes, seconds

**********************************************************/

#define SEC_PER_HR 3600.0
#define MIN_PER_HR 60.0
#define SEC_PER_MIN 60.0

double split(double original, int *whole_part);

void sec_to_hms(double total_sec, int *hr, int *min, double *sec)
{
    double total_hours;
    double frac_hour;

    total_hours = total_sec/SEC_PER_HR;

    frac_hour = split(total_hours, hr);

    *sec = SEC_PER_MIN * split(MIN_PER_HR * frac_hour, min);
}
```

(1) at the prototype line, (2) at the local variable declarations, (3) at the `frac_hour = split(...)` line, and (4) at the `*sec = ...` line.

Dissection of *shms.c*

(1) `double split(double original, int *whole_part);`

This is the prototype for the **split()** function that we wrote before. If this were omitted, the return value from **split()** would be treated as an **int**, not a **double**.

(2) `double total_hours;`
    `double frac_hour;`

The **sec_to_hms()** function needs two local variables, both of type **double**, to hold the time in hours and the fractional hours. These are not aliases, but variables belonging to **sec_to_hms()**.

(3) `frac_hour = split(total_hours, hr);`

Here again is the way we call **split()**. In this case, **hr** is the same as **&*hr**, so we could have written this function call as

```
frac_hour = split(total_hours, &*hr);
```

(4) `*sec = SEC_PER_MIN * split(MIN_PER_HR * frac_hour, min);`

Can you figure out what this statement does? Note that we used the shorthand **min** instead of **&*min**. Also note that three asterisks appear in this statement: The first is the dereferencing operator, the other two are multiplication operators.

Compiling and Testing the Complete Program

Once you are satisfied that the code is correct, close **shms.c**. Compile and link the files **timemain.c**, **shms.c**, and **split.c**. Run the executable file and try a test value:

```
How many seconds? 15732.89 RET
15732.89 sec = 4 hr, 22 min, & 12.89 sec
```

Try other values to assure yourself that the program is correct. (*Hint:* Use your time conversion program from the previous chapter to generate some test cases.)

HELPFUL HINTS

As we have seen, call by reference allows a function to alter the contents of variables that do not belong to it. Although this is useful, it is also dangerous. You must take care to ensure that the function changes only those variables you want it to change. This, of course, is not a problem with call by value. Therefore, we recommend that you use call by value whenever you can. We offer two guidelines:

* When writing a function that computes a single result, always use call by value to pass data to the function, and use the **return** statement to return the result.

* When writing a function that computes two or more results, you have no choice but to use call by reference. However, the function should be given pointers only to those variables that it is supposed to change. (Generally, this means variables that will be used to send values back to the calling function.) Use call by value for all other arguments.

SUMMARY

Function Header

`void swap(double *a, double *b)`   Declares ***a** and ***b** to be aliases for **double** variables. When called, **swap()** must receive pointers to the original **double** variables. The keyword **void** indicates that **swap()** returns no value.

Function Prototypes

`void swap(double *a, double *b);`   Declares **swap()** to be a **void** function that uses aliases for two **double** variables. Prototype must agree with the function header.

`void swap(double *, double *);`   As above; parameter names are optional in prototypes.

`double split(double x, int *y);`   Declares **split()** to be a function that takes a **double** value and the address of an **int** variable, and returns a **double** value.

Function Call

`swap(&in1, &in2);`   Calls **swap()** and sends it the pointers **&in1** and **&in2**.

Pointer to an Alias

`split(total_hours, &*hr);`   Calls **split()** and sends it the address of the alias ***hr**.

`split(total_hours, hr);`   As above, but uses **hr** as shorthand notation for **&*hr**.

- The **return** statement can send no more than one value at a time to the calling function. Call by reference is a way to circumvent this limitation. Using call by reference, a function is given access to a variable belonging to another function, allowing the two functions to share the same variable.

- A variable may be referred to by its name or by its address. The address of a variable is often called a pointer because it points the way to the variable. A pointer variable is a storage location that can hold the address of another variable.

- Once given a pointer to a variable, a function can use that variable just as if it were one of its own. However, the function uses an alias for the variable rather than its original name. An alias is distinguished from other identifiers in that the alias begins with an asterisk (*****). The asterisk is called the indirection or dereferencing operator.

- A function that uses call by reference can also employ the **return** statement to return a value to the calling function.

EXERCISES

1. *Define:* **a.** call by reference; **b.** pointer; **c.** alias; **d.** indirection operator; **e.** dereferencing operator.

2. *Errors.* Create a copy of *timemain.c* called *errors8a.c* and a copy of *shms.c* called *errors8b.c*. and introduce into the appropriate file the first error listed below. Compile and link *errors8a.c* and *errors8b.c*. If the compiler catches the error, write down both the error and the error message; if not, run the executable file with test data and make a note of any unexpected results. Correct the file, then repeat the process with the next error on the list. Continue until you have tried all of the errors.

    a. Remove the indirection operator (*) from one of the parameters in the prototype for **sec_to_hms()**.

    b. In the prototype for **sec_to_hms()**, change

```
double *sec  to  int *sec
```

    c. Omit the function prototype entirely.

    d. Remove the address operator (&) from one of the variables in the **sec_to_hms()** function call.

    e. In the header for **sec_to_hms()**, change

```
double *fract_part  to  int *fract_part
```

    f. Remove the indirection operator (*) from the last statement in the **sec_to_hms()** function.

3. Determine whether each of the following function prototypes is correct or incorrect; explain your reasoning.

```
int area(double &a, int size);
double area(double side1, *side2);
void read_data(double *width, int *repeat);
circle_area(radius, &area);
int selection();
int coord(double x, double y, double *phi, double *rho);
double zero((int)*x, (int)*y);
double register(double *a, int *b);
```

4. Consider the following program fragment:

```
int range(int *low, int *high);
double pyramid(int n, double *side, double *volume);

main()
{
   double a, b, c, d;
   int p, q, r, s;
```

Determine whether each of the following statements would be valid if written inside **main()**.

```
p = range(&r, &a);
a = pyramid(p, *b, *c);
c = pyramid(s, &a, &b, &c);
(int)b = p + range(&r, &q);
s = range(&pyramid(p, &c, &d), &s);
b = pyramid(range(&s, &q), &a, &b);
r = range(int &s, int &q);
range(&p, &q) = (int)pyramid(r, &c, &d);
```

5. *Degrees to degrees, minutes, seconds.* Write a function **deg_to_dms()** that takes an angle measured in degrees (a **double**) and computes its equivalent in degrees (an **int**), minutes (an **int**), and seconds (a **double**). For example, if the first argument is 27.72125 degrees, the function will compute 27 degrees, 43 minutes, and 16.5 seconds. For testing, write a **main()** function that calls this function.

6. *Arcsine.* Write an alternative trigonometric function **arcsine()** that takes the sine as an argument and returns the corresponding angle in degrees, minutes, and seconds. Write an appropriate **main()** function for testing arcsine(). (*Hint:* Use the function **radians_to_degrees()** [Exercise 20, Chapter 7], along with the math library function **asin()**.)

7. *Arccosine.* Write an alternative trigonometric function **arccosine()** that takes the cosine as an argument and returns the corresponding angle in degrees, minutes, and seconds. Write an appropriate **main()** function for testing **arccosine()**. (*Hint:* Use the function **radians_to_degrees()** [Exercise 20, Chapter 7], along with the math library function **acos()**.)

8. *Arctangent.* Write an alternative trigonometric function **arctangent()** that takes the tangent as an argument and returns the corresponding angle in degrees, minutes, and seconds. Write an appropriate **main()** function for testing **arctangent()**. (*Hint:* Use the function **radians_to_degrees()** [Exercise 20, Chapter 7], along with the math library function **atan()**.)

9. *Ounces to pounds.* Write a function **oz_to_lbs()** that takes total ounces and computes the equivalent weight in pounds and ounces.

10. *Cups to gallons, quarts, pints, and cups.* Write a function **cups_to_gqpc()** that receives the number of cups of an ingredient (such as flour) and converts this to gallons, quarts, pints, and cups (remember that 1 gallon = 16 cups, 1 quart = 4 cups, and 1 pint = 2 cups).

11. *Military to civilian time.* Write a function **mil_to_civ()** that receives the hour of the day on a 24-hour clock and converts it to the hour on a 12-hour clock. The function should also return an **int** code indicating whether the time is A.M. (−1) or P.M. (1). For example, if the function receives the value 21, it should compute 9 and return the value 1 to indicate P.M. Write a program that

prompts the user for the hours, minutes, and seconds on a 24-hour clock; calls **mil_to_civ()** to convert the time to the 12-hour clock; and prints the results.

12. *Civilian to military time.* Write a function **civ_to_mil()** that converts hours on the 12-hour clock to hours on the 24-hour clock. (See the previous problem.)

13. *Loan payment.* The Third Bank of Thistleborough wants a program that will compute auto loan information. Write a function that computes the monthly payment amount, the total interest that will be paid, and the total amount of money that will be paid over the life of the loan, given the loan amount (cost of the car), the yearly interest rate, and the number of years over which the loan must be repaid. The monthly payment can be computed as:

$$\frac{rP}{1 - \dfrac{1}{(1 + r)^n}}$$

where r is the monthly interest rate (yearly rate/12), P is the loan amount, and n is the number of payments (12 × number of years).

14. *Roots of a quadratic equation.* Write a program that finds the roots of a quadratic equation using the quadratic formula. Begin by writing a **main()** function that carries out the following tasks:

   a. Call **printf()** to prompt the user for the coefficients **a**, **b**, and **c**.

   b. Call **scanf()** to read the coefficients.

   c. Call **quadratic_formula()** to compute the roots.

   d. Call **printf()** to print the results to the standard output, properly labeled.

   Once **main()** is working, write **quadratic_formula()**. This function should return 0, 1, or 2, depending on whether there are no real roots (roots are imaginary), two equal real roots, or two distinct real roots. It should also compute any real roots and communicate them to **main()** using call by reference. The **main()** function should use the value returned by **quadratic_formula()** to determine how to label the output.

15. *Rational arithmetic: reduced form.* Write a function **rat_reduce()** that reduces a rational number to its lowest terms. Thus, for the numerator $n = 160$ and denominator $d = 640$, **rat_reduce()** would produce $n = 1$ and $d = 4$.

16. *Rational arithmetic: addition.* Write a function **rat_add()** that adds two rational numbers, and produces the sum as a rational number. You may recall that you were taught to add fractions this way:

$$\frac{n_1}{d_1} + \frac{n_2}{d_2} = \frac{d_2 n_1 + d_1 n_2}{d_1 d_2}$$

There are two drawbacks to this method: (1) the result will not be in reduced form; and (2) integer overflow can occur with large numerators or denominators. For example,

$$\frac{144}{864} + \frac{288}{576} = \frac{(576)(144) + (864)(288)}{(864)(576)} = \frac{331776}{497664}$$

In this case, both the numerator and denominator would overflow integer variables on some systems. There is a better way. First, use the **gcd()** function (see Exercise 27, Chapter 7) to compute the greatest common divisor of the denominators:

$$g = \gcd(d_1, d_2)$$

Next, divide the top and bottom by this value to reduce the size of the products:

$$\frac{n_1}{d_1} + \frac{n_2}{d_2} = \frac{n_1(d_2/g) + n_2(d_1/g)}{d_1(d_2/g)} = \frac{p}{q}$$

The last step is to divide p and q by their gcd:

$$\frac{\left(\dfrac{p}{\gcd(p,\,q)}\right)}{\left(\dfrac{q}{\gcd(p,\,q)}\right)}$$

17. *Rational arithmetic: subtraction.* Write a function **rat_subtr()** that subtracts two rational numbers. (See the previous problem.)

18. *Rational arithmetic: multiplication.* Write a function **rat_mult()** that multiplies two rational numbers. The usual method of multiplying fractions

$$\frac{n_1}{d_1}\,\frac{n_2}{d_2} = \frac{n_1 n_2}{d_1 d_2}$$

is unsatisfactory because it can produce overflow problems. A better method uses the **gcd()** function (see Exercise 27, Chapter 7) to reduce the size of the factors. First make sure that n_1/d_1 and n_2/d_2 are in reduced form. Then compute

$$g_1 = \gcd(n_1, d_2)$$

$$g_2 = \gcd(n_2, d_1)$$

Next, divide top and bottom by g_1 and g_2:

$$\frac{n_1}{d_1}\,\frac{n_2}{d_2} = \frac{(n_1/g_1)(n_2/g_2)}{(d_1/g_2)(d_2/g_1)} = \frac{p}{q}$$

The resulting rational number p/q will be in reduced form.

19. *Rational arithmetic: division.* Write a function **rat_div()** that divides two rational numbers. (See the previous problem.)

20. *Straight line: slope-intercept form.* The slope-intercept form of a line in the x-y plane is

$$y = mx + b$$

where m is the *slope* and b is the *y-intercept*. Write a function that receives the coordinates of two points P_1 and P_2, and calculates both the slope m and intercept b of the line going through those points. Write a **main()** to test this function.

21. *Straight line: general form.* The general form of a line in the *x-y* plane is

$$Ax + By + C = 0$$

where *A*, *B*, and *C* are constant coefficients. Write a function that receives the coordinates of two points P_1 and P_2, and calculates the coefficients *A*, *B*, and *C* of the line passing through those points. Write a **main()** to test this function.

22. *Straight line: general and slope-intercept forms.* Write a function that receives the coefficients *A*, *B*, and *C* of a straight line (see previous exercise) and computes the slope and intercept of the line. Write a **main()** to test this function.

23. *Three-phase circuit analysis—wye to delta.* In three-phase circuit analysis, delta and wye connections are commonly used. Sometimes it is necessary to convert from one configuration to another. Write a function that converts wye impedances Z_a, Z_b, and Z_c to delta impedances Z_{ba}, Z_{ac}, and Z_{cb}. Use the following conversion formulas:

$$Z = Z_a \cdot Z_b + Z_b \cdot Z_c + Z_c \cdot Z_a$$

$$Z_{ba} = \frac{Z}{Z_c} \qquad Z_{ac} = \frac{Z}{Z_b} \qquad Z_{cb} = \frac{Z}{Z_a}$$

If the function is able to calculate delta impedances, it should return 1, indicating success; otherwise, it should return 0, indicating failure. Test your function by writing an appropriate **main()** function.

24. *Three-phase circuit analysis—delta to wye.* Write a function that converts delta impedances Z_{ba}, Z_{ac}, and Z_{cb} to wye impedances Z_a, Z_b, and Z_c. Use the following conversion formulas:

$$Z = Z_{ba} + Z_{cb} + Z_{ac}$$

$$Z_a = \frac{Z_{ba}Z_{ac}}{Z} \qquad Z_b = \frac{Z_{cb}Z_{ba}}{Z} \qquad Z_c = \frac{Z_{ac}Z_{cb}}{Z}$$

If the function is able to calculate wye impedances, it should return 1, indicating success; otherwise, it should return 0, indicating failure. Test your function by writing an appropriate **main()** function.

25. *Coordinate transformations: Cartesian to cylindrical.* Write a function **cart_to_cyl()** that will convert Cartesian (rectangular) coordinates *x*, *y*, and *z* to cylindrical (polar) coordinates *r*, θ, and *z*. Cylindrical and Cartesian coordinates are related by

$$r = \sqrt{x^2 + y^2}$$

$$\theta = \tan^{-1}\left(\frac{y}{x}\right)$$

$$z = z$$

(*Hint:* The math library function **atan2()** is recommended for computing the arc tangent in this case.) Write an appropriate **main()** function to test **cart_to_cyl()**.

26. *Coordinate transformations: cylindrical to Cartesian.* Write a function **cyl_to_cart()** that will convert cylindrical (polar) coordinates r, θ, and z to Cartesian (rectangular) coordinates x, y, and z, using the relations

$$x = r\cos\theta$$

$$y = r\sin\theta$$

$$z = z$$

Write an appropriate **main()** function to test **cyl_to_cart()**.

27. *Coordinate transformation: Cartesian to spherical.* Write a function **cart_to_spher()** that will convert Cartesian (rectangular) coordinates x, y, and z to spherical coordinates ϕ, θ, and ρ. Spherical and Cartesian coordinates are related by

$$\phi = \cos^{-1}\left[\frac{z}{\sqrt{x^2 + y^2 + z^2}}\right]$$

$$\theta = \tan^{-1}\left(\frac{y}{x}\right)$$

$$\rho = \sqrt{x^2 + y^2 + z^2}$$

(*Hint:* The math library function **atan2()** is recommended for computing the arc tangent in this case.) Write an appropriate **main()** function to test **cart_to_spher()**.

28. *Coordinate transformations: cylindrical to spherical.* Write a function **cyl_to_spher()** that will convert cylindrical (polar) coordinates r, θ, and z to spherical coordinates ϕ, θ, and ρ. Cylindrical and spherical coordinates are related by

$$\phi = \cos^{-1}\left[\frac{z}{\sqrt{r^2 + z^2}}\right]$$

$$\theta = \theta$$

$$\rho = \sqrt{r^2 + z^2}$$

Write a **main()** function to test **cyl_to_spher()**.

29. *Coordinate transformation: spherical to Cartesian.* Write a function **spher_to_cart()** that will convert spherical coordinates ϕ, θ, and ρ to Cartesian (rectangular) coordinates x, y, and z. Spherical coordinates are related to Cartesian coordinates by

$$x = \rho\cos\theta\sin\phi$$

$$y = \rho\sin\theta\sin\phi$$

$$z = \rho\cos\phi$$

Write a **main()** function to test **spher_to_cart()**.

30. *Coordinate transformation: spherical to cylindrical.* Write a function
     spher_to_cyl() that will convert spherical coordinates ϕ, θ, and ρ to cylin-
     drical (polar) coordinates r, θ, and z. Cylindrical coordinates are related to
     spherical coordinates by

$$r = \rho \sin\phi$$

$$\theta = \theta$$

$$z = \rho \cos\phi$$

Write an appropriate **main()** function to test **spher_to_cyl()**.

9.

Arrays

With this chapter you will get your first taste of the general subject of data structures. A *data structure* is a collection of variables that are organized in a way that helps solve a particular problem. The simplest data structures are arrays, which are commonly used in a wide range of scientific and engineering applications. In this chapter you will see how to use arrays, focussing especially on arrays of **double** values.

What Are Arrays?

An *array* is a sequence of variables, all having the same type and sharing the same name. You can declare an array like this:

```
double x[8];
```

This creates an array of eight **double** variables sharing the name **x**, as shown in Figure 9–1. You might want to think of this as a list of eight **double** variables. The individual variables making up the list are called the *elements* of the array. Note that the array elements are stored one after another. The first element is designated **x[0]**; the last element is **x[7]**. (If you have previously used another programming language, you may be accustomed to arrays that begin numbering at 1.)

You can have arrays of any type. Thus, the declaration

```
int count[6];
```

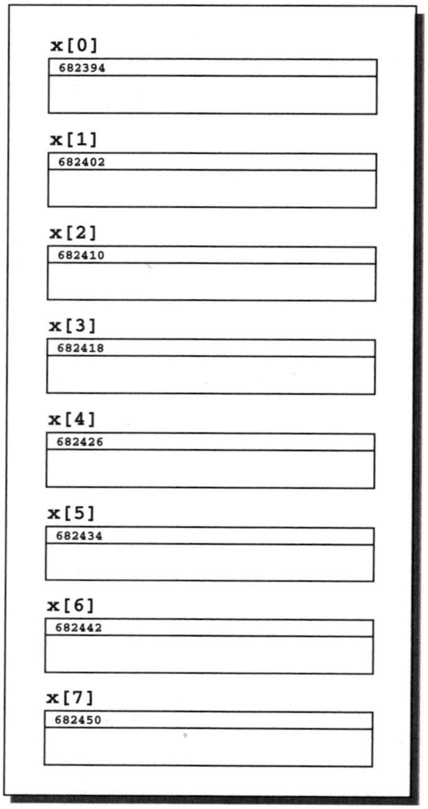

Figure 9–1 An array of **double** values. The declaration **double x[8]**; creates eight **double** variables, **x[0]**, **x[1]**, . . . , **x[7]**.

creates an array named **count** consisting of the six **int** variables **count[0]**, **count[1]**, **count[2]**, **count[3]**, **count[4]**, and **count[5]** (see Figure 9–2).

The individual elements of the array can be used just like any other variables. Thus, the statement

```
x[2] = 497.3;
```

assigns the value 497.3 to **x[2]**, the third element of the array **x**. The **int** value inside the brackets is called the *index* or *subscript* of the variable; arrays are sometimes referred to as *subscripted variables*. The subscript can also be an **int** variable or expression. Thus, if **j** is declared to be an **int**, the statements

```
j = 7;
x[j] = 83409.934;
x[j - 3] = 0.001;
```

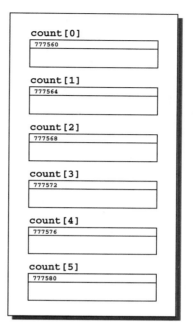

Figure 9–2 An array of **int** values. The declaration **int count[6];** creates six **int** variables, **count[0]**, **count[1]**, . . . , **count[5]**.

will assign 83409.934 to the array element **x[7]** and 0.001 to the array element **x[4]**. As we shall see shortly, this ability to use **int** variables and expressions as array indices accounts for much of the power of arrays.

Program: *upc2.c*

In Chapter 2, we showed you how to write a program to compute the check digit of a UPC bar code. That program required that you declare twelve separate **int** variables to hold the digits:

```
int dig1, dig2, dig3, dig4;      /* UPC digits 1 through 4 */
int dig5, dig6, dig7, dig8;      /* UPC digits 5 through 8 */
int dig9, dig10, dig11;          /* UPC digits 9 through 11 */
int dig12;                       /* The check digit */
```

The **scanf()** and **printf()** function calls used in the UPC program were somewhat intimidating:

```
scanf("%1d%1d%1d%1d%1d%1d%1d%1d%1d%1d%1d", &dig1, &dig2, &dig3,
   &dig4, &dig5, &dig6, &dig7, &dig8, &dig9, &dig10, &dig11);
```

```
printf("%d%d%d%d%d%d%d%d%d%d%d\n", dig1, dig2, dig3, dig4,
       dig5, dig6, dig7, dig8, dig9, dig10, dig11);
```

As we said in Chapter 2, there is a much easier way. Let's write an improved UPC program that uses an array to hold the digits. The C code for the new program is shown in Listing 9–1. Create a file named **upc2.c** and enter the code as shown.

Listing 9–1. *upc2.c*

```
/***********************************************
   Compute the check digit for a UPC.
***********************************************/

#include <stdio.h>

main()
{
    int digit[12];
    int j;
    int sum;

    for (j = 0; j < 11; j = j + 1) {
        scanf("%1d", &digit[j]);
    }

    for (j = 0; j < 11; j = j + 1) {              /* Echo print */
        printf("%d", digit[j]);
    }
    printf("\n");

    sum = 3 * (digit[0] + digit[2] + digit[4] + digit[6]
                  + digit[8] + digit[10]);

    sum = sum + (digit[1] + digit[3] + digit[5]
                  + digit[7] + digit[9]);

    digit[11] = (10 - sum % 10) % 10;

    printf("The check digit is %d\n", digit[11]);
}
```

Dissection of *upc2.c*

(1) `int digit[12];`

This is an array declaration. It creates twelve **int** array elements `digit[0]`, `digit[1]`, `digit[2]`,...,`digit[11]`. (You have to admit that this is easier than the way we declared twelve **int** variables before!)

(2)
```
for (j = 0; j < 11; j = j + 1) {
    scanf("%1d", &digit[j]);
}
```

This is how we read the first eleven UPC digits. Note that the counter `j` starts at 0 because the first element of the array is `digit[0]` (not `digit[1]`). Also note that the condition is `j < 11`, so the last element to be read will be `digit[10]`.

(3)
```
for (j = 0; j < 11; j = j + 1) {              /* Echo print */
    printf("%d", digit[j]);
}
printf("\n");
```

This is how we print the first eleven UPC digits. Again, the counter `j` starts at 0 and the loop continues as long as `j < 11`, with the result that the values in elements `digit[0]` through `digit[10]` will be printed.

(4)
```
sum = 3 * (digit[0] + digit[2] + digit[4] + digit[6]
              + digit[8] + digit[10]);
```

Compare this with the equivalent statement in the first program:

```
sum = 3 * (dig1 + dig3 + dig5 + dig7 + dig9 + dig11);
```

The most important difference is that the variables in the new program are numbered starting at 0, so that `digit[0]` in the new program corresponds to `dig1` in the old one.

Compiling and Testing *upc2.c*

Compile the program the usual way, and try out some test values:

UPC (first eleven digits)	Check Digit
0 8 9 4 0 8 0 1 5 9 2	2
0 1 9 2 0 0 0 2 8 3 6	3
0 7 1 8 1 5 2 6 1 8 9	4
0 4 8 8 9 8 0 9 1 7 5	5
0 7 1 6 4 1 8 2 0 7 4	6
0 1 1 1 1 1 4 0 1 2 9	7
0 7 9 4 0 0 7 6 5 2 0	8
0 8 9 4 0 8 0 3 0 5 2	9
0 3 6 6 0 0 8 1 5 0 1	0

Functions That Work on Arrays

Individually, each element of an array can be treated just as you would any ordinary variable. For example, imagine that **x** and **y** are declared to be arrays of type **double**:

```
double x[100], y[100];
```

You could take the square root of the tenth element of the array **x** and store the result in the tenth element of **y** like this:

```
y[9] = sqrt(x[9]);
```

sqrt() treats **x[9]** and **y[9]** as ordinary **double** variables. But now suppose you wanted to take the square root of *all* of the elements in the array **x** and store the results in the array **y**. You might want to write something like this:

```
y = sqrt(x);         /* Won't work. (x and y are arrays) */
```

Unfortunately, this will not work. It is not hard to understand why: The **sqrt()** library function expects just one **double** value as an argument, not an array of **double** values. Furthermore, the **return** mechanism in **sqrt()** can only **return** one value—it cannot return an entire array.

When passing an array to a function, we always use call by reference. In other words, we do not send a copy of the entire array to the function. Instead, it is more economical—requiring less time and storage space—to leave the array in place and let the function have access to it. This is done by passing the address of the first element of the array, along with the size of the array.

Suppose, for example, that we were to write a function named **sqrt_dbl_arr()** that takes the square root of each element of one array and places the results in a second array. This is how the arrays might be passed to the **sqrt_dbl_arr()** function:

```
sqrt_dbl_arr(&x[0], &y[0], n);    /* Call sqrt_dbl_arr() */
```

The first argument to **sqrt_dbl_arr()** is the starting address of the array **x**, the second argument is the starting address of the array **y**, and the third argument is the number of elements that are to be processed in each array. With these three quantities, **sqrt_dbl_arr()** has enough information to work on the arrays.

Because we so often refer to the starting address of an array, C provides a convenient shorthand notation for this address:

  x *is the same as* **&x[0]**

Using the shorthand notation, we would call **sqrt_dbl_arr()** this way:

```
sqrt_dbl_arr(x, y, n);     /* The easy way */
```

Once given the starting address of an array, a function uses an alias to refer to that array. To see how aliases are declared, consider how we might write the function header for the **sqrt_dbl_arr()** function:

```
void sqrt_dbl_arr(double in[], double out[], int size)
```

The keyword **void** indicates that **sqrt_dbl_arr()** does not use the **return** statement. There are three items inside the parentheses:

double in[]	Declares **in[]** to be an alias for a **double** array
double out[]	Declares **out[]** to be an alias for a **double** array
int size	Declares **size** to be an **int** variable

The function prototype must agree with the function header:

```
void sqrt_dbl_arr(double in[], double out[], int size);
```

However, when writing a prototype, we do not have to name the items in the parameter list:

```
void sqrt_dbl_arr(double [], double [], int);
```

Let's summarize array notation:

```
double array[100];          Declaration of a double array of 100 elements
double array[]              Declaration of an alias for a double array
array[2]                    Third element of an array
array                       Starting address of the array
```

Program: *arrays.c*

Our next program will show you how to write functions that work on arrays. The program will consist of **main()** and the following five functions:

get_dbl_arr()—read an array of **double** values from the standard input.

print_dbl_arr()—print an array of **double** values on the standard output.

ave_dbl_arr()—compute the average of an array of **double** values.

copy_dbl_arr()—copy one array of **double** values into another.

sort_dbl_arr()—sort an array of **double** values using a simple sort.

Following our usual practice, we will write and test this program in stages, beginning with **main()**, **get_dbl_arr()**, and **print_dbl_arr()**. While we are working on these functions, we will use stubs for the remaining functions. Eventually, we will replace the stubs by the actual functions. Here is the pseudocode for **main()**:

get array and return array size
print array and number of elements
compute and print average
copy original array to second array
sort second array
print second array

The C code for **main()** is shown in Listing 9–2.

Listing 9–2. *arrays.c*

```
/**********************************************************

    Demonstrate functions that work on arrays of doubles.

 **********************************************************/

    #include <stdio.h>
①  #define SIZE 100

②  int get_dbl_arr(double array[]);
    void print_dbl_arr(double array[], int n);
    double ave_dbl_arr(double array[], int n);
    void copy_dbl_arr(double array1[], double array2[], int n);
    void sort_dbl_arr(double array[], int n);

    main()
    {
③      double list[SIZE], sorted_list[SIZE];
        double ave_value;
        int n;

④      n = get_dbl_arr(list);
        printf("%d values read:\n", n);
⑤      print_dbl_arr(list, n);

        ave_value = ave_dbl_arr(list, n);
        printf("\nThe average is %g\n", ave_value);

        copy_dbl_arr(list, sorted_list, n);
        sort_dbl_arr(sorted_list, n);
        printf("\n The sorted array: \n");
        print_dbl_arr(sorted_list, n);
    }
```

> **Dissection of** *arrays.c*

① `#define SIZE 100`

It is good programming practice to set the size of the array with the **#define** preprocessor directive. This makes it easy to change the size of the array later if necessary.

② ```
int get_dbl_arr(double array[]);
void print_dbl_arr(double array[], int n);
double ave_dbl_arr(double array[], int n);
void copy_dbl_arr(double array1[], double array2[], int n);
void sort_dbl_arr(double array[], int n);
```

These are the prototypes for all of the functions that **main()** will call.

③ `double list[SIZE], sorted_list[SIZE];`

The preprocessor replaces **SIZE** with the value 100, producing the line

`double list[100], sorted_list[100];`

which is what the C compiler actually sees when it begins to work on the code. In this case, the arrays can handle as many as 100 entries. If you have more than 100 values, you must increase **SIZE** and recompile the program.

④ `n = get_dbl_arr(list);`

This is how we call the **get_dbl_arr()** function. As we shall see, **get_dbl_arr()** reads **double** values from the standard input and stores them in an array. As the numbers are read, they are also counted; this count is returned and stored in the variable **n**. Note the argument to the function:

`list`

Remember, passing an array to a function is always done by reference. The **get_dbl_arr()** function needs the address of the first element of the array to create an alias for the array.

⑤ `print_dbl_arr(list, n);`

This is how we call the **print_dbl_arr()** function. The function needs the address of the beginning of the array, as well as the number of elements to print.

## The get_dbl_arr() Function

The **get_dbl_arr()** function will fill an array with numbers read from the standard input. It has a simple outline:

*initialize counter*
*scan the standard input for the first number*
```

while there are numbers to be scanned
  increment the counter
  scan the standard input for another number
 return the number of elements read

The C code for this function is set out in Listing 9–3. Enter this code into the file *getarray.c*.

Listing 9–3. *getarray.c*

```
/*******************************************************************
    Read an array of double values from the standard input
*****************************************************************/
```

(1) `#include <stdio.h>`

(2)
```
int get_dbl_arr(double array[])
{
    int flag, count;

    count = 0;
```
(3) `flag = scanf("%lf", &array[count]);`
(4) `while (1 == flag) {`
```
        count = count + 1;
        flag = scanf("%lf", &array[count]);
    }
```

(5) `return (count);`
```
}
```

Dissection of *getarray.c*

(1) `#include <stdio.h>`

The standard header file *stdio.h* is included here because this function calls **scanf()**.

(2) `int get_dbl_arr(double array[])`

The **get_dbl_arr()** function returns an **int** value: the number of elements read and stored in the array. Inside the parentheses,

```
double array[]
```

tells the compiler that **array[]** is an alias for an array declared in the **main()** function. *Note that there is nothing inside the square brackets.* Remember, this is the way we declare an alias for an array. To use this alias, **get_dbl_arr()** will need the starting address of the array.

③ ```
flag = scanf("%lf", &array[count]);
```

This **scanf()** statement attempts to read a **double** value from the standard input. It also returns a value that is assigned to **flag**. When this statement is finished, **flag** can end up with one of three possible values:

| flag | Meaning |
| --- | --- |
| 1 | One **double** scanned and stored |
| 0 | No value scanned or stored (error) |
| EOF | "End of File" |

④  ```
while (1 == flag) {
    count = count + 1;
    flag = scanf("%lf", &array[count]);
}
```

As long as **flag** equals 1, the **while** loop will be executed. Two things happen inside the loop: The number of items is counted, and the items themselves are read from the standard input. The loop is repeated until there is an error in the scanning or the end of file is reached.

⑤ ```
return (count);
```

The number of elements is passed back to the **main()** function by the **return** mechanism. The array itself is not passed back because there is no need. Remember, **array[]** is an alias for an array that belongs to **main()**. Every time you assign a value to the array element **array[n]**, it is put directly in the original array element in **main()**.

## The print_dbl_arr() Function

The function that prints an array is very simple:

*for each element of the array*
  *print the value on the standard output*

The C code that implements this outline is shown in Listing 9–4. Put this code in the file *prnarray.c.*
```

Listing 9–4. *prnarray.c*

```
/*************************************************************

    Print an array of double values on the standard output

*************************************************************/
```

① `#include <stdio.h>`

②
```
void print_dbl_arr(double array[], int size)
{
    int j;

    for (j = 0; j < size; j = j + 1) {
        printf("%g\n", array[j]);
    }
}
```

Dissection of *prnarray.c*

① `#include <stdio.h>`

We need to include *stdio.h* in this file because **print_dbl_arr()** uses **printf()**.

② `void print_dbl_arr(double array[], int size)`

print_dbl_arr() is declared to be of type **void** because it does not return a value. The first expression inside the parentheses indicates that `array[]` is an alias for an array of **double** values. As before, **print_dbl_arr()** will need to receive the address of the first element of the array.

Stub Functions

Before you can compile **main()**, **get_dbl_arr()**, and **print_dbl_arr()** for testing, you must provide stubs for the remaining functions. The stubs are shown in Listings 9–5 through 9–7. Create a file for each of these functions, and enter the stubs as shown in the listings.

Listing 9–5. *avearray.c*

```
/*************************************************

   Stub for the ave_dbl_arr() function

*************************************************/

double ave_dbl_arr(double array[], int count)
{
   return(1234567.0);    /* Replace later. */
}
```

Listing 9–6. *copy.c*

```
/*************************************************

   Stub for the copy_dbl_arr() function

*************************************************/

void copy_dbl_arr(double array1[], double array2[], int n)
{
   /* Do nothing for now. */
}
```

Listing 9–7. *sort.c*

```
/*************************************************

   Stub for the sort_dbl_arr() function

*************************************************/

void sort_dbl_arr(double array[], int count)
{
   /* Do nothing for now. */
}
```

Compiling and Testing the Complete Program

Compile and link the files *arrays.c*, *getarray.c*, *prnarray.c*, *avearray.c*, *copy.c*, and *sort.c*. Then execute the program.

The **get_dbl_arr()** function reads values from the standard input until it receives an EOF signal (or some other nonnumeric input). You could enter numbers at the keyboard, generating an EOF signal (CONTROL+d on most UNIX systems, CONTROL+z on DOS systems) when the list is complete. However, this program is really designed to take its input from a file employing redirection. Create a file named *testdata* and put ten **double** values into the file (any ten values will do):

```
324.00
-132.99
0.5645
-0.009
-234.67
8796.650
99.33
-766.77
0.001239
0.00
```

Run the executable file, redirecting the standard input to come from *testdata*:

> a.out < testdata`RET`   or   arrays < testdata`RET`

If your program is working correctly, it should print the number of values read, a list of the values themselves, their "average," and the "sorted array":

```
10 values read:
324
-132.99
0.5645
-0.009
-234.67
8796.65
99.33
-766.77
0.001239
0

The average is 1.234567e + 06

The sorted array:
```

We haven't shown you the output from the "sorted array" because there is no telling what it might look like—we haven't assigned any values to that array yet. If the output looks something like this, your **main()**, **get_dbl_arr()**, and **print_dbl_arr()** functions are probably correct. If not, be sure to correct any errors before proceeding further.

The ave_dbl_arr() Function

Our next function returns the arithmetic mean of an array of n elements. The pseudocode is straightforward:

initialize sum to 0

for each element of the array

    add the value of that element to the sum

calculate and return the arithmetic mean

The C code for this function is shown in Listing 9–8. Add this code to the *avearray.c* file, replacing the stub function.

Listing 9–8. *avearray.c* (Revised)

```
/**************************************************

    Compute the average of an array.

**************************************************/
```

①
```
double ave_dbl_arr(double array[], int count)
{
    double sum;
    int i;

    sum = 0.0;
    for (i = 0; i < count; i = i + 1) {
        sum = sum + array[i];
    }
```

②
```
    return (sum/(double)count);
}
```

Dissection of *avearray.c*

① `double ave_dbl_arr(double array[], int count)`

Reading from left to right, we see that **ave_dbl_arr()** returns a **double** value. Inside the parentheses, we see that **ave_dbl_arr()** uses an alias for an array of **double** values. To connect this alias with the existing array, **ave_dbl_arr()** will need to receive the address of the array from the **main()** function. Finally, we see the declaration **int count** that creates an **int** variable that will receive the number of array elements to be processed.

② `return (sum/(double)count);`

What would this statement do if **count** happens to be 0?

Compiling and Testing the Complete Program

Close the *avearray.c* file and compile the files together in the usual way. Run the executable program with *testdata* as the input file, just as you did before. You should see something like this:

```
10 values read:
324
-132.99
0.5645
-0.009
-234.67
8796.65
99.33
-766.77
0.001239
0

The average is 808.611

The sorted array:
```

Again, we do not show the output from the "sorted" array because no values have been assigned to that array. Does your **ave_dbl_arr()** function give the right result? If not, correct the function before going on.

The copy_dbl_arr() Function

Our next function copies one **double** array of *n* elements into a second **double** array. The pseudocode is simple:

for each element of the first array
> *copy the element into the corresponding place in the second array*

The C code for this function is shown in Listing 9–9. Add this code to the ***copy.c*** file, replacing the stub function.

Listing 9–9. *copy.c*

```
/*************************************************

    Copy first array into second array.

*************************************************/
void copy_dbl_arr(double array1[], double array2[], int n)
{
    int i;

①  for (i = 0; i < n; i = i + 1) {
        array2[i] = array1[i];
    }
}
```

Dissection of *copy.c*

```
① for (i = 0; i < n; i = i + 1) {
    array2[i] = array1[i];
  }
```

Array-processing functions don't get much simpler than this. We use a **for** loop rather than a **while** loop because we know that there are *n* elements to process. Inside the body of the loop, we copy each element of the first array into the corresponding position in the second array. Keep in mind that **array1[]** and **array2[]** are actually aliases for arrays that belong to **main()**.

Compiling and Testing the Complete Program

Recompile the program, and run it with ***testdata*** as an input file. If your program is correct, you should see something like this:

```
10 values read:
324
-132.99
0.5645
-0.009
-234.67
8796.65
99.33
-766.77
0.001239
0

The average is 808.611

The sorted array:
324
-132.99
0.5645
-0.009
-234.67
8796.65
99.33
-766.77
0.001239
0
```

The second array looks just like the first one because the **sort_dbl_arr()** function is not working yet. If your program's output is similar, your functions are probably correct. If not, try to figure out where the problem might be, and correct it. (Begin with the **copy_dbl_arr()** function.)

The sort_dbl_arr() Function

Our next function sorts the values in a **double** array, putting the smallest value in the first element, the next smallest value in the second element, and so on. The function employs a *selection sort*. The idea behind the selection sort is simple:

1. *Put the smallest value in the first element of the array.* Search through the array from the first element to the last to find the smallest value. Swap this value with the value currently in the first element.

2. *Put the second smallest value in the second element.* Search through the array from the second element to the last to find the second smallest value. Swap this value with the one currently in the second element.

3. *Put the third smallest value in the third element.* Search through the array from the third element to the last to find the third smallest value. Swap this with the value in the third element.

And so on. By now, you should be able to see the pattern:

j. *Put the jth smallest value in the jth element.* Search through the array from the *j*th element to the last element to find the *j*th smallest value. Swap this with the value in the *j*th element.

This scheme cries out for a **for** loop. Here is the pseudocode outline for the selection sort:

for 0 ≤ j < size − 1

   find the next smallest value and its index

   swap the next smallest value with the value in `array[j]`

This outline is not complete; it does not explain the method of finding the next smallest value in the array. Suppose we are trying to fill the *j*th element of the array. Here is how we would find the *j*th smallest value to put in that element:

0. To start, select the current value in the *j*th element as the *j*th smallest value. (We do this so that we will have a value to compare with succeeding values.) Select *j* as the index of the *j*th smallest value.

1. Examine the next value (in element *j* + 1). If it is smaller than the value selected before as the *j*th smallest, select the new value as the *j*th smallest.

2. Examine the next value (in element *j* + 2). If it is smaller than the value selected before as the *j*th smallest, select the new value as the *j*th smallest.

3. Examine the next value (in element *j* + 3). If it is smaller than the value selected before as the *j*th smallest, select the new value as the *j*th smallest.

And so on. The pattern should be evident, as should the need for another loop. Here is how we would revise the pseudocode for the sorting function:

for 0 ≤ j < size − 1

   select `array[j]` *as the next smallest value*

   select j as the index of the next smallest value

   for j ≤ k < size

      if `array[k]` *is smaller than the next smallest value,*

      make `array[k]` *the next smallest value*

   swap the next smallest value with the value in `array[j]`

We will use the **swap_doubles()** function from the previous chapter to do the swapping. Create a file and enter the C code shown in Listing 9–10.

Listing 9–10. *sort.c*

```c
/******************************************************

    Sort an array of doubles using a selection sort.

******************************************************/

void swap_doubles(double *first, double *second);

void sort_dbl_arr(double array[], int size)
{
    int j, k;
    int index_next_smallest;
    double next_smallest;

    for (j = 0; j < size - 1; j = j + 1) {

        next_smallest = array[j];
        index_next_smallest = j;

        for (k = j; k < size; k = k + 1) {
            if (array[k] < next_smallest) {
                next_smallest = array[k];
                index_next_smallest = k;
            }
        }

        swap_doubles(&array[j], &array[index_next_smallest]);
    }
}
```

(1) (2) (3) (4) are circled markers in the left margin corresponding to the code lines.

Dissection of *sort.c*

(1) `void sort_dbl_arr(double array[], int size)`

sort_dbl_arr() does not return a value. It works on an array alias (**array[]**), and it needs the number of elements (**size**).

(2) `for (j = 0; j < size - 1; j = j + 1) {`

Note that the condition controlling the outer loop is

$$j < size - 1; \quad not \quad j < size;$$

In other words, the outer loop stops just before reaching the last element of the array. Why? If all the values but the very last one have been put in their proper places, the last value must be in its proper place as well.

③ `for (k = j; k < size; k = k + 1) {`

Note that the condition controlling the inner loop is different from that of the outer loop:

$$k < size; \quad \text{not} \quad k < size - 1;$$

The inner loop begins at **array[j]** and searches all of the elements from there down to and including the last element.

④ `swap_doubles(&array[j], &array[index_next_smallest]);`

This is how we call the **swap_doubles()** function to swap two elements of the array. Note that we send the addresses of the elements, just as we would with any other **double** variable.

Compiling and Testing the Complete Program

Recompile all of the files making up the program, and run the executable code with *testdata* as an input file. This time, the "sorted array" output should indeed be properly sorted:

```
The sorted array:
-766.77
-234.67
-132.99
-0.009
0
0.001239
0.5645
99.33
324
8796.65
```

Program: *diving.c*

The Take-A-Dive Aquatics and Boxing Center needs a computer program for scoring springboard and platform diving competitions. Diving events are judged by a panel of either five or seven judges. (The Olympics and world championships require seven judges.) Each judge evaluates the technique and execution of a dive, assigning a score on a scale that runs from 0 to 10 in half-point increments. The highest and lowest scores of the panel are discarded, then the remaining scores are added. The resulting sum is multiplied by an official "degree of difficulty" factor that depends on the particular dive. Some typical degrees of difficulty are shown in the following table:

Dive	1-meter Tuck	Pike	Layout	3-meter Tuck	Pike	Layout
Forward Dive	1.2	1.3	1.4	1.2	1.3	1.4
Forward 2½ Somersault	2.2	2.4	—	2.1	2.3	—
Back Double Somersault	2.2	2.3	—	2.0	2.2	2.4
Reverse 2½ Somersault	—	—	—	2.8	—	—
Reverse 3½ Somersault	—	—	—	3.4	—	—
Inward 1½ Somersault	2.2	2.4	—	2.0	2.2	—
Forward Dive 1 Twist	—	2.1	2.0	—	2.1	2.0
Back Dive ½ Twist	—	2.0	1.7	—	1.9	1.6
Reverse Somersault 1½ Twist	2.1	2.1	—	—	2.2	2.2
Inward Somersault ½ Twist	1.9	1.9	—	2.0	2.0	—

At the 1984 Olympics, Greg Louganis attempted a Reverse 3½ Somersault Tuck* (degree of difficulty: 3.4), for which he received the following scores from the seven judges:

$$9.0 \quad 10.0 \quad 9.0 \quad 9.5 \quad 9.0 \quad 9.0 \quad 9.0$$

To compute Louganis's overall score on this dive, first sort the scores:

$$9.0 \quad 9.0 \quad 9.0 \quad 9.0 \quad 9.0 \quad 9.5 \quad 10.0$$

After discarding the highest score (10.0) and lowest score (9.0), sum the remaining scores and multiply by the degree of difficulty (3.4):

$$(9.0 + 9.0 + 9.0 + 9.0 + 9.5) \times 3.4 = (45.5) \times 3.4 = 154.7$$

Let's write a program that will perform this computation. The pseudocode for **main()** is

prompt for the degree of difficulty
read the degree of difficulty
prompt for the scores (end with EOF)
call **get_dbl_arr()** *to read scores*
call **sort_dbl_arr()** *to sort array of scores*
sum all but the first and last scores
multiply the sum by the degree of difficulty
print results

---

* This is sometimes known as the "Dive of Death" because at least one diver has been killed attempting it.

Create a file named ***diving.c*** and enter the C code as shown in Listing 9–11.

Listing 9–11. ***diving.c***

```
/**********************************************************

    Compute overall score in a diving event.

**********************************************************/

#include <stdio.h>
#define MAX_JUDGES 7

int get_dbl_arr(double array[]);
void sort_dbl_arr(double array[], int n);

main()
{
    double difficulty;
    double scores[MAX_JUDGES];
    double sum;
    double result;
    int n;
    int j;

    sum = 0.0;

    printf("Degree of difficulty: ");
    scanf("%lf", &difficulty);

    printf("Scores (end with EOF): ");
    n = get_dbl_arr(scores);

    sort_dbl_arr(scores, n);

/* Sum all but the first and last scores */

    for (j = 1; j < n - 1; j = j + 1) {
        sum = sum + scores[j];
    }

    result = difficulty * sum;
    printf("Overall score: %.2f\n", result);
}
```

Dissection of *diving.c*

(1) `#define MAX_JUDGES 7`

Normally, we would expect no more than seven judges; however, this can be updated easily should the rules change in the future.

(2)
```
int get_dbl_arr(double array[]);
void sort_dbl_arr(double array[], int n);
```

The **main()** function will call two array functions, **get_dbl_arr()** and **sort_dbl_arr()**, which we declare here using function prototypes.

(3) `n = get_dbl_arr(scores);`

The array **scores** is passed to a function by passing the address of the first element of the array. You will remember that C provides a shorthand notation for the address of the start of an array:

scores   *has the same value as*   **&scores[0]**.

(4) `/* Sum all but the first and last scores */`

```
for (j = 1; j < n - 1; j = j + 1) {
    sum = sum + scores[j];
}
```

The comment is put here to warn any future reader of the program that there is something unusual about the way the sum is being computed in the loop, namely that the first and last scores are not to be included. Hence, the loop counter is initialized to 1 (not 0), and the loop condition is written as `j < n - 1` (not `j < n`). Whenever you do something out of the ordinary in a program, be sure to explain it with a comment.

Compiling and Testing the Complete Program

Compile and link the files *diving.c*, *getarray.c*, *sort.c*, and *swapdbl.c*, then run the program on some test cases. What happens if you try to enter more than seven scores? Is there any way to signal the end of the data other than generating an EOF?

What Are Arrays Good For?

Some beginning programmers have difficulty deciding when to use an array. To a certain extent, this is something that one learns with experience, but we can offer some rules of thumb. Use an array whenever

- *You have a set of related data, all of the same type.* The larger the set, the more convenient is the use of an array. But the data must all be of the same type: You cannot store both floating-point and integer quantities in the same **int** array, for example.

- *You wish to process the data using a loop.* Closely related data will likely be processed similarly, using the same operations over and over—obviously a situation calling for a loop.

- *You do not know ahead of time exactly how many items will be in the data set.* Proper use of the **#define** preprocessor directive makes it a simple matter to change the size of an array. Moreover, loops can be written to process data sets of any size.

- *You want to search, sort, or reuse the entire data set.* Simple operations—such as reading and summing data—can often be done without an array. But more complicated operations such as sorting almost always require an array.

You might want to examine **upc2.c** and ***diving.c*** to see how the guidelines apply to these programs. Can you think of a way to write ***diving.c*** without using an array? (It would be very difficult.)

HELPFUL HINTS

We end this chapter with a warning about two errors that can cause serious trouble when you are working with arrays. Suppose we have declared an array to hold ten **double** values:

```
double array[10];
```

The first point to keep in mind is this:

>   **array[0]** *is the first element of the array.*

In C, array elements are indexed beginning with 0. This can cause difficulties for programmers who are accustomed to languages that begin numbering at 1 (or some other number). Such programmers may make the mistake of specifying the element that follows the one they really want. They fall victim to the *off-by-one error.*

A related error is that of *overrunning the end of the array.* Referring again to our example, the point to note is this:

>   **array[9]** *is the last element of the array.*

In this case, *there is no element named* **array[10]**. The programmer who tries to assign a value to **array[10]** could be in for a nasty surprise.

If you are having trouble with a program that uses an array, you should check that you have not overrun the bounds on the array. Be sure to examine the conditions in any **for** loops that process the array. If you are working with an array that has been declared to have **SIZE** elements, you should not try to refer to element **array[SIZE]**. Thus this loop might cause trouble:

```
for(j = 0; j <= SIZE; j = j + 1) {        /* Trouble! */
```

The condition should be **j < SIZE** rather than **j <= SIZE**.

● ▬▬▬▬▬ SUMMARY

Array Declaration

`double list[100];`   Declares **list** to be a **double** array of 100 elements.

Array Element

`list[2]`   Specifies the third element of the array **list**. The **int** value in the brackets is the variable's index or subscript.

Function Header

`int get_dbl_arr(double x[])`   Declares **x[]** to be an alias for an array of **double**s. When called, **get_dbl_arr()** must receive the address of the original **double** array. The keyword **int** indicates that **get_dbl_arr()** returns an integer value.

Function Prototypes

`int get_dbl_arr(double x[]);`   Declares **get_dbl_arr()** to be an **int** function that uses an alias for a **double** array. The prototype must agree with the function header.

`int get_dbl_arr(double []);`   As above; parameter names are optional in prototypes.

Function Calls

`n = get_dbl_arr(&list[0]);`   Calls **get_dbl_arr()** and sends it the pointer to the array **list**. The function returns an **int** value.

`n = get_dbl_arr(list);`   As above, but uses **list** as shorthand notation for the address of the array.

- A data structure is a collection of variables that are organized to facilitate the solution of a problem. Arrays are the simplest data structures.
- An array is a sequence of variables, all having the same type and sharing the same name; it can be thought of as a list of related variables.
- The individual variables making up the array are called the elements of the array, and are stored one after another in memory. Each element is designated by an integer index. Unlike most other programming languages, C numbers the elements of an array beginning at zero.
- Arrays are passed to functions using call by reference: The address of the first element of the array is passed to the function. Many functions also require the size of the array.
- Arrays are especially useful when (1) you have a large set of related data of the same type; (2) you wish to process the data using a loop; (3) you do not know ahead of time exactly how many items will be in the data set; and (4) you want to search, sort, or reuse the entire data set.

EXERCISES

1. *Define:* **a.** data structure; **b.** array; **c.** index; **d.** subscript; **e.** subscripted variable; **f.** array element.

2. *Errors.* Create a copy of ***arrays.c*** called ***errors9.c***. Simplify the **main()** function so that it calls only **get_dbl_arr()** and **print_dbl_arr()**, then introduce into the file the first error listed below. Compile and link ***errors9.c***, ***getarray.c***, and ***prnarray.c***. If the compiler catches the error, record both the error and the error message; if not, run the executable file with test data and make a note of any unexpected results. Correct the file, then repeat the process with the next error on the list. Continue until you have tried all of the errors.

    a. Remove the square brackets from the first function prototype so that it reads

      ```
      int get_dbl_arr(double array);
      ```

    b. Change **int** to **void** in the first function prototype so that it reads

      ```
      void get_dbl_arr(double array[]);
      ```

    c. Remove `[SIZE]` from the declaration `double list[SIZE]`.

    d. Remove `#define SIZE 100` from the top of the program.

    e. Remove the square brackets from the function header, so that it reads

      ```
      int get_dbl_arr(double array)
      ```

    f. Remove the address operator (**&**) from the **scanf()** call, changing

      ```
      flag = scanf("%lf", &array[count]);
      ```

      to

      ```
      flag = scanf("%lf", array[count]);
      ```

g. Remove the address operator and square brackets from the **scanf()** call, changing

```
flag = scanf("%lf", &array[count]);
```

to

```
flag = scanf("%lf", array);
```

h. Replace the square brackets with parentheses, changing

```
flag = scanf("%lf", &array[count]);
```

to

```
flag = scanf("%lf", &array(count));
```

i. Remove **count** from the **scanf()** call, changing

```
flag = scanf("%lf", &array[count]);
```

to

```
flag = scanf("%lf", &array[]);
```

3. Consider the following program fragment:

```
double funct(double a);

main()
{
    double b[10];
```

a. How would you call the function **funct** to pass the fifth element of the array **b** and store the result in the seventh element of the array **b**?

b. What is the index of the first element of the array **b**? The last element?

c. How would you indicate the address of the first element of array **b**? The last element?

4. Consider the following program fragment:

```
int count(double arr[], int size, double *value);
double measure(int arr[], int *size, double *code);
main()
{
    double b[10], error, volume;
    int n[10], size, j;
```

a. Which of the following function calls would be valid in **main()**? Explain.

```
j = (int)measure(b, &size, &error);

volume = measure(n, *size, *error);

j = measure(&error, n, b);

measure(n, &size, &volume);
```

```
volume = measure(n, &j, &b[5]);
n[7] = (int)measure(n, &size, &error);
j = (int)measure(n, &j, volume);
measure(n, &size, &volume);
```

b. Which of the following would be valid assignment statements? Explain.

```
measure = n;
b = (void)n[7];
error = (double)size + b[5];
n = (int)b;
count = (double)measure;
*size = j;
&j = n[5];
b[error] = 3.4;
```

5. Which of the following function prototypes are valid? Explain.

```
(void) funct(double a[], int b, int c);
a = funct(double c, int k);
double funct(int a[], b, c);
int funct(int a[], int *b, int *p);
```

6. *Improved* **get_dbl_arr()** *function.* There is a problem with the **get_dbl_arr()** function as it appears in Listing 9–3: It will continue to read numbers from the standard input and store them in the array even when the array is not big enough. For example, if you have an array of 100 elements and a data file containing 200 numbers, the **get_dbl_arr()** function will try to read all 200 values and store them in the array. This can cause serious errors. Modify **get_dbl_arr()** so that it takes the maximum allowable array size as a second argument and quits when the array is full. Modify **main()** so that it calls **get_dbl_arr()** correctly. Test your modifications.

7. *Maximum value in an array.* Write an **int** function **max_dbl_arr()** that will find the maximum value of a one-dimensional array of **doubles**. The function should return the index of the array element that has the maximum value (using the **return** statement) and pass the maximum value back through the parameter list. Modify the **main()** function from Listing 9–2 so that it calls **max_dbl_arr()** and prints the maximum value and its index on the standard output.

8. *Minimum value in an array.* Write an **int** function **min_dbl_arr()** that will find the minimum value of a one-dimensional array of **doubles**. The function should return the index of the array element that has the minimum value (using the **return** statement) and pass the minimum value back through the parameter list. Modify the **main()** function from Listing 9–2 so that it calls

min_dbl_arr() and prints the minimum value and its index on the standard output.

9. *Square roots of array values.* Write the **sqrt_dbl_arr()** function described earlier in this chapter (p. 239).

10. *Variance.* Write a **double** function **var_dbl_arr()** that returns the *variance* of a one-dimensional array of **double** values. The variance of the n values x_1, $x_2, \ldots, x_n$ is given by

$$\text{var}(x_1, x_2, \ldots, x_n) = \frac{n \sum\limits_{i=1}^{n} (x_i)^2 - \left(\sum\limits_{i=1}^{n} x_i \right)^2}{n(n-1)}$$

Write a **main()** function that calls **var_dbl_arr()** and prints the result on the standard output.

11. *Mean and variance.* Write a **void** function **mean_var_dbl_arr()** that takes a one-dimensional array of **double** values and computes both the arithmetic mean and the variance of these values (see previous exercise). Write a **main()** function that calls **mean_var_dbl_arr()** and prints the results on the standard output.

12. *Geometric mean.* Write a **double** function named **geomean_dbl_arr()** that returns the *geometric mean* of a one-dimensional array of positive **double** values (see Exercise 16, Chapter 6):

$$\text{Geometric mean} = \overline{G} \equiv \sqrt[n]{x_1 x_2 \ldots x_n}$$

Note that the data should be positive; if any value is negative or zero, the function should print an appropriate error message, then return -1. For testing, write a suitable **main()** function.

13. *Harmonic mean.* Write a **double** function named **harmean_dbl_arr()** that returns the *harmonic mean* of a one-dimensional array of **double** values (see Exercise 17, Chapter 6):

$$\text{Harmonic mean} = \overline{H} \equiv \frac{n}{\left(\dfrac{1}{x_1} + \dfrac{1}{x_2} + \ldots + \dfrac{1}{x_n} \right)} = \frac{n}{\sum\limits_{i=1}^{n} \dfrac{1}{x_i}}$$

What conditions, if any, will cause an error in this calculation? (If such an error occurs, the function should print an appropriate message on the standard output, then return 0.) For testing, write a suitable **main()** function.

14. *Quadratic mean.* Write a **double** function named **quadmean_dbl_arr()** that returns the *quadratic mean* of a one-dimensional array of **double** values (see Exercise 18, Chapter 6):

$$\text{Quadratic mean} = \overline{Q} \equiv \sqrt{\frac{x_1^2 + x_2^2 + \ldots + x_n^2}{n}} = \sqrt{\frac{\sum\limits_{i=1}^{n} x_i^2}{n}}$$

What conditions, if any, will cause an error in this calculation? (If such an error occurs, the function should print an appropriate message on the standard output, then return −1.) For testing, write a suitable **main()** function.

15. *Median.* In some situations, the *median* is used instead of the average or mean for measuring the center of a set of data. Suppose you have n data, sorted in order of magnitude. If n is odd, the median is defined as the value that occurs in the middle of the set. For example,

$$2, 4, 4, 6, 8, 10, 10 \quad \Rightarrow \quad \text{median} = 6$$

If n is even, the median is defined as the arithmetic mean of the two middle values. For example,

$$17, 17, 28, 37, 72, 81, 81, 90 \quad \Rightarrow \quad \text{median} = \frac{37 + 72}{2} = 54.5$$

Write a **double** function **median_dbl_arr()** that returns the median of a one-dimensional array of **double** values. For testing, write an appropriate **main()** function.

16. *Mean absolute deviation.* Write a **double** function **mad_dbl_arr()** that returns the *mean absolute deviation* (MAD) of a one-dimensional array of **double** values. The MAD of the n values $x_1, x_2, \ldots, x_n$ is given by

$$\text{MAD} \equiv \frac{\sum\limits_{i=1}^{n} |x_i - \overline{x}|}{n}$$

where $\overline{x}$ is the arithmetic mean of the values. (*Hint:* Have **mad_dbl_arr()** call the **ave_dbl_arr()** function to compute the arithmetic mean.)

17. *Standard deviation.* Write a **double** function **stdev_dbl_arr()** that returns the standard deviation of a one-dimensional array of **double** values. The standard deviation, often denoted as σ, is calculated as the square root of the variance. (*Hint:* Make use of the function **var_dbl_arr()**, described in Exercise 10.)

18. *Vector operations.* Vectors are often represented as one-dimensional arrays of three elements each. For example, the vectors **a** and **b** can be written in terms of their components:

$$\mathbf{a} = (a_1, a_2, a_3) \quad \text{and} \quad \mathbf{b} = (b_1, b_2, b_3)$$

There are a number of useful operations that can be performed on vectors. (You should assume throughout that all quantities are **doubles**.)

a. *Vector equality.* The two vectors **a** and **b** are considered equal if and only if their corresponding elements are equal:

$$\mathbf{a} = \mathbf{b} \Leftrightarrow \begin{cases} a_1 = b_1 \\ a_2 = b_2 \\ a_3 = b_3 \end{cases}$$

Write an **int** function **vector_equality()** that takes two vectors as arguments and returns 1 if the vectors are equal, 0 otherwise. For testing, write a program that (1) prompts for and reads the elements of the two input vectors, (2) calls **vector_equality()**, and (3) prints the result on the standard output.

b. *Multiplication by a scalar.* If **a** is a vector and s is a scalar (constant), the product of **a** and s is a vector given by

$$s\,\mathbf{a} \equiv (sa_1,\ sa_2,\ sa_3)$$

Write a function **mult_by_scalar()** that returns the scalar product of a vector. For testing, write a program that (1) prompts for and reads the scalar factor and the elements of the vector, (2) calls **mult_by_scalar()**, and (3) prints the result on the standard output.

c. *Vector addition.* The sum of two vectors **a** and **b** is another vector given by

$$\mathbf{a} + \mathbf{b} \equiv (a_1 + b_1,\ a_2 + b_2,\ a_3 + b_3)$$

Write a function **vector_sum()** that adds two vectors and puts the result into a third vector. For testing, write a program that (1) prompts for and reads the elements of the vectors, (2) calls **vector_sum()**, and (3) prints the result on the standard output.

d. *Vector magnitude.* The magnitude or length of the vector **a**, denoted $|\mathbf{a}|$, is given by

$$|\mathbf{a}| \equiv \sqrt{a_1^2 + a_2^2 + a_3^2}$$

Write a **double** function **vector_mag()** that returns the magnitude of a vector. For testing, write a program that (1) prompts for and reads the elements of the vectors, (2) calls **vector_mag()**, and (3) prints the result on the standard output.

e. *Vector dot product.* The dot product of two vectors **a** and **b** is the sum of the products of the corresponding components of the vectors:

$$\mathbf{a} \cdot \mathbf{b} \equiv a_1 b_1 + a_2 b_2 + a_3 b_3$$

Write a **double** function **dot_prod()** that returns the dot product of two vectors. For testing, write a program that (1) prompts for and reads the elements of the vectors, (2) calls **dot_prod()**, and (3) prints the result on the standard output.

f. *Vector cross product.* The cross product of two vectors **a** and **b** is another vector:

$$\mathbf{a} \times \mathbf{b} \equiv (a_2 b_3 - a_3 b_2,\ a_3 b_1 - a_1 b_3,\ a_1 b_2 - a_2 b_1)$$

Write a **double** function **cross_prod()** that that returns the cross product of two vectors. For testing, write a program that (1) prompts for and reads the elements of the vectors, (2) calls **cross_prod()**, and (3) prints the result on the standard output.

19. *Grading curve.* A question commonly asked of professors is, "Will this course be graded on the curve?" Contrary to popular student opinion, "curving" of grades will not necessarily increase an individual student's letter grade. Several curving schemes exist that assign letter grades to numeric scores. One such scheme is given by

Grade	Numeric score (x)
A	$\mu + 1.5\sigma \leq x$
B	$\mu + 0.5\sigma \leq x < \mu + 1.5\sigma$
C	$\mu - 0.5\sigma \leq x < \mu + 0.5\sigma$
D	$\mu - 1.5\sigma \leq x < \mu - 0.5\sigma$
F	$x < \mu - 1.5\sigma$

where x is a student's score, μ is the mean score for all students enrolled in the class, and σ is the standard deviation of all scores.

Write a program that reads student scores from the standard input into a **double** array, then prints a letter grade for each student. Use the **double** functions **ave_dbl_arr()** (Listing 9–8) and **stdev_dbl_arr()** (Exercise 17) to calculate the mean and standard deviation of the scores. Write a function **curve_grades()** to compute the appropriate grade for each student. Test your program on the following scores:

Student	1	2	3	4	5	6	7	8	9	10	11	12	13	14
Score	61.0	87.0	72.0	82.0	99.0	79.0	90.0	89.0	92.0	77.0	63.0	78.0	82.0	81.0

How will this grading scheme compare to grading on a straight scale (i.e., 90 to 100 = A, 80 to 90 = B, etc.)?

20. *Bar chart.* A bar chart is a graph that represents data frequencies by the relative lengths of rectangles or other symbols. Write a function that prints a simple bar chart on the standard output, using lines of asterisks (*). Suppose, for example, that you have the following array of data frequencies:

```
array[0] = 3
array[1] = 2
array[2] = 7
array[3] = 5
```

The function would print the following bar chart:

```
0: ***
1: **
2: *******
3: *****
```

21. *Integer array functions.* Most of the functions discussed thus far in this chapter work on **double** arrays. Write the following functions that work on arrays of **int** values, and write appropriate **main()** functions for testing:

    a. **get_int_arr()**—reads data from the standard input into an **int** array until an EOF signal is received or the array is full; returns the number of elements read. (See Exercise 6.)

    b. **print_int_arr()**—prints contents of an **int** array on the standard output.

    c. **ave_int_arr()**—returns the average of the values in an **int** array. (Note that the average should be a **double** value.)

    d. **sort_int_arr()**—sorts the values in an **int** array.

    e. **var_int_arr()**—returns the variance of the values in an **int** array. (See Exercise 10. Note that the variance should be a **double** value.)

    f. **median_int_arr()**—returns the median of the values in an **int** array. (See Exercise 15.)

    g. **mad_int_arr()**—returns the mean absolute deviation (MAD) of the values in an **int** array. (See Exercise 16. Note that the MAD should be a **double** value.)

22. *Searching an array.* Write a function **find_int_value()** that will search an array of integers for a particular value. If the value is found, the function will return the index of the first element containing that value; otherwise, it will return −1. Write an appropriate **main()** function for testing.

10

Two-Dimensional Arrays

In the previous chapter we worked with one-dimensional arrays of **int** and **double** variables. Such arrays may be thought of as lists or columns of numbers:

357
−22
−13
99
110

In this chapter, we will see how to use *two-dimensional arrays*, which may be considered *tables* of numbers:

−7	41	13	90
33	17	−6	4
55	0	83	98

The data in this table might be stored in a two-dimensional array of type **int**. Note that, whereas a one-dimensional array may be considered a column of numbers, a two-dimensional array is arranged in both rows and columns.

● ▬▬▬▬▬ # Creating Two-Dimensional Arrays

Two-dimensional arrays must be declared before they can be used. When declaring a two-dimensional array, you must specify its type (e.g., **int** or **double**), its name, and the numbers of rows and columns it has. Thus, the declaration

```
double table[5][3];
```

causes the compiler to create an array of **double** variables named **table**, having five rows and three columns (Figure 10–1).

Of course, we would follow our usual practice and set the array size using the **#define** directive. At the top of the file, we might put the lines

```
#define ROWS 5
#define COLS 3
```

Then, to declare the array, we could write

```
double table[ROWS][COLS];
```

As usual, this approach allows us to change the array size by simply modifying the **#define** directive, and, as usual, **ROWS** and **COLS** are chosen to be at least as large as the largest array that the program is likely to encounter.

Once a two-dimensional array has been properly declared, you can work with any element by specifying its row and column. Thus, the element in the second row and third column of the array **table** would be specified by

```
table[1][2]
```

Note carefully that the row index **[1]** comes first, followed by the column index **[2]**. Note too that each index is enclosed in its own set of square brackets. It would be an error to write

```
table[1,2]          /* Wrong! */
```

Just as with one-dimensional arrays, the row and column indices start at 0, so the first element in the array is **table[0][0]**.

Program: *array2D.c*

This chapter's first sample program will read numbers from the standard input into an array, then print the data from the array to the standard output. In designing the program, we will assume that the data comes by redirection from a file and

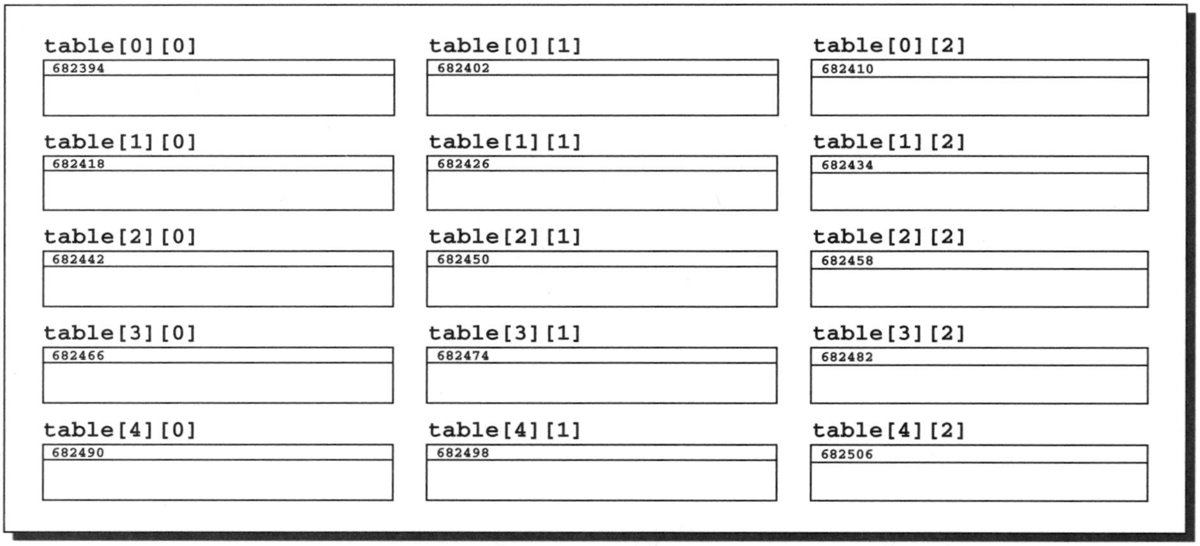

table[0][0]	table[0][1]	table[0][2]
682394	682402	682410
table[1][0]	table[1][1]	table[1][2]
682418	682426	682434
table[2][0]	table[2][1]	table[2][2]
682442	682450	682458
table[3][0]	table[3][1]	table[3][2]
682466	682474	682482
table[4][0]	table[4][1]	table[4][2]
682490	682498	682506

Figure 10–1 A two-dimensional array of **double** values. This array has five rows and three columns.

that the first two entries in the file give the number of rows and the number of columns, respectively. For example, the data file might look something like this:

```
3
4
11.7   32.02   0.17   −10.9998
−47.60   78.1  3.6   −0.11
2.0   −3.245   73.4   −0.0013
```

The first entry in the file gives the number of rows (3); the second entry gives the number of columns (4). We will use this arrangement for all of our data files in this chapter.

The pseudocode for the program is quite simple:

read nrows, ncols

read two-dimensional array

print two-dimensional array

Actually, this outline is *too* simple—it leaves out the important details about how the two-dimensional array is read and printed. Each of these operations requires two loops, one inside the other. The outer loop controls the row index; the inner loop controls the column index. Thus, the pseudocode for reading the array might be

for each row j

 for each column k

  read `table[j][k]`

The pseudocode for printing the array is similar:

for each row j

 for each column k

  print `table[j][k]`

Create a source file named *array2D.c* and enter the C code shown in Listing 10–1.

Listing 10–1. *array2D.c*

```
/**************************************************

   Read numerical data from the standard input
   into a two-dimensional array of type double,
   then print the data on the standard output.

**************************************************/
```

① ```
#include "array2D.h"
```

```
main()
{
```
② ```
   double array[ROWS][COLS];
   int nrows, ncols;
   int j, k;
```

③ ```
   scanf("%d %d", &nrows, &ncols);
```

④ ```
   for (j = 0; j < nrows; j = j + 1) {
      for (k = 0; k < ncols; k = k + 1) {
         scanf("%lf", &array[j][k]);
      }
   }
```

⑤ ```
   for (j = 0; j < nrows; j = j + 1) {
      for (k = 0; k < ncols; k = k + 1) {
         printf("%g ", array[j][k]);
      }
      printf("\n");   /* Start a new line for each row */
   }
}
```

**Dissection of** *array2D.c*

① `#include "array2D.h"`

The header file ***array2D.h*** will contain all of the preprocessor directives needed for working with two-dimensional arrays. This is not a standard header file, but one that you will create yourself. (We will show you what to put in ***array2D.h*** shortly.) The double quotes around the file name tell the preprocessor to look for the file in the current directory.
```

② `double array[ROWS][COLS];`

This declares **array** to be a two-dimensional array of **double**s.

③ `scanf("%d %d", &nrows, &ncols);`

The first two entries in the data file should be integers specifying the number of rows and columns.

④
```
for (j = 0; j < nrows; j = j + 1) {
    for (k = 0; k < ncols; k = k + 1) {
        scanf("%lf", &array[j][k]);
    }
}
```

The elements of a two-dimensional array are filled using nested loops. The outer **for()** loop selects the row; the inner loop selects the column.

⑤
```
for (j = 0; j < nrows; j = j + 1) {
    for (k = 0; k < ncols; k = k + 1) {
        printf("%g ", array[j][k]);
    }
    printf("\n");      /* Start a new line for each row */
}
```

Again we use nested **for()** loops to print the elements of the array. Note that we print a newline character after each row.

Creating Your Own Header File

In every program you have written thus far, you have used the **#include** preprocessor directive to include one or more of the following standard header files:

`stdio.h`	Standard input/output header file
`limits.h`	Integer limits header file
`float.h`	Floating-point limits header file
`math.h`	Mathematics header file
`stdlib.h`	Standard library header file

Most of the functions presented in this chapter will use at least one of the standard header files, as well as some **#define** directives setting the array size. To save yourself the trouble of having to type these directives into every source file, create the header file shown in Listing 10–2.

Listing 10–2 *array2D.h*

```
/***********************************************

    Header file for functions that work on
    two-dimensional arrays of type double.

***********************************************/
```

①   `#include <stdio.h>`
     `#include <math.h>`
     `#include <float.h>`

②   `#define ROWS 100`
     `#define COLS 100`

Dissection of *array2D.h*

①   `#include <stdio.h>`
     `#include <math.h>`
     `#include <float.h>`

Normally, we would include the standard header files *stdio.h*, *math.h*, and *float.h* in every source file that needs them. By putting these preprocessor directives in *array2D.h*, we need only include this one header file in the source file.

②   `#define ROWS 100`
     `#define COLS 100`

As it stands, this program can handle an array as large as 100 rows by 100 columns. That should be more than enough for our needs. However, should we wish to change this, we can easily modify the **#define** lines in the header file and recompile the program.

Compiling and Testing *array2D.c*

To test the program, you will need a data file. Create a file named ***testdata*** and enter the following lines into the file:

```
4
3
−6.0 −5.0 −4.0 −3.0 −2.0 −1.0
1.0 2.0 3.0 4.0 5.0 6.0
```

The arrangement and spacing of the entries in the file are not important, so long as the first two entries are integers giving the number of rows and columns.

Compile *array2D.c* in the usual way. Then run the executable program, redirecting the input from the file *testdata*. You should see output that looks like this:

```
-6  -5  -4
-3  -2  -1
 1   2   3
 4   5   6
```

Regardless of how the input data was arranged, the *array2D.c* program prints the data in the form of a two-dimensional array, with four rows and three columns. You can change this by specifying a different arrangement of rows and columns. Edit the *testdata* file to specify six rows and two columns:

```
6
2
-6.0 -5.0 -4.0 -3.0 -2.0 -1.0
1.0 2.0 3.0 4.0 5.0 6.0
```

Run the program on *testdata* now, and you should see the new arrangement:

```
-6 -5
-4 -3
-2 -1
1 2
3 4
5 6
```

Functions That Work on Two-Dimensional Arrays

Our first program showed us how to fill a two-dimensional array with data taken from the standard input and how to print the data to the standard output. These operations are so commonly performed that it would be convenient to have some functions to carry them out.

Two-dimensional arrays (like one-dimensional arrays) are passed to functions using the call-by-reference mechanism. A function that works on a two-dimensional array needs the address of the array, together with the number of rows and columns in the array. Suppose, for example, that we were to write a function named **print_dbl_2D()** that prints the contents of a two-dimensional array. Here is how we would call this function to print an array named **x**:

```
print_dbl_2D(x, nrows, ncols);
```

The function header would look like this:

```
void print_dbl_2D(double array[][COLS], int nrows, int ncols)
```

The keyword **void** indicates that the function returns no value. There are three parameters inside the parentheses:

`double array[][COLS]`	Declares **array** to be an alias for a two-dimensional array
`int nrows`	Declares **nrows** to be an **int** variable
`int ncols`	Declares **ncols** to be an **int** variable

Note how we declare the alias for the two-dimensional array:

```
double array[][COLS]
```

The first set of braces is left empty to indicate that this is an array alias. However, *you must insert the maximum number of columns (COLS) inside the second set of brackets.* The compiler requires this information.

The function prototype must agree with the function header (although the parameter names need not be the same):

```
void print_dbl_2D(double array[][COLS], int nrows, int ncols);
```

Again, notice how we indicate an alias for a two-dimensional array:

```
double array[][COLS]
```

Program: Reading and Printing an Array

Our next program, like the previous one, will read data from the standard input into a two-dimensional array, then print the data on the standard output. The difference is that the new program will consist of the three functions **main()**, **get_dbl_2D()**, and **print_dbl_2D()**. Create three source files named *main.c*, *get2D.c*, and *print2D.c*, and enter the code as shown in Listings 10–3, 10–4, and 10–5, respectively.

Listing 10–3 *main.c*

```
/*****************************************************

    Call functions to read numerical data from the standard
    input into a two-dimensional array of type double, then
    print the data on the standard output.

*****************************************************/
```

1 `#include "array2D.h"`

2 `void get_dbl_2D(double array[][COLS], int *nrows, int *ncols);`
   `void print_dbl_2D(double array[][COLS], int nrows, int ncols);`

```
main()
{
    double array[ROWS][COLS];
    int nrows, ncols;
```

3 `    get_dbl_2D(array, &nrows, &ncols);`
   `    print_dbl_2D(array, nrows, ncols);`
```
}
```

Dissection of *main.c*

1 `#include "array2D.h"`

You will recall that the header file *array2D.h* contains (among other things) the **#define** directives for ROWS and COLS. For now, both constants are defined to be 100, but this can easily be changed. (If you do change them, be sure to recompile any files that use *array2D.h*.)

2 `void get_dbl_2D(double array[][COLS], int *nrows, int *ncols);`
   `void print_dbl_2D(double array[][COLS], int nrows, int ncols);`

As usual, we could have omitted the parameter names from these function prototypes:

`void get_dbl_2D(double [][COLS], int *, int *);`
`void print_dbl_2D(double [][COLS], int, int);`

Note, however, that the number of columns in the array (COLS) is required even if the parameter names are omitted.

③
```
get_dbl_2D(array, &nrows, &ncols);
print_dbl_2D(array, nrows, ncols);
```

These are calls to the **get_dbl_2D()** and **print_dbl_2D()** functions. The **get_dbl_2D()** function takes the addresses of **nrows** and **ncols**, whereas **print_dbl_2D()** takes the values of these variables.

Listing 10–4 *get2D.c*

```
/***************************************************

    Read numerical data from the standard input
    into a two-dimensional array of type double.

***************************************************/
```

①
```
#include "array2D.h"
```

②
```
void get_dbl_2D(double array[][COLS], int *nrows, int *ncols)
{
    int j, k;
```

③
```
    scanf("%d %d", nrows, ncols);

    for (j = 0; j < *nrows; j = j + 1) {
        for (k = 0; k < *ncols; k = k + 1) {
            scanf("%lf", &array[j][k]);
        }
    }
}
```

Dissection of *get2D.c*

①
```
#include "array2D.h"
```

The header file ***array2D.h*** is included here to provide the prototype for the **scanf()** function and the value of the symbolic constant **COLS**.

②
```
void get_dbl_2D(double array[][COLS], int *nrows, int *ncols)
```

The **get_dbl_2D()** function header declares three aliases:

`double array[][COLS]`	Alias for **double** array (**COLS** is required)
`int *nrows`	Alias for **int**
`int *ncols`	Alias for **int**

You will recall that we use call by reference to pass arrays to functions—hence the array alias. But why the aliases *nrows and *ncols? The function will read the number of rows and the number of columns from the standard input and supply these values to main(). Since the **return** statement cannot return more than one value, call by reference is required.

③ scanf("%d %d", nrows, ncols);

At first glance, you might think there has been a mistake: Where are the address operators (&)? But this function call is correct as written. Remember, *nrows and *ncols are aliases for **int** variables, so nrows and ncols are pointers to those variables.

Listing 10–5 *print2D.c*

```
/**************************************************

    Print contents of a two-dimensional array
    of type double on the standard output.

**************************************************/
#include "array2D.h"

void print_dbl_2D(double array[][COLS], int nrows, int ncols)
{
    int j, k;

    for (j = 0; j < nrows; j = j + 1) {
        for (k = 0; k < ncols; k = k + 1) {
            printf("%g ", array[j][k]);
        }
        printf("\n");        /* Start a new line for each row */
    }
}
```

Compiling and Testing the Complete Program

Compile *main.c*, *get2D.c*, and *print2D.c* in the usual way. Then run the executable program, redirecting the input from the file *testdata*. You should see the following output:

```
−6 −5
−4 −3
−2 −1
1 2
3 4
5 6
```

More Two-Dimensional Array Functions

We are going to show you three more functions that work on two-dimensional arrays of **double**s:

`ave_dbl_2D()`	Returns the average of the values in a two-dimensional array
`ave_row_dbl_2D()`	Returns the average of the values in one row of a two-dimensional array
`swap_rows_dbl_2D()`	Interchanges the data in two rows of a two-dimensional array

The definitions of these functions are given in Listings 10–6, 10–7, and 10–8. These functions are fairly simple, so we will forgo the dissections. We leave it to you to modify **main()** to call these functions and print the results.

Listing 10–6 *ave2D.c*

```
/*************************************************

    Average the contents of a two-dimensional
    array of type double.

*************************************************/

#include "array2D.h"

double ave_dbl_2D(double array[][COLS], int nrows, int ncols)
{
    int j, k;
    double sum;

    sum = 0.0;

    for (j = 0; j < nrows; j = j + 1) {
        for (k = 0; k < ncols; k = k + 1) {
            sum = sum + array[j][k];
        }
    }
    return (sum/(double)(nrows * ncols));
}
```

Listing 10–7. *averow.c*

```
/**************************************************

   Average the values in one row of a two-dimensional
   array of type double.

**************************************************/

#include "array2D.h"

double ave_row_dbl_2D(double array[][COLS], int row, int ncols)
{
    int k;
    double sum;

    sum = 0.0;

    for (k = 0; k < ncols; k = k + 1) {
        sum = sum + array[row][k];
    }

    return (sum/(double)(ncols));
}
```

Listing 10–8 *swaprows.c*

```
/*****************************************************

   Swap values in one row of a two-dimensional array
   with the values in another row. Swapping is done
   by calling the swap_doubles() function that was
   written in Chapter 8.

 *****************************************************/

#include "array2D.h"

void swap_doubles(double *first, double *second);

void swap_rows_dbl_2D(double array[][COLS], int row1,
                      int row2, int ncols)
{
    int k;

    for (k = 0; k < ncols; k = k + 1) {
        swap_doubles(&array[row1][k], &array[row2][k]);
    }
}
```

Matrices*

In mathematics, a two-dimensional array is called a *matrix*. An $m \times n$ matrix is one having m rows and n columns. Matrices are typically designated by boldface roman letters; individual elements are designated by subscripts:

$$\mathbf{A} = [a_{ij}] = \begin{bmatrix} a_{11} & a_{12} & a_{13} & a_{14} \\ a_{21} & a_{22} & a_{23} & a_{24} \\ a_{31} & a_{32} & a_{33} & a_{34} \end{bmatrix}$$

In most mathematics texts, rows and columns are numbered beginning at one, but we will follow the C practice of numbering from zero. Thus, we would represent the array $\mathbf{A}$ like this:

---

* This section is optional, and may be skipped on first reading.

$$\mathbf{A} = [a_{ij}] = \begin{bmatrix} a_{00} & a_{01} & a_{02} & a_{03} \\ a_{10} & a_{11} & a_{12} & a_{13} \\ a_{20} & a_{21} & a_{22} & a_{23} \end{bmatrix}$$

Appendix C summarizes matrices, including the elementary operations of matrix algebra.

Matrix Multiplication*

Let's write a function that performs matrix multiplication. As shown in Appendix C, the product of the matrices **A** and **B** is a matrix **C** whose elements are computed by

$$c_{ij} = \sum_{k=0}^{p} a_{ik}b_{kj}$$

For this product to exist, **A** must be of order $m \times p$, and **B** must be of order $p \times n$; arrays that meet this requirement are said to be *conformable* for multiplication. As is our custom, we begin by computing a couple of examples by hand:

$$\begin{bmatrix} 2 & 3 & 4 \\ 1 & 4 & 6 \\ 9 & 5 & 2 \end{bmatrix} \begin{bmatrix} 1 \\ 2 \\ 3 \end{bmatrix} = \begin{bmatrix} (2)(1) + (3)(2) + (4)(3) \\ (1)(1) + (4)(2) + (6)(3) \\ (9)(1) + (5)(2) + (2)(3) \end{bmatrix} = \begin{bmatrix} 20 \\ 27 \\ 25 \end{bmatrix}$$

$$\begin{bmatrix} 5 & -3 \\ 1 & 6 \end{bmatrix} \begin{bmatrix} 1 & 4 \\ -2 & -2 \end{bmatrix} = \begin{bmatrix} (5)(1) + (-3)(-2) & (5)(4) + (-3)(-2) \\ (1)(1) + (6)(-2) & (1)(4) + (6)(-2) \end{bmatrix} = \begin{bmatrix} 11 & 26 \\ -11 & -8 \end{bmatrix}$$

Listing 10–9 shows a C function that will perform matrix multiplication on two arrays of **doubles**, putting the results in a third **double** array. Before attempting the multiplication, the function checks to see that the original arrays are conformable for multiplication, and that the third array is large enough to hold the product.

---

* This section is optional, and may be skipped on first reading.

Listing 10–9 *mult2D.c*

```
/***************************************************************

    Multiply two matrices (a and b), and put the result in
    a third matrix (c).

    This function returns -1 if matrices a and b are not
    conformable, 0 if matrix c is too small to store the
    product, and 1 otherwise.

****************************************************************/

#include "array2D.h"

int mult_matrix(double a[][A_COLS], int a_rows, int a_cols,
                double b[][B_COLS], int b_rows, int b_cols,
                double c[][C_COLS], int *c_rows, int *c_cols)
{
    int i, j, k;

    if (a_cols != b_rows) {
        return (-1);
    }

    if (C_COLS < b_cols || C_ROWS < a_rows) {
        return (0);
    }

    *c_rows = a_rows;
    *c_cols = b_cols;

    for (i = 0; i < *c_rows; i = i + 1) {
        for (j = 0; j < *c_cols; j = j + 1) {
            c[i][j] = 0.0;
            for (k = 0; k < a_cols; k = k + 1) {
                c[i][j] = c[i][j] + a[i][k] * b[k][j];
            }
        }
    }
    return (1);
}
```

Dissection of *mult2D.c*

① ```
int mult_matrix(double a[][A_COLS], int a_rows, int a_cols,
                double b[][B_COLS], int b_rows, int b_cols,
                double c[][C_COLS], int *c_rows, int *c_cols)
```

The **mult_matrix()** function uses three **double** array aliases: **a**, **b**, and **c**. (The symbolic constants **A_COLS**, **B_COLS**, and **C_COLS** should be defined in *array2D.h*.) It also uses the aliases **\*c_rows** and **\*c_cols**, as well as the local integer variables **a_rows**, **a_cols**, **b_rows**, and **b_cols**.

② ```
if (a_cols != b_rows) {
    return (-1);
}
```

If the arrays to be multiplied are not conformable, the function returns control back to the calling function, along with the error code −1.

③ ```
if (C_COLS < b_cols || C_ROWS < a_rows) {
    return (0);
}
```

If the array **c** does not have enough rows or columns to hold the product, the function returns control back to the calling function with the error code 0. Note that **C_ROWS** and **C_COLS** must be defined in *array2D.h*.

④ ```
for (i = 0; i < *c_rows; i = i + 1) {
    for (j = 0; j < *c_cols; j = j + 1) {
        c[i][j] = 0.0;
        for (k = 0; k < a_cols; k = k + 1) {
            c[i][j] = c[i][j] + a[i][k] * b[k][j];
        }
    }
}
```

You should take a moment to convince yourself that these nested loops do indeed compute the following sum of products for every element of matrix **C**:

$$c_{ij} = \sum_{k=0}^{p} a_{ik} b_{kj}$$

Compiling and Testing mult_matrix()

We leave it as an exercise for you to write an appropriate **main()** function that will call **mult_matrix()** (see Exercise 8). Be sure to define the following symbolic constants in the header file *array2D.h*:

```
A_ROWS
A_COLS
B_ROWS
B_COLS
C_ROWS
C_COLS
```

Higher-Dimensional Arrays

Having worked with one- and two-dimensional arrays, you might be wondering if there is such a thing as a three-dimensional array in C. The answer is yes—in fact, the C standard puts no limits on the number of dimensions an array may have. Three-, four-, and even higher-dimensional arrays are possible, although they are not as commonly used as one- or two-dimensional arrays.

We will focus on three-dimensional arrays here. If a one-dimensional array can be thought of as a list, and a two-dimensional array as a table, then a three-dimensional array is a book of tables. With that in mind, suppose we were to define the following symbolic constants

```
#define ROWS 10
#define COLS 6
#define PAGES 5
```

Then, to declare **book** to be a three-dimensional array of **double**s, you could write

```
double book[ROWS][COLS][PAGES];
```

This declaration creates a three-dimensional array having $10 \times 6 \times 5 = 300$ **double** elements. The first element is

```
book[0][0][0]
```

The last element is

```
book[9][5][4]
```

A three-dimensional array is passed to a function using call by reference. The function takes the address of the array, together with the number of rows, columns, and pages in the array. If we had a function named **print_dbl_3D()** that prints the contents of a three-dimensional array, we would call it this way:

```
print_dbl_3D(book, nrows, ncols, npages);
```

The function header would look like this:

```
void print_dbl_3D(double book[][COLS][PAGES], int nrows,
                  int ncols, int npages)
```

Note how we declare the alias for the three-dimensional array:

```
double book[][COLS][PAGES]
```

The first set of braces is left empty to indicate that this is an alias. However, the function must know how many columns and pages are in the array.

The function prototype must agree with the function header in the number and types of parameters:

```
void print_dbl_3D(double book[][COLS][PAGES], int nrows,
                  int ncols, int npages);
```

As always, the parameter names are optional in the prototype:

```
void print_dbl_3D(double [][COLS][PAGES], int, int, int);
```

● ▬▬▬▬▬▬ **HELPFUL HINTS**

In the previous chapter, we warned you that programmers accustomed to other programming languages often fall victim to the "off-by-one" error. They forget that in C, array elements are numbered beginning at zero, not one. This same warning applies to two-dimensional arrays as well, except that you must worry about the rows as well as the columns of the arrays. For example, suppose we have the following declaration:

```
double array[10][10];
```

In C, the rows and columns of a two-dimensional array are indexed beginning with 0. Consequently,

   `array[0][0]` *is the first element of the array.*

   `array[9][9]` *is the last element of the array.*

   There is no element named `array[10][10]`.

If you have trouble with a program that uses a two-dimensional array, check that the program is not overrunning either the end of a row or the end of a column. Be sure to examine the conditions in any loops that process the array. For example, consider these loops from the **ave_dbl_2D()** function:

```
for (j = 0; j < nrows; j = j + 1) {
   for (k = 0; k < ncols; k = k + 1) {
      sum = sum + array[j][k];
   }
}
```

It would be a mistake to write `<=` rather than `<` in the loop conditions:

```
for (j = 0; j <= nrows; j = j + 1) {        /* Error! */
   for (k = 0; k <= ncols; k = k + 1) {     /* Error! */
      sum = sum + array[j][k];
   }
}
```

Another common error is to switch the order of the row and column indices. Consider this version of the nested **for** loops from the **ave_dbl_2D()** function:

```
for (j = 0; j < nrows; j = j + 1) {
   for (k = 0; k < ncols; k = k + 1) {
      sum = sum + array[k][j];               /* Error! */
   }
}
```

Remember, the row index is written before the column index. Writing them the other way around can cause bugs that are hard to find.

SUMMARY

Preprocessor Directive

`#include "array2D.h"`

Instructs the preprocessor to insert the contents of the file *array2D.h*. The double quotes tell the preprocessor to look in the current directory.

Array Declarations

`double table[10][5];`

Declares **table** to be a two-dimensional **double** array having ten rows and five columns.

`int book[4][6][3];`

Declares **book** to be a three-dimensional **int** array having $4 \times 6 \times 3 = 72$ elements.

Array Element

`table[3][2]`

Specifies the element in the fourth row and third column of the array **table**.

Function Header

```
void func(double x[][COLS],
          int nrows, int ncols)
```

Declares an alias for a two-dimensional **double** array, as well as two **int** variables. When called, **func()** must receive the address of the original array, as well as the number of rows and number of columns in the array. **void** indicates that **func()** returns no value.

Function Prototypes

```
void func(double x[][COLS],
          int nrows, int ncols);
```

Declares **func()** to be a **void** function that uses an alias for a **double** array and takes two integer arguments. The prototype must agree with the function header.

```
void func(double [][COLS],
          int, int);
```

As above; parameter names are optional in prototypes.

Function Calls

```
func(&list[0][0], nrows, ncols);
```

Calls **func()** and sends it the pointer to the array **list**, as well as the number of rows and number of columns in the array. The function returns no value.

```
func(list, nrows, ncols);
```

As above, but uses **list** as shorthand notation for the address of the array.

- A two-dimensional array is a data structure consisting of variables having the same type and sharing the same name; it can be thought of as a table of data arranged in rows and columns.
- The individual elements of a two-dimensional array are designated by two integer indices. Unlike most other programming languages, C numbers the rows and columns of a two-dimensional array beginning at zero.
- Two-dimensional arrays are passed to functions using call by reference: The address of the first element of the array is passed to the function. In most cases, the function also requires the number of rows and the number of columns in the array.
- C allows programmers to create their own header files, which can be included in a program using the **#include** preprocessor directive. Such files may hold other **#include** and **#define** directives.
- Three-, four-, and higher-dimensional arrays can be created, although they are not commonly used.

EXERCISES

1. *Define:* **a.** two-dimensional array; **b.** matrix.

2. *Errors.* Create a copy of **main.c** called **err10a.c** and a copy of **get2D.c** called **err10b.c**, then introduce into the appropriate file the first error listed below. Compile and link **err10a.c**, **err10b.c**, and **print2D.c**. If the compiler catches the error, write down both the error and the error message; if not, run the executable file with test data and make a note of any unexpected results. Correct the file, then repeat the process with the next error on the list. Continue until you have tried all of the errors.

   a. In **main()**, remove **#include "array2D.h"**.
   b. In **main()**, remove **COLS** from the prototype for **print_dbl_2D()**.
   c. In **main()**, remove **COLS** from the square brackets in the declaration for **array**.
   d. In **main()**, change the call to **get_dbl_2D()** to read

      ```
      get_dbl_2D(array, &ncols, &nrows);
      ```

   e. In **main()**, change the call to **print_dbl_2D()** to read

      ```
      print_dbl_2D(array, &nrows, &ncols);
      ```

   f. In **get_dbl_2D()**, remove **COLS** from the square brackets.
   g. In **get_dbl_2D()**, in the inner **for** loop, change all occurrences of **k** to **j**.
   h. In **get_dbl_2D()**, in the outer **for** loop, change the condition

      ```
      j < *nrows   to   j <= *nrows
      ```

3. *Array functions.* Write and test the following functions that work on two-dimensional arrays of type **double**:

   a. **copy_dbl_2D()**—copies the elements of a two-dimensional array into another two-dimensional array.
   b. **zero_dbl_2D()**—fills the elements of a two-dimensional array with zeroes.
   c. **max_dbl_2D()**—finds the maximum element of an entire two-dimensional array and sends the value of this element and its indices to the calling function.
   d. **min_dbl_2D()**—finds the minimum element of an entire two-dimensional array and sends the value of this element and its indices to the calling function.

4. *Row functions.* Write and test the following functions that work on two-dimensional arrays of type **double**:

   a. **sum_row_dbl_2D()**—returns the sum of the values in a specified row.
   b. **row_max_dbl_2D()**—finds the maximum value of a specified row and sends the value of this element and its index to the calling function.

    c.   **row_min_dbl_2D()**—finds the minimum value of a specified row and sends the value of this element and its index to the calling function.

5. *Column functions.* Write and test the following functions that work on two-dimensional arrays of type **double**:

    a.   **sum_col_dbl_2D()**—returns the sum of a specified column.

    b.   **swap_cols_dbl_2D()**—swaps two columns.

    c.   **col_max_dbl_2D()**—finds the maximum value of a specified column and sends the value of this element and its index to the calling function.

    d.   **col_min_dbl_2D()**—finds the minimum value of a specified column and sends the value of this element and its index to the calling function.

6. *Row maxima.* Write a function **all_row_maxima()** that receives a two-dimensional array of type **double**, finds the maximum element in *each* row, and stores the index of that element in the corresponding position of a one-dimensional **int** array (e.g., stores the index of the maximum element from row 2 in element 2 of the one-dimensional array).

7. *Column maxima.* Write a function **all_col_maxima()** that receives a two-dimensional array of type **double**, finds the maximum element in *each* column, and stores the index of that element in the corresponding position of a one-dimensional **int** array (e.g., stores the index of the maximum element from column 4 in element 4 of the one-dimensional array).

8. *Matrix multiplication program.* Write a program that calls the **mult_matrix()** function (Listing 10–9) to multiply two matrices.

9. *Matrix operations.* Multiplication is not the only operation permitted on matrices; Appendix C describes a number of others. Write and test the following matrix functions to process matrices of type **double**:

    a.   **scalar_mult_matrix()**—multiplies a matrix of **double** values by a constant and stores the result in another matrix.

    b.   **add_matrix()**—adds two matrices and stores the result in a third matrix. Note that you must check to see that the two matrices are of the proper order.

    c.   **transpose_matrix()**—computes the transpose of a matrix.

    d.   **trace_matrix()**—returns the trace of a matrix.

10. *Tic-Tac-Toe.* Write a program to allow two persons play tic-tac-toe. Use a 3×3 array of integers to represent the game board. (*Hint:* Use 0 to represent an empty space on the board, 1 to represent the token for the first player, and 2 to represent the token for the second player.)

11. *Tic-Tac-Toe II.* Modify the previous program so that the computer will play tic-tac-toe against the user. The computer should select its moves randomly. The program should give the user the option of playing first or second.

12. *Tic-Tac-Toe III.* Modify the previous program so that the computer uses an optimal strategy to select its moves.

13. *Employee compensation.* The Crayfish Computer Company wants a program that will compile a year-end report of the earnings of its sales representatives. Each sales rep earns a base salary of $1000 per month and a commission that is a percentage of sales:

Monthly Sales ($)	Commission
0 to 50,000	4.0%
50,000 to 100,000	5.0%
100,000+	6.0%

The company also awards an additional 0.5% commission each month to the employee with the highest sales.

Your program will read the monthly sales figures for all members of the sales staff into a two-dimensional array. For each month in the year, print a message indicating which employee (by number, based on his/her position in the array) had the highest sales record in that month. Calculate and print the total monthly pay (salary + appropriate commission) for each employee for each month. Finally, calculate and print the total pay for the year for each employee.

14. *Course grades.* Write a program that will calculate the final percentage score in a course that consists of four parts that are weighted differently:

laboratory reports—20%   homework—20%

exams—50%   quizzes—10%

The program should read the students' scores for the four parts of the course, taking the data by redirection from a file. The program should print a table showing the class average and standard deviation for each of the four parts of the course, as well as a final score for each student. Assume, for now, that there will be a maximum of 100 students in the course.

15. *Olympic long jump.* In the long jump, the competitor runs down a runway and jumps from a takeoff board into a sand-filled landing area. The distance jumped is measured from the front edge of the board to the nearest edge of any impression in the sand made by any part of the jumper's body. The jump is considered a failure if the jumper's toe touches the runway beyond the front edge of the board.

Competitors draw lots to determine the order in which they will compete. The first competitor makes one attempt, then waits until each of the other competitors has taken a jump before taking his second jump. This continues until everyone has taken a total of six jumps. The winner is the competitor with the longest jump out of all six trials.

Write a program that will allow the judges to keep track of the distances during the long-jump competition. The program should first prompt for the total number of jumpers (assume a maximum of eight). Then it should prompt for and read the distances until every competitor has made six attempts. At the end of the last jump, the program should print a table showing all distances, then a list of the longest jump made by each competitor.

16. *Olympic shooting.* In Olympic smallbore rifle events, competitors fire 5.9-mm (.22-caliber) rifles at paper targets placed 50 meters away. Printed on the target are a series of concentric scoring rings. For each shot fired, 0 to 10 points are awarded, depending on the scoring ring where the bullet strikes the target:

Outside Diameters (OD) of Scoring Rings			
Scoring	OD (mm)	Scoring	OD (mm)
10 ring	12.40	5 ring	95.73
9 ring	29.07	4 ring	112.40
8 ring	45.73	3 ring	129.07
7 ring	62.40	2 ring	145.73
6 ring	79.07	1 ring	162.40

There is also an "inner 10" circle, 1 mm in diameter, that is used to break ties. If a bullet hole touches any part of the line separating two scoring areas, the higher score is awarded. (Note that the diameter of the bullet is 5.9 mm.)

Write a program that will permit a shooter to compute his or her score. The program will prompt for the (x, y) coordinates of as many as 120 shots. When all shots have been recorded (as indicated by the EOF signal), the program will print a table showing, for each shot, the (x, y) coordinates, the radial distance of the center of the bullet hole from the center of the target, the scoring ring in which the shot landed, and the point value of the shot. Finally, the program will print the total score.

17. *Bingo.* Compu-Games Inc. has hired you to write a prototype for their new BINGO game. Here are the rules of the game:

- Each player has a card with five columns labelled B-I-N-G-O
- Each of the five columns contains five rows of randomly chosen numbers that lie within the ranges shown below:

Column	1	2	3	4	5
Letter	B	I	N	G	O
Number	1–15	16–30	31–45	46–60	61–75

- No two players will have identical cards.
- Numbers are selected at random, one at a time. If a player's card contains the selected number, that number is marked off on the card.
- The first player to mark off an entire row or column wins the game.

Your program should do the following:

a. Set up the cards for any number of players (assume a maximum of 5 for now) using a random-number generator (see Chapter 4 and Appendix B). Print the cards on the screen.

b. Randomly select a number to be marked off on the cards. Clear the screen and print the newly selected number. Search all cards; wherever the selected number is found, replace it with its negative (e.g., 16 would become −16). Print the updated cards, as well as a list of all letter/number combinations that have been drawn previously. Finally, prompt the user for an integer (0 to quit the game, 1 to continue).

c. Repeat part **b** until a winner is found.

18. *Bowling.* Write a program that will keep score of a bowling game for one player. A bowling game consists of ten "frames." In each frame, the player has two chances to knock down ten pins with a ball. If all ten pins are knocked down by the first ball, this is called a "strike" and the frame ends. If all ten pins are knocked down in two tries it is called a "spare."

The scoring proceeds as follows: Unless the player bowls a spare or a strike, a player's score in a frame equals the number of pins knocked down in that frame. If a spare is thrown in a frame, the player scores 10 points plus the number of pins knocked down by his next ball. If a strike is bowled in a frame, the player scores 10 points plus the number of pins knocked down by his next two balls. Finally, if a spare is bowled in the tenth frame, the player gets one extra ball; if a strike is bowled, the player gets two extra balls. Any pins knocked down by the extra ball(s) are added to the player's total score.

The frame scores are recorded cumulatively. Thus, the score for frame 3 equals the score for frame 1, plus that for frame 2, etc. At the end of the game, the program should print a table that might look something like this:

Frame	1	2	3	4	5	6	7	8	9	10	Extra
First ball	10	5	6	9	10	10	10	9	8	10	8
Second ball	0	3	4	0	0	0	0	1	1	0	2
Frame score	18	26	45	54	84	113	133	151	160	180	

In this example, the bowler's final score is 180. (The maximum possible score is 300, for which the player must bowl strikes in all ten frames, plus two strikes in the extra frame.)

19. *Team bowling.* The program described in the previous problem will compute the score for one bowler. Write a program that will keep score for a team of bowlers. (For now, assume five players on a team.)

20. *Battleship.* The game of Battleship requires two players. Each player arranges four ships on a 12 × 12 grid, out of sight of the other player. The players take turns "firing" shots at the opponent's ships, in an effort to sink them. Listed below are the type, size, and number of ships per player, and the number of shots each ship can fire per salvo.

Vessel Type	Number per Side	Spaces Occupied	Shots per Salvo
Battleship	1	4	4
Cruiser	1	3	3
Destroyer	2	2	2

The game proceeds as follows:

a. Each player secretly sets up his ships within a 12 × 12 array. The parts of a ship must be placed in a straight line—horizontally, vertically, or diagonally—in adjacent array elements. All ships must be separated by at least one empty space.

b. Player 1 has eleven shots available from all four ships; he fires them at Player 2's array, calling out the shot locations by row and column. He records all shots attempted on the enemy's fleet to avoid re-shooting a spot.

c. Player 2 reports the number of hits made on his fleet but does not indicate which of the shots were successful. A "hit" is made when a shot's coordinates match one of the ship's indices.

d. Player 2 fires eleven shots at his opponent's array, and Player 1 reports the damage.

e. The players continue to exchange fire until all the ships on one side are sunk. (A ship is "sunk" if every space it occupies is hit.) When a ship sinks, it can no longer fire shots, and the player's available shots are reduced accordingly.

Write a program that will play Battleship against the user. The computer should set up and initialize the appropriate arrays, allow the user to place his ships, keep track of all shots, etc., as well as act as the second player.

Character Data

Until now, we have dealt exclusively with numerical data—integers and floating-point quantities. In this chapter, you will learn how C treats nonnumerical data such as letters, punctuation, and mathematical symbols. As you will see, even non-numerical characters must be converted to numerical form because

To the computer, everything is a number.

The trick is to devise a numerical code to represent any symbol or character we need. There are two such codes in widespread use: ASCII (read "Ask-key") and EBCDIC ("EBB-see-dick"). Of these, ASCII is the more commonly used. It is the code that we will feature throughout this chapter.

ASCII

ASCII is an acronym for American Standard Code for Information Interchange. The complete ASCII code is listed in Table D–1 in Appendix D. There are a number of points to note about this code:

- Characters are represented as integers in the range 0 to 127.
- There is no apparent connection between an ASCII value and the character it represents. For example, the capital letter *A* has the ASCII value 65; the digit *9* has the value 57.

- The ASCII values are nonnegative—thus −1 is not an ASCII value for anything. (To represent −1 in ASCII you would use 45 for the minus sign and 49 for the *1*.)

- The uppercase letters (*A* through *Z*) are contiguous and in alphabetical order in the ASCII table, as are the lowercase letters (*a* through *z*). Likewise, the digits (*0* through *9*) are contiguous and in numerical order.

- The ASCII values 0–31 and 127 are *nonprinting*—they do not cause anything to appear on the screen. These are often called *control characters*. Some of the more interesting control characters are listed below, along with their ASCII representations:

0	NUL	Null character (\0)
7	BEL	Audible bell or alert (\a)
8	BS	Backspace (\b)
9	HT	Horizontal tab (\t)
10	LF	Line feed
12	FF	Form feed (\f)
13	CR	Carriage return (\r)
27	ESC	Escape
127	DEL	Delete

- The ASCII value 32 stands for the blank.
- There is no ASCII value for EOF ("End of File").

The latter point bears repeating:

There is no ASCII value for the EOF signal.

Most systems use a negative value (such as −1) for the EOF signal. This ensures that an EOF signal cannot be generated accidentally by an ASCII character because all ASCII values are nonnegative.

EBCDIC

Although we will deal almost exclusively with ASCII in this book, you should know something about the other major scheme for representing characters numerically. It is EBCDIC, which is short for Extended Binary-Coded Decimal Interchange Code. This code has traditionally been used by IBM mainframe computers (but not IBM personal computers). Table D–2 in Appendix D shows the entire EBCDIC code. This code has some important features:

- Characters are represented as integers in the range 0 to 255, but not all of the values are currently assigned a meaning. For example, EBCDIC values 81–89 are not used to represent any characters.

- There is no apparent connection between the EBCDIC value and the character it represents. For example, the capital letter *A* has the EBCDIC value 193; the digit *9* has the value 249.

- The uppercase letters (*A* through *Z*) occur in alphabetical order in the table, but there are gaps between some of the letters. For example, the uppercase letter *R* has the EBCDIC value 217, but the letter *S* has the value 226. The lowercase letters (*a* through *z*) also occur in alphabetical order with gaps. In contrast, the digits (*0* through *9*) are listed contiguously and in numerical order.

- Like the ASCII values, the EBCDIC values are nonnegative. (To represent −1 in EBCDIC you would use 95 for the minus sign and 241 for the *1*.)

- EBCDIC values 0–64 are nonprinting control characters. Some of these are listed below, along with their EBCDIC values.

0	NUL	Null character (\0)
5	HT	Horizontal tab (\t)
7	DEL	Delete
12	FF	Form feed (\f)
13	CR	Carriage return (\r)
22	BS	Backspace (\b)
37	LF	Line feed
39	ESC	Escape
47	BEL	Audible bell or alert (\a)

- The EBCDIC value 64 stands for the blank.

- As with ASCII, there is no EBCDIC value for EOF ("End of File").

Program: *ascii.c*

Throughout the rest of this chapter, we will assume that your computer uses ASCII to represent characters. Let's write a program that prints out the ASCII values and the characters they stand for. The pseudocode outline for this program is shown below:

for i = 32 to 126

    print ASCII value and character

This is a very simple program; it is shown in Listing 11–1.

Listing 11–1. *ascii.c*

```
/***********************************

   Print the ASCII values for the
   printable characters.

 ***********************************/

#include <stdio.h>

main()
{
    int i;

    printf("ASCII    Prints\n");

    for (i = 32; i < 127; i = i + 1) {
        printf("%d    %c\n", i, i);
    }
}
```

① `int i;`

② `printf("ASCII    Prints\n");`

③ `for (i = 32; i < 127; i = i + 1) {`

④ `printf("%d    %c\n", i, i);`

Dissection of *ascii.c*

① `int i;`

The variable i will hold the ASCII values. We declare it to be an **int** because ASCII values are integers.

② `printf("ASCII    Prints\n");`

This command prints a heading for the output.

③ `for (i = 32; i < 127; i = i + 1) {`

The ASCII values run from 0 to 127, but values 0–31 and 127 represent nonprinting characters. Since we know how many ASCII values we want to print before the loop begins, we use a **for** loop rather than a **while** loop.

④ `printf("%d    %c\n", i, i);`

This **printf()** prints the current value of i twice, first as a decimal integer (**%d**), then as a character (**%c**). The %c format causes **printf()** to convert an ASCII value to its character equivalent.

Compile and run the program as usual. If it contains no errors, you should see a listing of the ASCII codes representing printing characters and the characters themselves. We leave it as an exercise for you to revise this program so that it prints the ASCII table in multiple columns (see Exercise 4).

The Data Type char

The standard ASCII values run from 0 to 127, for a total of 128 values. C has a special integer data type—the **char** type—that holds (at least) 128 values. You can declare a variable of type **char** in your program this way:

```
char symbol;
```

This creates a **char** variable named **symbol**, as shown in Figure 11–1. Note that a **char** box is much smaller than either an **int** or a **double** box. This is true of many systems: A **char** variable only needs to be big enough to hold integer values from 0 to 127. (The symbolic constant **CHAR_MAX**, defined in *limits.h*, equals the maximum integer that a **char** variable can hold.)

The rules for naming **char** variables are exactly the same as for **int** or **double** variables.

You can use the assignment operator to put a value in a **char** variable. To see how this is done, suppose you have the following line in your program:

```
char c1, c2;
```

This tells the compiler to create two **char** variables named **c1** and **c2** (Figure 11–2). Let's put the ASCII value for the letter *A* into these two variables. One way to do this is to look up the ASCII value (65) and assign it to the variable:

```
c1 = 65;
```

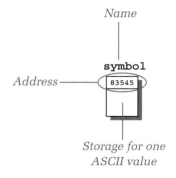

Figure 11–1   A character variable. On most systems, a variable of type **char** takes up less storage space than either an **int** or a **double**.

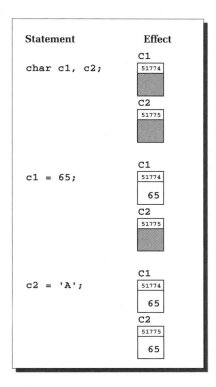

Figure 11–2 Declaration and assignment to **char** variables. When the variables are first declared, they hold no values (except perhaps some "garbage" values left over from a previous program).

However, this requires that you either memorize the ASCII code or always have a table of ASCII values handy. There is a better way:

```
c2 = 'A';
```

The **'A'** is a *character constant*. It has the integer value 65 in ASCII (193 in EBCDIC). Note that a character constant is written with single quotes, not double quotes.

Program: *echoline.c*

The **echoline.c** program will get characters one at a time from the standard input and print them on the standard output, very much like the UNIX **echo** utility. The outline for this program is quite simple:

get next character from the standard input
while (next character is not a newline)

print next character out on the standard output
get next character from the standard input
put a newline on the standard output

The C code that implements this is shown in Listing 11–2.

Listing 11–2. *echoline.c*

```
/*********************************************

    Read a line from the standard input
    and echo it on the standard output.

 *********************************************/

#include <stdio.h>

main()
{
    char next_char;

    scanf("%c", &next_char);

    while (next_char != '\n') {
        printf("%c", next_char);
        scanf("%c", &next_char);
    }
    printf("%c", next_char);       /* Print new line */
}
```

① ② ③ ④

Dissection of *echoline.c*

① `char next_char;`

We'll need one variable, of type **char**, to hold the characters as they are read in from the standard input. We call the variable **next_char** because the name is descriptive.

② `scanf("%c", &next_char);`

This statement shows how the **%c** format may be used with **scanf()** to read a single character from the standard input.

```
3   while (next_char != '\n') {
        printf("%c", next_char);
        scanf("%c", &next_char);
    }
```

Characters are to be read from the standard input, one by one, until a newline character (`'\n'`) is encountered in the input line. After each character is read, it is printed immediately on the standard output.

```
4   printf("%c", next_char);       /* Print new line */
```

The **while** loop terminates when **next_char** receives a new line character. We still want the new line to be printed, so we need one last **printf()** function call.

Compiling and Testing *echoline.c*

Compile the program in the usual way and run the executable file:

a.out `RET` or **echoline** `RET`

At this point you should see no activity on the screen because the program is waiting for you to enter some characters. *Watch carefully what happens as you type;* the output on the screen can tell you a lot about how your computer processes input. Try typing the following line:

Take that, you beast! `RET`

On most systems, the program will echo back this line after you press RETURN:

Take that, you beast!

If this is how your system acts, it uses *buffered* input. On some systems, however, you might observe something like this

TTaakkee tthhaatt yyoouu bbeeaasstt!!

In other words, the program echoes each character as you type it, not waiting for you to press RETURN. If your system acts this way, it uses *unbuffered* input.

A system that employs buffered input collects the characters you type in a temporary storage location called a *line buffer*. When you press RETURN, that is the signal for the program to begin reading characters from the line buffer. (The maximum number of characters the line buffer can hold is given by the symbolic constant **BUFSIZ**, which is defined in *stdio.h*.)

In contrast, on a system that uses unbuffered input, the program takes each character directly from the keyboard and immediately prints it to the standard output before getting the next character. There is no input buffer.

Standard Character Functions

The C library includes a number of useful functions for processing **char** data. These functions are listed in Tables 11–1 and 11–2. To use one of these functions in your program, you must include the *ctype.h* header file:

```
#include <ctype.h>
```

The functions listed in Table 11–1 allow you to classify ASCII arguments. Notice the names of these functions: **isalnum()**, **isalpha()**, **isspace()**, etc. Each of these is asking a question: Is the argument alphanumeric? Is it alphabetic? Is it a space? For example, suppose that **c** and **m** have been declared as **int** variables and that your program contains the statement

```
m = isalnum(c);
```

If **c** contains the ASCII value for an alphanumeric character (*a–z, A–Z, 0–9*), **isalnum()** returns a nonzero value. Otherwise the function returns a 0. The value of **c** is unchanged by this function call. Likewise, the statement

```
m = isspace(c);
```

puts a nonzero value into **m** if **c** is a white-space character—a carriage return, form feed, horizontal tab, space, or vertical tab character. Otherwise, **m** receives a 0. (Remember, in C, zero means "FALSE," and nonzero means "TRUE.")

Table 11–1   Character Classification Functions

Prototype	Returns a Nonzero Value if c Is . . .
int isalnum(int c)	alphanumeric (*a–z, A–Z, 0–9*)
int isalpha(int c)	alphabetic (*a–z, A–Z*)
int iscntrl(int c)	a control character*
int isdigit(int c)	a digit (*0–9*)
int isgraph(int c)	a printable character, except the space
int islower(int c)	a lowercase letter (*a–z*)
int isprint(int c)	a printable character, including the space
int ispunct(int c)	a punctuation mark or space
int isspace(int c)	white space[†]
int isxdigit(int c)	a valid hexadecimal digit (*0–9, A–F, a–f*)

* Control characters have the ASCII values 0–31 and 127.

† The category "white space" includes the carriage return, form feed, horizontal tab, space, and vertical tab characters.

Table 11–2   Character Conversion Functions

Prototype	Purpose
`int tolower(int c)`	If c contains ASCII for an uppercase letter, returns the value for the corresponding lowercase letter; otherwise, returns the value in c
`int toupper(int c)`	If c contains ASCII for a lowercase letter, returns the value for the corresponding uppercase letter; otherwise, returns the value in c

The standard library also includes the two character conversion functions shown in Table 11–2. These functions convert uppercase letters to lowercase letters and vice versa. For example, if c is an **int** variable containing the ASCII value 75 (the character `'K'`), the statement

```
c = tolower(c);
```

puts the ASCII value 107 (the character `'k'`) into c. If c contains the ASCII value for something other than an uppercase letter, **tolower()** returns the value of c, unchanged.

Program: *countlds.c*

Our next program will use several of the functions in *ctype.h* to count the letters, digits, and spaces in the standard input. Here is the pseudocode for this program:

initialize counters for letters, digits, spaces

*read **next_char** from the standard input and set the flag*

while (flag != EOF)
    if character is alphabetical
        add 1 to letter counter
    else if character is a digit
        add 1 to digit counter
    else if character is white space
        add 1 to space counter
print total letters, digits, spaces.

The C code for this program is shown in Listing 11–3.

Listing 11–3. *countlds.c*

```
/***************************************************
    Count letters, numbers and spaces in a file.

 ***************************************************/

#include <stdio.h>
#include <ctype.h>

main()
{
    char next_char;
    int flag;
    int letter_count, digit_count, space_count;

    letter_count = 0;
    digit_count = 0;
    space_count = 0;

    flag = scanf("%c", &next_char);

    while (flag != EOF) {

        if (isalpha(next_char) != 0) {
            letter_count = letter_count + 1;
        }
        else if (isdigit(next_char) != 0) {
            digit_count = digit_count + 1;
        }
        else if (isspace(next_char) != 0) {
            space_count = space_count + 1;
        }

        printf("%c", next_char);
        flag = scanf("%c", &next_char);
    }

    printf("Total letters: %d\n", letter_count);
    printf("Total digits: %d\n", digit_count);
    printf("Total spaces: %d\n", space_count);
}
```

Dissection of *countlds.c*

① ```
if (isalpha(next_char) != 0) {
    letter_count = letter_count + 1;
}
```

If **next_char** contains the ASCII value for an alphabetic character, **isalpha()** returns a nonzero value, and **letter_count** is increased by 1.

② ```
else if (isdigit(next_char) != 0) {
    digit_count = digit_count + 1;
}
```

If **next_char** contains the ASCII value for a digit, **isdigit()** returns a nonzero value, and **digit_count** is increased by 1.

③ ```
else if (isspace(next_char) != 0) {
    space_count = space_count + 1;
}
```

If **next_char** contains the ASCII value for a carriage return, form feed, horizontal tab, space, or vertical tab, **isspace()** returns a nonzero value—you know the rest.

Note that the **if/else** structure does not have a default case. Therefore, if **next_char** does not contain the ASCII value for either a letter, digit, or space, none of the **if** conditions is satisfied, and none of the counters is changed.

## Compiling and Testing *countlds.c*

Although *countlds.c* takes its input from the standard input, it is really designed to echo characters taken by redirection from a file. Create a file named *testdata* containing the following lines:

```
The different branches of arithmetic:
Ambition
Distraction
Uglification
Derision
```

Compile and run *countlds.c*, using the redirection operator (<) so that the program will take its input from the *testdata* file. You should see output that looks something like this:
```

```
The different branches of arithmetic:
Ambition
Distraction
Uglification
Derision

Total letters: 71
Total digits: 0
Total spaces: 9
```

Note that the total number of spaces may be 8 rather than 9, depending on the way you set up your data file: If you placed a newline at the end of the data file, the number will be 9; if not, it will be 8.

Functions: get_int() and clear_buffer()

A good interactive program will protect the user from errors. We have already examined what happens when a program encounters a nonnumerical character when attempting to read a number from the standard input. You will recall that **scanf()** leaves the erroneous character in the buffer, where it can cause difficulties should **scanf()** attempt to read the standard input again.

Let's write a function named **get_int()** that will prompt for an integer and attempt to read the user's response. If the input is not an integer, **get_int()** will clear the buffer and repeat the prompt. Here is the pseudocode for the **get_int()** function:

prompt for integer
read standard input and set the flag

while (flag is not 1)
    clear buffer
    prompt for integer
    read standard input and set the flag

clear buffer
return integer value.

To clear the standard input buffer, we will use a function named **clear_buffer()**. Here is the pseudocode for this function:

read a character from the standard input

while (character is not a newline)
    read another character from the standard input

The C code for the **get_int()** and **clear_buffer()** functions are shown in Listings 11–4 and 11–5, respectively. These functions are fairly simple, so we will dispense with the dissections.

Listing 11–4. *getint.c*

```
/*********************************************************

    Prompt for an integer on the standard output;
    read the value from the standard input.

    In case of an error, clear the buffer and prompt
    again for an integer.

*********************************************************/

#include <stdio.h>

void clear_buffer(void);

int get_int(void)
{
    int input;
    int flag;

    printf("Please enter an integer: ");
    flag = scanf("%d", &input);

    while (1 != flag) {
       clear_buffer();
       printf("Please enter an integer: ");
       flag = scanf("%d", &input);
    }

    clear_buffer();
    return (input);
}
```

Listing 11–5. *clearbuf.c*

```
/********************************************************

    Clear the input buffer up to and including
    a newline character.

********************************************************/

#include <stdio.h>

void clear_buffer(void)
{
    char discard;

    scanf("%c", &discard);

    while ('\n' != discard) {
        scanf("%c", &discard);
    }
}
```

Compiling and Testing get_int() **and** clear_buffer()

To test the **get_int()** and **clear_buffer()** functions, you will need to write a **main()** function. We suggest that your **main()** function call **get_int()** at least twice to make sure that the buffer is being cleared completely after erroneous data is entered.

call **get_int()** *to get first integer*
call **get_int()** *to get second integer*
print first integer
print second integer

Compile and link **get_int()**, **clear_buffer()**, and **main()**, then run the executable file. Does the program work as it should? Can you find input that will cause the program to fail?

● ▬▬▬▬   **HELPFUL HINTS**

There are a few points to keep in mind when working with **char** data:

- Do not write **"A"** when you mean **'A'**. They are not the same: **'A'** is a character constant; **"A"** is a string constant. As we will see in the next chapter, the C language treats these very differently.

- When using a data file, remember that EOF is a signal generated by the operating system, not something that you must put in the file yourself.
- In general, do not attempt to read numerical values using the **%c** format. The reason is that **%c** causes **scanf()** to treat numbers as collections of individual characters. Thus, for example, the integer -12 would be treated as three separate characters: $-$(ASCII value 45), *1* (ASCII value 49), and *2* (ASCII value 50).
- Finally, do not waste your time memorizing the ASCII table or require that readers of your code know the table. For instance, you may recall that there are two ways to assign the ASCII value 65 to a **char** variable:

```
c1 = 65;

c2 = 'A';
```

The second method is much better because it requires no knowledge of the ASCII table and it works without modification on machines that use EBCDIC or some other code.

● ▬▬▬▬ SUMMARY

Preprocessor Directive

```
#include <ctype.h>
```

Instructs the preprocessor to insert the contents of the standard header file, *ctype.h*. Angle brackets, **<** and **>**, tell the preprocessor to look in the "usual place" (which is system-dependent).

Variable Declaration

```
char next_char;
```

Declares **next_char** to be a variable of type **char**.

Character Input

```
scanf("%c", &next_char);
```

Calls the library function **scanf()** to read a character (**%c**) from the standard input and store it in the variable **next_char**.

Assignment

```
next_char = 'A';
```

Assigns **'A'** (ASCII value 65 or EBCDIC value 193) to the variable **next_char**.

Character Output

```
printf("%c", next_char);
```

Calls the library function **printf()** to print the contents of **next_char** as a character.

- To the computer, everything is a number. Consequently, all data must be converted to numerical form to be processed by the computer.

- The American Standard Code for Information Interchange (ASCII) represents characters as nonnegative integers in the range 0 to 127. Of these, values 0–31 and 127 are nonprinting. In general, there is no apparent connection between the ASCII code and the character it represents.

- The Extended Binary-Coded Decimal Interchange Code (EBCDIC) represents characters as nonnegative integers in the range 0 to 255, although not all of the values are currently assigned a meaning. Values 0–64 represent nonprinting control characters.

- Neither ASCII nor EBCDIC contains a value for EOF ("End of File"). This ensures that an EOF signal cannot be generated accidentally by an ASCII or EBCDIC value. Most systems use a negative value such as –1 for the EOF signal.

- A variable of type **char** is designed to hold a single integer character code. On most systems, **char** variables are smaller than **int** variables, although the C standard does not require this. The maximum integer value that can be stored in a **char** variable is given by the symbolic constant **CHAR_MAX**, which is defined in *limits.h*.

- A character enclosed by single quotes (e.g., **'A'**) is a character constant. The actual value of this constant depends on the code used (ASCII or EBCDIC).

- Input from the keyboard may be buffered or unbuffered. A system using buffered input collects characters in a line buffer until the RETURN key is pressed. On a system that uses unbuffered input, a program takes each character as it is entered at the keyboard.

- The C library includes a number of functions for classifying and converting **char** data. The prototypes for these functions are found in the standard header file *ctype.h*.

EXERCISES

1. *Define:* **a.** ASCII; **b.** EBCDIC; **c.** control character; **d.** character constant; **e.** white space; **f.** alphanumeric; **g.** line buffer.

2. *Errors.* Make a copy of *countlds.c* called *errors11.c* and introduce into the new file the first error listed below. Run your compiler on the file. If the compiler catches the error, write down both the error and the error message; if not, run the executable file with test data and make a note of any unexpected results. Correct the file, then repeat the process with the next error on the list. Continue until you have tried all of the errors.

    a. Remove `#include <ctype.h>`.

    b. Change the type of `next_char` from **char** to **int**.

    c. Change the character conversion specification from `%c` to `%d` in the first `scanf()` call.

    d. Remove both parentheses around **next_char** in the first **if** statement.

    e. Change the character conversion specification from **%d** to **%c** in the first **printf()** call.

3. *Limits.* The standard header file ***limits.h*** contains the **#define** directive for the symbolic constant **CHAR_MAX** (the maximum value that can be stored in a **char** variable); ***stdio.h*** contains the definition of **BUFSIZ** (the maximum number of characters that the buffer can hold). Modify your ***prlimits.c*** program so that it will print the values of **CHAR_MAX** and **BUFSIZ**, properly labeled.

4. *Improved ASCII table.* The table produced by the ***ascii.c*** program (Listing 11–1) will not fit entirely on the typical computer screen. Revise the program so that it will print the ASCII table in 20 rows (including headings) and 10 columns:

ASCII	Prints	ASCII	Prints	ASCII	Prints	ASCII	Prints	ASCII	Prints
32		51	3	70	F	89	Y	108	l
33	!	52	4	71	G	90	Z	109	m
34	"	53	5	72	H	91	[	110	n
35	#	54	6	73	I	92	\	111	o
36	$	55	7	74	J	93	]	112	p
37	%	56	8	75	K	94	^	113	q
38	&	57	9	76	L	95	_	114	r
39	'	58	:	77	M	96	`	115	s
40	(	59	;	78	N	97	a	116	t
41	)	60	<	79	O	98	b	117	u
42	*	61	=	80	P	99	c	118	v
43	+	62	>	81	Q	100	d	119	w
44	,	63	?	82	R	101	e	120	x
45	–	64	@	83	S	102	f	121	y
46	.	65	A	84	T	103	g	122	z
47	/	66	B	85	U	104	h	123	{
48	0	67	C	86	V	105	i	124		
49	1	68	D	87	W	106	j	125	}
50	2	69	E	88	X	107	k	126	~

5. *Extended ASCII table.* Standard ASCII includes 128 integer values (0 to 127); however, many systems extend ASCII to include 256 or more values. Modify the program you wrote for the previous exercise so that it also prints a second table of ASCII values from 127 through 256. What kind of characters (if any) do the extended codes represent on your system?

6. *Echoing input.* Write a program named ***echofile.c*** that reads characters from the standard input and prints them on the standard output until it receives an EOF signal. (*Hint:* Make a copy of the ***echoline.c*** file and modify the code as needed.)

7. *Counting words.* Write a program ***mywc.c*** that mimics the UNIX ***wc*** ("word count") command. The program will count the number of characters, words, and lines in the standard input, until it receives an EOF signal. (*Hint:* Treat any group of characters followed by white space to be a "word.")

8. *Capitalize.* Write a program ***caps.c*** that reads characters from a text file, converts lowercase letters to uppercase letters (leaving other characters unchanged), and echoes the characters to the screen. Thus, if the input text includes the line

   ```
   Out, out %$@#% spot!
   ```

   the output from ***caps.c*** would be

   ```
   OUT, OUT %$@#% SPOT!
   ```

9. *Line adjustment.* Write a program, named ***adjust.c***, that reads text from the standard input and prints it on the standard output, adjusting the output lines to be about *N* characters long. The program will read and count characters from the standard input. So long as the current line is less than *N* characters long, the program will change any newline character to a space before writing it to the standard output. However, as soon as the line exceeds *N* characters, the program will change the next white space it encounters to a newline character. The program will terminate when it receives an EOF signal.

10. *Double spacing.* Write a program ***dblspace.c*** that reads text from the standard input and prints it double-spaced on the standard output, stopping at an EOF signal.

11. *Counting pairs.* Write a program ***pairs.c*** that reads text from the standard input and counts each (a) opening parenthesis; (b) closing parenthesis; (c) opening brace; (d) closing brace; (e) opening bracket; (f) closing bracket; (g) double quote; (h) single quote. The program will print out the totals, properly labeled.

12. *Checking quotes.* Write a program ***chquotes.c*** that checks each line of a C program for pairs of double quote characters. ***chquotes.c*** will print the line number of any line of code that contains a double quote without a matching double quote.

13. *Vowels.* Write an **int** function **isvowel()** that returns 1 if the argument is the ASCII value for a vowel, and 0 otherwise. For testing, modify the ***countlds.c*** program so that it calls **isvowel()** and prints the total number of vowels in the input.

14. *Consonants.* Write an **int** function **isconsonant()** that returns 1 if the argument is the ASCII value for a consonant, and 0 otherwise. For testing, modify the ***countlds.c*** program so that it calls **isconsonant()** and prints the total number of consonants in the input.

15. *English without vowels.* Some ancient languages were written without symbols for the vowel sounds. It has been said that English is quite understandable when the vowels are omitted. Check this by writing a program that reads text from the standard input and prints it to the standard output, omitting the vowels.

16. *Other integer-input functions.* The **get_int()** function presented in Listing 11–4 will accept any integer input. In some situations, however, it is convenient to limit the input to integers in a given range. Write and test the following functions:

   a. **get_pos_int()**—like **get_int()**, but returns positive integers only.

   b. **get_neg_int()**—like **get_int()**, but returns negative integers only.

   c. **get_int_between()**—like **get_int()**, but returns integers in the range a to b, where a and b are specified as arguments to the function.

17. *Menu input.* The function **get_int()** is especially useful in interactive programs written for general public use, because it helps to guard against input errors. Modify the McDowell Restaurant menu (Exercise 19, Chapter 6) to use **get_int()**. Better yet, use the **get_int_between()** function described in the previous exercise.

18. *Yes or no?* Many interactive programs require the user to answer "yes" or "no" to a question. Write and test a function named **get_YorN()** that will ask the user to enter a y or n. The program should accept any one of the characters y, Y, n, or N; it should clear the buffer and repeat the prompt if any other input character is entered.

19. *Quit or continue?* Write and test a function named **get_QorC()** that will ask the user to enter Q (or q) to indicate "quit," and C (or c) to indicate "continue." The program should clear the buffer and repeat the prompt if any other input character is entered.

20. *Floating-point input.* Write and test the following input functions:

   a. **get_dbl()**—works like **get_int()**, but returns a **double** value.

   b. **get_pos_dbl()**—like **get_dbl()**, but returns positive values only.

   c. **get_neg_dbl()**—like **get_dbl()**, but returns negative values only.

   d. **get_dbl_between()**—like **get_dbl()**, but returns values in the range a to b, where a and b are specified as arguments to the function.

21. *Quiz scores.* A professor wants a program to help her enter quiz scores interactively. If she should mistakenly enter a nonnumerical character, or a value outside a specified range, the program should clear the standard input and prompt for the score again. When all the scores have been entered, the program should display the class average. (*Hint:* You may wish to use **get_dbl_between()**, described in the previous exercise.)

22. *Improved quiz scoring.* Modify the previous program so that after each score has been entered, the program checks to see that the score is correct. For example,

```
The score for student number 7 was 95.6.
Is this correct? (y or n)
```

   If the user enters **n**, the program should prompt for the correct score. (*Hint:* Use **get_YorN()**, described in Exercise 18.)

23. *Encryption—rot 13.* Many Internet news groups deal with controversial issues. To protect users from accidentally reading articles they might prefer not to see, it is customary to encrypt such articles using the "rot13" cipher. This is a simple scheme in which each letter of the alphabet is "rotated" thirteen letters (leaving other characters unchanged):

Original	a	b	c	d	...	w	x	y	z
Rotated	n	o	p	q	...	j	k	l	m

Original	A	B	C	D	...	W	X	Y	Z
Rotated	N	O	P	Q	...	J	K	L	M

Applying rot13 again to the encrypted message restores the original message. Write a program named ***rot13.c*** that will read characters from the standard input, encrypt them using the rot13 cipher, and print the encrypted characters on the standard output.

24. *Roman numeral conversion.* Write a program that converts Roman numerals to their decimal equivalents:

Roman	M	D	C	L	X	V	I
Decimal	1000	500	100	50	10	5	1

The order in which the numerals are written matters. In particular, if a numeral immediately precedes another of greater value, the lower value is subtracted from the total. Hence,

$$\text{MIX} = 1000 - 1 + 10 = 1009$$

$$\text{MCMLXLVIII} = 1000 - 100 + 1000 + 50 - 10 + 50 + 5 + 1 + 1 + 1 = 1998$$

25. *Musical notes.* Beginning at the left side of the piano keyboard, the notes corresponding to the white keys are designated by the seven letters

A, B, C, D, E, F, G

The black keys are named according to the nearest white keys. Thus, the black key between A and B is designated either as A# ("A-sharp") or as B♭ ("B-flat"). Altogether, the lowest twelve notes on the piano keyboard (also called the lowest octave) are as follows:

A, A# (or B♭), B, C, C# (or D♭), D, D# (or E♭), E, F, F# (or G♭), G, G# (or A♭)

The pitch of a musical note depends on the frequency of the sound: the greater the frequency, the higher the pitch. Adjacent notes on the musical scale differ in frequency by the ratio

$$\sqrt[12]{2} \approx 1.05946$$

For example, the lowest A has a frequency of 27.50 Hz; A# (B♭) has the frequency 29.135 Hz (29.135/27.50 = 1.05946).

Write a program ***music.c*** that reads a series of notes within the lowest octave (with or without spaces between notes) and prints their frequencies

on the standard output, until it receives an EOF signal. Use the pound sign
(#) to represent sharps and the lowercase *b* to represent flats. For example,
given the input

F#GBbA CD# DbEbF [RET] [CNTRL] + [z]   or   [CNTRL] + [d]

the program should produce the output

```
46.249
48.999
29.135
27.500
32.703
38.891
34.648
38.891
43.654
```

26. *Musical notes—octaves.* The ***music.c*** program described in the previous
exercise computes the frequency of the 12 lowest notes of the piano. The
remaining 76 keys produce frequencies that are multiples of these 12. Thus,
for example, there are eight A notes, whose frequencies differ from each other
by factors of 2:

Note	A_0	A_1	A_2	A_3	A_4	A_5	A_6	A_7
(Hz)	27.5	55	110	220	440	880	1760	3520

Any two frequencies that differ by a factor of 2 are said to span an *octave*.
Here we have designated the octaves by a subscript. Thus, the notes B_0, C_0,
D_0, etc., lie between A_0 and A_1; the notes B_1, C_1, D_1, etc., lie between A_1 and
A_2; and so on. (Other notations are used as well.)

Modify ***music.c*** so that the user can specify the octave of the note by an
integer (after the sharp or flat symbol, if any). If the number is omitted, the
program should assume that octave 4 is intended. Thus, given the input

F#1 G2Bb4A CD# Db7Eb7F4 [RET] [CNTRL] + [z]   or   [CNTRL] + [d]

the program should produce the output

```
92.499
195.998
466.164
440.000
523.251
622.254
4434.922
4978.032
698.456
```

Chapter *12.*

Strings

In the previous chapter we saw how to process character data—one character at a time. Although this is adequate for many purposes, there are times when it is necessary to work with groups of characters. For this we use character *strings*, which are treated in C as arrays of type **char**. In this chapter we will see how to store and manipulate string constants and string variables.

String Constants

We have said that a *string constant* (also called a *string literal*) is any character or group of characters enclosed by double quotes. Thus, the following would all be string constants:

```
"A"
"%lf"
"The answer is %d.\n"
"A fine mess"
```

The computer stores string constants in arrays of type **char**. For example, the string constant

```
"A fine mess"
```

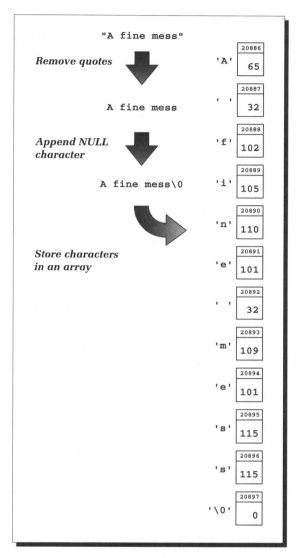

Figure 12–1 A string constant. The compiler stores string constants in arrays of type **char**. Note that this array does not have a name.

would be stored in an array of 12 **char** elements, as shown in Figure 12–1. There are four things to note about this array:

- The array has no name. That means you cannot refer to a string constant by name.
- Although there are eleven characters in the string, including two spaces, there are twelve **char** elements in the array. In general, if there are *n* characters between the double quotes, the C compiler will create a **char** array having (*n* + 1) elements.

- The double quotes are not stored in the array. The quotes serve only to mark the beginning and the end of the string. If you want to include a double quote as part of a string constant, you must put a backslash (\) in front of it:

```
"he said \"Phooey!\""
```

- The last element of the array holds the null character '\0' (ASCII value 0). This was not part of the original string, but was inserted by the compiler to mark the end of the string. When used this way, the null character is called the *string delimiter* or *end-of-string sentinel*.

The end-of-string sentinel ('\0') is the key to understanding how C processes strings. It is also the reason we said that 'A' and "A" are different: 'A' is a character (ASCII value 65) and "A" is a two-element **char** array containing characters 'A' and '\0'.

String Variables

Although string constants are useful, they have one important limitation: Once the program is compiled, you cannot alter a string constant. (That is why it is called a constant.) If you want to modify a string while the program is running, you must use a *string variable*. Let's see how to create and fill a string variable.

C stores strings in arrays of **char** variables, so the first step is to declare a **char** array:

```
char str[10];
```

This declaration creates an array of ten **char** variables named **str** (see Figure 12–2).

How big should the array be? Always declare the array to be at least as large as the largest string you anticipate it will need to hold—and remember to include one element to hold the null character that serves as the end-of-string sentinel.

Filling the Array

Once the **char** array is declared, you will need a way to put characters into the array. Unfortunately, you cannot do this:

```
str = "Hot car";      /* Won't work! */
```

You could assign the characters one by one to the elements of the array, making sure to insert a null character at the end:

```
str[0] = 'H';
str[1] = 'o';
str[2] = 't';
str[3] = ' ';
```

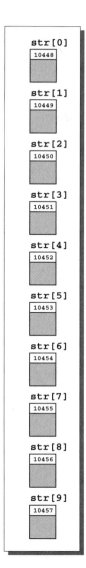

Figure 12–2 A string variable. String variables are arrays of type **char**. Unlike a string constant, a string variable has a name: this one is called **str**.

```
str[4] = 'c';
str[5] = 'a';
str[6] = 'r';
str[7] = '\0';
```

This is tedious, but it will work. The end result of these assignment statements is shown in Figure 12–3. Note that the array has ten elements, but we only needed eight of them to hold the string. The null character in the eighth element marks the end of the string.

As we said, it is tedious to put a string into a **char** array using multiple assign-

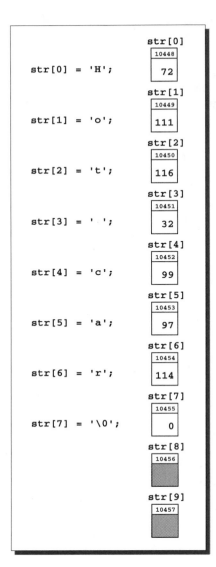

Figure 12–3 Assigning values to a string variable. The end of the string is marked by the null character (ASCII value 0).

ment statements. In most cases, we would use the **scanf()** function and a **while** loop to get each character of the string. Here is an example:

```
j = 0;

scanf("%c", &string[j]);

while (string[j] != '\n') {
    j = j + 1;
    flag = scanf("%c", &string[j]);
}
```

This is precisely what we will do in the **get_line()** function for our next program. Before writing that function, however, we need to say something about how strings are passed to functions.

Strings as Function Arguments

A string variable is an array, and like other arrays, is passed to a function using call by reference. Recall that an array name written by itself gives the address of the array. Thus, the function **print_line()** would receive the string **line** this way:

```
print_line(line);
```

Compare this with the way we called the **print_dbl_arr()** function to print the contents of the **double** array **list** in Chapter 9 (Listing 9–2):

```
print_dbl_arr(list, n);
```

Here, **list** gives the address of the start of the array, and **n** gives the number of elements that are to be processed. A function that works on an **int** or **double** array typically requires both the array's address and its length. In contrast, a function that works on a string gets the address of the string, but not its length. Why the difference?

Whenever an array is processed by a function, the function needs to know where the array ends. If it is an **int** or **double** array, we must provide that information explicitly by passing the array length as an argument to the function. If the array is a string variable, the null character (**'\0'**) serves to mark the end of the string, making it unnecessary to pass the length of the string. Hence,

Pass the address of a string variable, but not its size.

Program: **User-Defined String Functions**

Our next program will show you how to write functions that work on strings. The program will consist of **main()** and the following five functions:

get_line()—reads a line of characters from the standard input into a string variable.

print_line()—prints a line of characters from a string variable to the standard output.

string_length()—returns the length of a string, not counting the null character.

copy_string()—copies the contents of one string into another string variable.

reverse_string()—reverses the order of the characters in a string variable.

Following our usual practice, we will write and test this program in stages, beginning with **main()**, **get_line()**, and **print_line()**. The definitions for these functions are shown in Listings 12–1, 12–2, and 12–3. Create files having the appropriate names to hold the code for these functions.

Listing 12–1. *main.c*

```
/*********************************************************

    Demonstrate various functions that work on strings.

*********************************************************/

#include <stdio.h>
#define MAXSTR 100

void get_line(char string[]);
void print_line(char string[]);

main()
{
    char line[MAXSTR];
    char copy[MAXSTR];

    printf("Enter a line: \n");
    get_line(line);

    printf("You typed: \n");
    print_line(line);
}
```

Listing 12–2. *getline.c*

```c
/*****************************************************

    Read a line from the standard input into a string.

******************************************************/

#include <stdio.h>

void get_line(char string[])
{
    int j;

    j = 0;

    scanf("%c", &string[j]);

    while (string[j] != '\n') {
        j = j + 1;
        scanf("%c", &string[j]);
    }
    string[j] = '\0';        /* Replace newline with NULL. */
}
```

Listing 12–3. *prntline.c*

```c
/*****************************************************

    Print a line from a string to the standard output.

******************************************************/

#include <stdio.h>

void print_line(char string[])
{
    int j;

    j = 0;

    while (string[j] != '\0') {
        printf("%c", string[j]);
        j = j + 1;
    }
    printf("\n");
}
```

Compiling and Testing the Complete Program

Before proceeding further, you should test the program as it exists thus far. Compile and link *main.c*, *getline.c*, and *prntline.c*, and run the executable file. Enter an appropriate line of text at the prompt:

```
Enter a line:
Here in the Twilight Zone. RET
```

If the program is working correctly, the input line will be echoed on the standard output:

```
You typed:
Here in the Twilight Zone.
```

More String Functions

Once you are satisfied that **main()**, **get_line()**, and **print_line()** are working as they should, you are ready to complete the remaining functions. Here are their proto-types, which you should insert in the proper place in the *main.c* file:

```
int string_length(char string[]);
void copy_string(char original[], char copy[]);
void reverse_string(char string[]);
```

You will also want to modify **main()** to call these functions, perhaps like this:

```
printf("\nYou entered %d characters.\n", string_length(line));

copy_string(line, copy);
printf("\nHere is a copy of that string: \n");
print_line(copy);

reverse_string(copy);
printf("\nBackwards, this reads: \n");
print_line(copy);
```

Determining the Length of a String

The **string_length()** function takes a string and returns the number of characters in that string *not including the null character at the end*. The pseudocode for this function is extremely simple:

initialize counter j
while **string[j]** *!= NULL character*
    increment j
return j

The C code is also very simple, as you can see from Listing 12–4.

Listing 12–4. *strleng.c*

```
/*************************************************
   Return the length of a string (not including the
   terminating NULL character).
*************************************************/
int string_length(char string[])
{
    int j;

    j = 0;

    while (string[j] != '\0') {
       j = j + 1;
    }

    return (j);
}
```

Copying a String

The **copy_string()** function copies a string from one **char** array into another. The pseudocode for this function is quite simple:

initialize counter j
while **original[j]** *!= NULL character*
    copy[j] = original[j]
    increment j
put NULL character into **copy[j]**

The C code that implements this outline is shown in Listing 12–5.

Listing 12–5. *copystr.c*

```
/*********************************************************

    Copy one string into another.

*********************************************************/

void copy_string(char original[], char copy[])
{
    int j;

    j = 0;

    while (original[j] != '\0') {
        copy[j] = original[j];
        j = j + 1;
    }

    copy[j] = '\0';
}
```

Reversing a String

The **reverse_string()** function takes a string and reverses the order of the characters. Thus, if the string variable originally held the characters

`No stinkin' badges.\0`

reverse_string() will change this to

`.segdab 'niknits oN\0`

Note that the null character remains at the end of the reversed string. The C code that accomplishes this is shown in Listing 12–6. Note that **reverse_string()** calls the **string_length()** function to determine how many characters are in the string.

Listing 12–6. *revstr.c*

```
/*****************************************************

   Reverse a string.

*****************************************************/

int string_length(char string[]);

void reverse_string(char string[])
{
   int j;
   int length;
   char temp;

   length = string_length(string);

   for (j = 0; j < length/2; j = j + 1) {
      temp = string[j];
      string[j] = string[length - 1 - j];
      string[length - 1 - j] = temp;
   }
}
```

Compiling and Testing the Complete Program

Compile and link *main.c*, *getline.c*, *prntline.c*, *strleng.c*, *copystr.c*, and *revstr.c*. Run the executable file and enter a line of text at the prompt:

```
Enter a line:
Go ahead, make my day. RET

You typed:
Go ahead, make my day.

You entered 22 characters.

Here is a copy of that string:
Go ahead, make my day.

Backwards, this reads:
.yad ym ekam ,daeha oG
```

String Functions and *string.h*

The C library includes a number of standard functions for processing strings, some of which are shown in Table 12–1. The standard header file **string.h** contains the prototypes for these functions; you should include this file whenever you want to use them:

```
#include <string.h>
```

You will undoubtedly notice that some of the functions listed in the table resemble functions we have previously written in this chapter. The standard library function **strlen()**, for example, is similar to the function **string_length()** shown in Listing 12–4.

Which should you use, the library string functions or your own versions of these functions? The answer depends on your purpose. When you are first learning

Table 12–1   Standard String Functions

Function Call*	Effect
strlen(string)	Returns the length of the string (not counting the null character).
strcat(str1, str2)	Appends **str2** to **str1**.
strncat(str1, str2, n)	Appends exactly **n** characters of **str2** to **str1**. (If **str2** has fewer than **n** characters, null characters are written into **str1** until exactly **n** characters have been written.)
strcmp(str1, str2)	Returns **0** if **str1** is the same as **str2**; returns a positive **int** if **str1** is lexicographically greater than **str2**; returns a negative **int** if **str1** is lexicographically less than **str2**.
strncmp(str1, str2, n)	Like **strcmp()**, but only compares first **n** characters of the strings.
strcpy(str1, str2)	Copies the contents of **str1** into **str2** (including the null character).
strncpy(str1, str2, n)	Like **strcpy()**, but only copies the first **n** characters of string **str1** into **str2**.

* In these examples, assume **string**, **str1**, and **str2** to be strings, and **n** to be an **int**.

to program in C, it is instructive to write your own string functions. However, once you have learned how to process strings, it is usually better to use the library functions—they are likely to be more efficient. (Of course, if the library does not have the function you need, you will have to write your own.)

● ▬▬▬▬ **HELPFUL HINTS**

Programming with strings is relatively straightforward, but there are some pitfalls to be avoided:

- When declaring a string variable, make sure it is long enough to hold the string *and the terminating null character*. To be safe, it is usually a good idea to declare an array that is slightly longer than you expect to need.
- Do not forget to insert the null character into the **char** array to mark the end of the string. (It is surprising how often programmers forget this.)
- Whenever possible, use the standard C library functions for processing strings (and when you do, be sure to include the *string.h* header file).
- Finally, remember that string variables are arrays, and pose some of the same problems as other arrays. In particular, beware of the off-by-one error.

● ▬▬▬▬ **SUMMARY**

Preprocessor Directive

`#include <string.h>`

Instructs the preprocessor to insert the contents of the standard header file, *string.h*, containing prototypes for the library string functions. Angle brackets, `<` and `>`, tell the preprocessor to look in the "usual place" (which is system-dependent).

String Constant

`"This is a string"`

Causes the compiler to store the characters `'T'`, `'h'`, `'i'`, etc., in a **char** array. The null character `'\0'` is inserted to mark end of the string.

Variable Declaration

`char str1[20];`

Declares `str1` to be a string variable.

Assignment

`str1[0] = 'T';`

Assigns `'T'` (ASCII value 84 or EBCDIC value 227) to the first element of the string variable `str1`.

Function Prototypes

`int string_length(char str[]);`	Declares **string_length()** to be an **int** function that uses an alias for a **char** array. The prototype must agree with the function header.
`int string_length(char []);`	As above; parameter names are optional in prototypes.

Function Call

`length = string_length(str1);`	Calls **string_length()** and sends it the pointer to the array **str1**. The function returns an **int** value.

- String constants, also called string literals, consist of one or more characters enclosed by double quotes. The compiler stores string constants in arrays of type **char**, placing a null character (`'\0'`) in the last element to mark the end of the string. This null character is the string delimiter or end-of-string sentinel.
- String constants and character constants are different. Whereas `'A'` is a character constant having the ASCII value 65, `"A"` represents a two-element string constant consisting of the characters `'A'` and `'\0'`.
- String variables are **char** arrays. It is up to the programmer to declare an array large enough to hold the string, including the end-of-string null character.
- Characters may be assigned one by one to the elements of a string variable. Alternatively, the characters may be read into the array using the **scanf()** function in a loop.
- The C library contains functions for processing strings. The prototypes for these functions are found in the standard header file *string.h*.

EXERCISES

1. *Define:* **a.** string constant; **b.** string literal; **c.** end-of-string sentinel; **d.** string delimiter; **e.** null character; **f.** string variable.

2. *Errors.* Create a copy of *getline.c* (Listing 12–2) called *errors12.c* and introduce into the new file the first error listed below. Compile and link *main.c*, *errors12.c*, *prntline.c*, etc. If the compiler catches the error, write down both the error and the error message; if not, run the executable file with test data and make a note of any unexpected results. Correct the file, then repeat the process with the next error on the list. Continue until you have tried all of the errors.

   a. Initialize the counter **j** to the value 1 rather than zero.

   b. Change the condition of the **while** loop from

   ```
   string[j] != '\n'    to    string[j] != '\0'
   ```

    c. Change the last executable line of ***getline.c*** from

        `string[j] = '\0';`   to   `string[j] = '\n';`

3. *Calling* **reverse_strings().** Write a **main()** function that calls the **reverse_strings()** function shown in Listing 12–6.

4. *Improved* **get_line()** *function.* The **get_line()** function presented in Listing 12–2 does no error-checking. In particular, if the user enters a string that is too long for the **char** array that is supposed to hold it, the function will over-fill the array. Modify **get_line()** so that it stops reading characters when the array is full. You should be able to call the improved **get_line()** this way:

`get_line(line, MAXSTR);`

5. *Reading a string.* Write a function **get_string()** that reads characters from the standard input into a string variable until either the variable is full or the function receives an EOF. This function should read and store any character, including new lines.

6. *The* **%s** *format.* We wrote the functions **get_line()** and **get_string()** to read characters from the standard input into a string. It is also possible to read a string using the **%s** format with **scanf()**, but it works a bit differently from either **get_line()** or **get_string()**. Suppose **str** is a string variable. To read characters from the standard input and store them in **str**, you might write

`scanf ("%s", str);`

The **%s** format causes **scanf()** to read characters until it encounters white-space. To print the contents of **str**, write

`printf ("%s", str);`

Write a program named ***sformat.c*** to determine how the **%s** format works.

7. *Erasing a string.* A string function such as **string_length()** will process a string until it encounters a null character. Therefore, a string variable that has a null character in the first element will appear to the function to have zero length. Write a function **string_erase()** that puts a null character in the first element of a string variable. What does this do to the rest of the string?

8. *Comparing strings.* Write an **int** function **compare_strings()** that takes two strings and returns 0 if there is no difference between the strings, 1 if there is a difference. Modify **main()** as needed to test this function.

9. *Reading a word.* Write a function **get_word()** that reads a word of text from the standard input and stores it in a string. For now, consider a word to be any sequence of characters followed by white space.

10. *Reading a word—revised.* Modify the previous exercise so that it strips off punctuation that immediately precedes or follows the word (such as quotes, commas, semicolons, etc.).

11. *Printing a word.* Write a function **put_word()** that prints a word on the standard output. Use the function **get_word()**, described in the previous two exercises, to test **put_word()**.

12. *Double words.* When typing or editing text (a term paper, for example) you may occasionally introduce a double occurrence of a word, such as in "I came, I saw saw, I conquered." There is an extra "saw" in the text, but most spell-checking software will not catch this error. Write a function **dbl_word_check()** that will check for double words in a file and print all words that occur as double words. You may wish to make use of the functions **get_word()**, **put_word()**, and **compare_strings()**, described in previous exercises.

13. *Palindromes.* A palindrome is a string that reads the same backward or forward. This includes words such as bib, madam, dad, and phrases such as "Able was I ere I saw Elba."

    Write a program that prompts for a string, calls the function **pal_test()** to determine whether the string is a palindrome, and prints an appropriate message. All punctuation and spaces must match backwards and forwards. However, ignore capitalization (e.g., *A* and *a* should be considered the same letter).

14. *More palindromes.* Modify the previous exercise to ignore spaces and punctuation. For example, it should recognize "Madam, I'm Adam" as a palindrome.

15. *Roman numeral conversion.* Write an **int** function that converts Roman numerals to their decimal equivalents. (See Exercise 24, Chapter 11.) The function should take a string containing the Roman numeral and return the decimal value.

13

Simple File I/O

By now, you are familiar with the input and output redirection operators (< and >) that permit a C program to communicate with data files. Redirection is convenient and adequate for most purposes—but not all. For instance, you might have to write a program to run under an operating system that does not support redirection. Or your program might require multiple data files. Or perhaps your program is intended for users who are not comfortable using redirection.

In this chapter you will see how to work with input and output files—how to open a file, read from (or write to) the file, and close the file when you are finished.

Sequential vs. Random Access

There are two ways a program can read a data file. The simplest is to start at the top and read the data in order, one after another, until the bottom of the file is reached. This is called *sequential access*. The alternative is *random access*, in which the file's contents may be read in any order.

In this chapter, we will employ sequential access exclusively because it is (1) easier to program, and (2) sufficient for most problems that a scientist or engineer will encounter.

The FILE Data Type

The C language has a special data type—the **FILE** type—that is designed for working with data files. For example, suppose you wish to deal with two files, one for input and another for output. You might put the following declarations in your program:

```
FILE *infile;
FILE *outfile;
```

The asterisks indicate that **infile** and **outfile** are intended to hold *pointers* to files.

Why do we need file pointers? Bear in mind that a data file is not part of the C program, and that a C program does not have direct access to it. Just as we previously used pointers to manipulate variables that exist outside a particular function, we use pointers to manipulate files that exist outside a particular program.

Incidentally, three **FILE** pointers are declared for you in the standard header file *stdio.h*:

```
FILE *stdin;      /* Standard input */
FILE *stdout;     /* Standard output */
FILE *stderr;     /* Standard error */
```

The standard input and output are already familiar to you. The *standard error*, as the name suggests, is the place where error messages are sent. Usually this is the terminal screen.

Opening Files

After a **FILE** pointer variable has been declared, it still remains to associate it with a specific file. Data files are managed by the computer's operating system. C programs use the **fopen()** function to request that the operating system open a file and connect it to a **FILE** pointer. For example, the statement

```
infile = fopen("testdata", "r");
```

asks the operating system to open the file *testdata* for reading by the C program. If this is successful, **fopen()** returns a pointer to that file, and this pointer is stored in **infile**. From this point onward, the C program will refer to the file by the pointer in **infile**.

Note that the two arguments to the **fopen()** function are both strings. The first gives the name of the file as it is known to the operating system. The second argument is called the *mode*; it indicates how the file is to be used. We will employ three modes in this chapter:

Mode	Meaning
"r"	Open text file for reading only.
"w"	Open or create a text file for writing (discard its previous contents, if any).
"a"	Open or create a text file for appending (add new text to the end of the file).

The statement

```
outfile = fopen("outdata", "w");
```

asks the operating system to open the file ***outdata*** to receive output from the C program. The new output will replace anything already in the file. If there is no file named ***outdata***, the operating system will create one. Similarly, the statement

```
outfile = fopen("outdata", "a");
```

asks the operating system to open the file ***outdata*** to receive output from the program. The new data will be added to the end of the file, preserving anything already in the file. As before, if there is no file named ***outdata***, the operating system will create one.

Note that you do not have to open the standard input (**stdin**), standard output (**stdout**), or standard error (**stderr**); these are opened and closed for you automatically when the program begins executing.

Closing Files

After you are finished with a file, you should close it. This is done with the **fclose()** function:

```
fclose(infile);
fclose(outfile);
```

If you forget to close a file explicitly, the operating system will do it for you once the program finishes. Nevertheless, it is a good idea to develop the habit of always closing files that you no longer need because most systems impose a limit on how many files can be open at one time. (This limit is given by the symbolic constant **FOPEN_MAX**, defined in ***stdio.h***. We leave it as an exercise for you to print this number [see Exercise 3].)

The fscanf() and fprintf() Functions

Once a file has been opened for reading, you can use the **fscanf()** function to get data from the file. For example, the statement

```
fscanf(infile, "%c", &next_char);
```

causes the program to read a character (**"%c"**) from the file pointed to by **infile**, and to store the character in the variable **next_char**.

You probably noticed the resemblance of **fscanf()** to **scanf()**. The two functions are very similar, differing only in that the first argument to **fscanf()** must be a pointer to a file. In fact, this can even be a pointer to the standard input, so that the following statements have the same effect:

```
fscanf(stdin, "%c", &next_char);    /* Scan the stdin */
scanf("%c", &next_char);            /* Scan the stdin */
```

The **fprintf()** function is used to print to a file. Thus, to print the contents of the **char** variable **next_char** into the file designated by **outfile**, you could write

```
fprintf(outfile, "%c", next_char);
```

As you might expect, **fprintf()** and **printf()** are very similar. The following statements would have the same effect of printing a character on the standard output:

```
fprintf(stdout, "%c", next_char);    /* Print to the stdout */
printf("%c", next_char);             /* Print to the stdout */
```

Program: Copying Files

Our next program will copy the contents of one file into another. The program will consist of the functions **main()** and **copy_file()**. Here is the pseudocode for **main()**:

prompt for the name of the original file
read the file name
open the original file for reading

prompt for the name of the copy
read the file name
open the copy for writing

call **copy_file()**

close the files

The pseudocode for **copy_file()** is quite simple:

read next character from the infile and set the flag

while (flag does not equal EOF)
    print next character to the outfile
    read next character from the infile and set the flag

The C code for **main()** and **copy_file()** are shown in Listings 13–1 and 13–2, respectively.

Listing 13–1. *copymain.c*

```
/**********************************************

    Copy a file.

**********************************************/

#include <stdio.h>

void copy_file(FILE *original, FILE *copy);

main()
{
    char filename[FILENAME_MAX];
    FILE *infile;
    FILE *outfile;

    printf("This program copies files.\n");

    printf("Original file: ");
    scanf("%s", filename);
    infile = fopen(filename, "r");

    printf("Copy: ");
    scanf("%s", filename);
    outfile = fopen(filename, "w");

    copy_file(infile, outfile);

    fclose(infile);
    fclose(outfile);
}
```

Dissection of *copymain.c*

(1) `char filename[FILENAME_MAX];`

We need a string to hold the file name entered by the user. The symbolic constant **FILENAME_MAX**, defined in *stdio.h*, gives the maximum number of characters allowed in a file name on your system. (If there is no set maximum, **FILENAME_MAX** gives an "appropriate" length of a file name.)

(2) `FILE *infile;`
`FILE *outfile;`

This program will use two files, one for input and the other for output. Therefore, we must declare two variables to hold the file pointers.

(3) `printf("Original file: ");`
`scanf("%s", filename);`

This is how we prompt for a file name, then read the name into the string using the **%s** format. (Refer to Exercise 6, Chapter 12 for a discussion of the **%s** format.) Note that we do not need the address operator with **filename**—remember, the name of a string variable gives the address of the string.

(4)
`infile = fopen(filename, "r");`

The input file is to be opened for reading only (mode **"r"**). Once this is done, the program will refer to the file by the pointer value stored in **infile**.

(5)
`outfile = fopen(filename, "w");`

This statement opens the output file with mode **"w"**. Consequently, if the file already exists, its contents will be lost when the data are written into it.

(6)
`copy_file(infile, outfile);`

This is how we call the function to copy the files. Note that **infile** and **outfile** are both pointer variables.

Listing 13–2. *copyfile.c*

```
/**************************************************

    Copy the contents of one file into another.

**************************************************/

#include <stdio.h>

void copy_file(FILE *original, FILE *copy)
{
    char next_char;
    int flag;

    flag = fscanf(original, "%c", &next_char);

    while (EOF != flag) {
        fprintf(copy, "%c", next_char);
        flag = fscanf(original, "%c", &next_char);
    }
}
```

Dissection of *copyfile.c*

① `void copy_file(FILE *original, FILE *copy)`

The keyword **void** shows that **copy_file()** does not return a value. Inside the parentheses, **original** and **copy** are declared to be pointers to files.

② `flag = fscanf(original, "%c", &next_char);`

Because the first argument to **fscanf()** should be a pointer to a file, we write it as **original** rather than ***original**.

Compiling and Testing the Program

To test the program, you will need an input file. For convenience, use the **testdata** file from the previous chapter, which contains the following lines:

```
The different branches of arithmetic:
Ambition
Distraction
Uglification
Derision
```

Compile and link **copymain.c** and **copyfile.c**, then run the executable file. At the prompt, specify **testdata** as the original file:

```
This program copies files.
Original file: testdata RET
```

Name the copy **copy1**:

```
Copy: copy1 RET
```

If your program is working correctly, there should now be a file named **copy1** in your directory. Examine this file to make sure that its contents are the same as the original:

```
The different branches of arithmetic:
Ambition
Distraction
Uglification
Derision
```

What happens if you try to copy a nonexistent file? Try it. Run the program and give it two fictitious file names:

```
This program copies files.
Original file: xxxx RET
Copy: zzzz RET
```

On some systems, the program will produce an output file containing gibberish. On other systems, the program will crash:

```
Segmentation fault (core dumped).
```

The problem is that **fscanf()** tried to read a file that had not been opened. To correct this problem, you will need to know something about what **fopen()** does when it cannot open a file. That is the topic of the next section.

File-Opening Errors

Let's look again at the statement used in *copymain.c* to open the input file for reading:

```
infile = fopen(filename, "r");
```

If the file is opened successfully, a pointer to that file is stored in the pointer variable **infile**. But what is stored in **infile** if the file cannot be opened? The answer is that **fopen()** will return what is called a *null pointer*, which is an address equal to zero. (You might think of this as a pointer to nothing.) We should test for this pointer before trying to read from the file:

```
if (NULL == infile) {
    printf("Cannot open %s\n", filename);
}
else {
    [Prompt for the output file, open the file, etc.]
}
```

Note the symbolic constant **NULL**. This constant is defined in the *stdio.h* header file to have the integer value zero.

Improved main() Function

Let's improve the **main()** function we wrote for the file-copying program. Listing 13–3 shows the revised version. We have made three changes:

1. **main()** now checks for a **NULL** file pointer after trying to open the input file with **fopen()**. If the file contains a **NULL** address, **main()** will print an error message on the standard error.
2. The output file is opened with mode **"a"** rather than mode **"w"**. This is a safety feature, preventing the loss of the file's contents should the user specify the name of an existing file.
3. **main()** now calls **copy_file()** twice, first to echo the input file on the standard output, then to copy the file.

Listing 13–3. *copymain.c* (Improved)

```
/****************************************************

    Improved main() for file-copying program. This
    version checks for errors in opening the original
    file. It also echoes the original on the stdout.

****************************************************/

#include <stdio.h>

void copy_file(FILE *original, FILE *copy);

main()
{
    char filename[FILENAME_MAX];
    FILE *infile;
    FILE *outfile;

    printf("This program copies files.\n");

    printf("Original file: ");
    scanf("%s", filename);
    infile = fopen(filename, "r");

    if (NULL == infile) {        /* Check for fopen() error */
        fprintf(stderr, "Cannot open %s\n", filename);
    }
    else {
        printf("Copy: ");
        scanf("%s", filename);
        outfile = fopen(filename, "a");

        copy_file(infile, stdout);      /* Echo infile on stdout */
        copy_file(infile, outfile);     /* Copy infile to outfile */

        fclose(infile);
        fclose(outfile);
    }
}
```

Compiling and Testing the Program

Compile and link *copyfile.c* and the new *copymain.c*. Then run the executable file using *testdata* as the input file:

```
This program copies files.
Original file: testdata RET
```

Name the copy *copy2*:

```
Copy: copy2 RET
```

The contents of *testfile* will appear on the standard output:

```
The different branches of arithmetic:
Ambition
Distraction
Uglification
Derision
```

You will also find a new file named *copy2* in your directory. However, if you examine the contents of this file, you will discover that it is empty. What went wrong?

There is a subtle flaw in the **copy_file()** function. To understand what it is, you need to know something about how a file is read.

The File Position Indicator

When **fopen()** first opens a file for reading, a *file position indicator* is set at the beginning of the file. This indicator marks the place where **fscanf()** will start reading. Each time **fscanf()** reads from the file, the position indicator is advanced, always marking the place that is to be read next.

The problem with the **copy_file()** function is that it leaves the file position indicator at the bottom of the input file. In the revised program, **copy_file()** is called twice, like this:

```
copy_file(infile, stdout);      /* Echo infile on stdout */
copy_file(infile, outfile);     /* Copy infile to outfile */
```

The first call to **copy_file()** leaves the file position indicator at the end of the input file. The second time **copy_file()** is called, it starts at the end of the input file, where of course there is nothing left to copy.

What is needed is a way to reset the position indicator at the beginning of the file after **copy_file()** finishes. You could do this by closing and reopening the file.

However, a better solution is to use the **rewind()** function, which resets the file position indicator without closing the file. This is how you would call **rewind()** to reset the input file:

```
rewind(infile);
```

Listing 13–4 shows a revised **copy_file()** function. Note that it rewinds the input file twice, before copying and afterwards. (Why?) Note too that it does not rewind the output file. (Why?)

Listing 13–4. *copyfile.c* (Improved)

```
/****************************************************

   Copy the contents of one file into another.
   This version rewinds the original file before
   and after copying.

****************************************************/

#include <stdio.h>

void copy_file(FILE *original, FILE *copy)
{
    char next_char;
    int flag;

    rewind(original);

    flag = fscanf(original, "%c", &next_char);

    while (EOF != flag) {
        fprintf(copy, "%c", next_char);
        flag = fscanf(original, "%c", &next_char);
    }

    rewind(original);
}
```

Function: reverse_lines()

Our next example shows the function **reverse_lines()**, which reverses the lines in a file and puts the reversed lines in another file. Thus, if the input file contains the lines

```
The different branches of arithmetic:
Ambition
Distraction
Uglification
Derision
```

the output file will contain the lines

```
:citemhtira fo sehcnarb tnereffid ehT
noitibmA
noitcartsiD
noitacifilgU
noisireD
```

The pseudocode for **reverse_lines()** is given below:

read a line from the infile and set the flag

while (flag does not equal EOF)
    call **reverse_string()** *to reverse the line*
    put the line into the output file
    read a line from the infile and set the flag

The C code that implements this outline is shown in Listing 13–5. Note that **reverse_lines()** calls the function **reverse_string()** that we showed you in the previous chapter, as well as two functions that you have not yet written, **fget_line()** and **fput_line()**. We leave it (see Exercise 4, 7, and 8) for you to write these functions and a **main()** function for this program.

Listing 13–5. *revfile.c*

```
/**************************************************

    Reverse the contents of one file and print
    into another file.

**************************************************/

#include <stdio.h>

void reverse_string(char string[]);
int fget_line(FILE *infile, char line[], int line_length);
void fput_line(FILE *outfile, char line[]);


void reverse_lines(FILE *infile, FILE *outfile)
{
    int flag;
    char line[BUFSIZ];

    rewind(infile);

    flag = fget_line(infile, line, BUFSIZ);

    while (EOF != flag) {
        reverse_string(line);
        fput_line(outfile, line);
        flag = fget_line(infile, line, BUFSIZ);
    }
    rewind(infile);
}
```

① (next to `char line[BUFSIZ];`)
② (next to `fput_line(outfile, line);`)

Dissection of *revfile.c*

① `char line[BUFSIZ];`

The symbolic constant **BUFSIZ** is defined in *stdio.h* to equal the maximum number of characters that the input buffer can hold. This is a good size for the string **line**, which will receive each line as it is read from the buffer.

② `fput_line(outfile, line);`
`flag = fget_line(infile, line, BUFSIZ);`

These lines show how the **fput_line()** and **fget_line()** functions are called. You will need to write these functions accordingly.

Function: encipher_file()

For our next example we will write a function that uses a simple cipher to conceal the meaning of a file's contents. For example, suppose we wish to encrypt the following line of text:

Pack your bags.

We will use "Eureka!" as the password. Write the password underneath the message, so that each character of the message corresponds to a character of the password:

Pack your bags.
Eureka!Eureka!E

Note that we repeat the password as necessary to make it as long as the original message, including any blanks or punctuation. Next convert each character to its ASCII value:

'P'	'a'	'c'	'k'	' '	'y'	'o'	'u'	'r'	' '	'b'	'a'	'g'	's'	'.'
80	97	99	107	32	121	111	117	114	32	98	97	103	115	46

'E'	'u'	'r'	'e'	'k'	'a'	'!'	'E'	'u'	'r'	'e'	'k'	'a'	'!'	'E'
69	117	114	101	107	97	33	69	117	114	101	107	97	33	69

Finally, add the ASCII value of each character to that of the character beneath it. The result is

149 214 213 208 139 218 144 186 231 146 199 204 200 148 115

Anyone looking at the message now would see only a meaningless series of numbers. Knowing the proper password, however, we can easily convert these numbers back into the original message. (How?)

In this example, we used the ASCII values of the letters, but the method will work just as well with EBCDIC. The major drawback with this method is that the enciphered message requires more storage than the original.

The pseudocode for the enciphering function is as follows:

rewind input file

get character from the input file

select first character of password

while (not at the end of file)

    add integer values of message character and password character

    print the sum as an integer to the output file.

    get next character from the input file

    select next character of password

    if (at end of password)

        reset counter to beginning of the password

insert new line at bottom of output file

rewind input file

The C code for **encipher.c** is shown in Listing 13–6. We leave it as an exercise for you to write the necessary **main()** function to make this into a complete program (see Exercise 5).

Listing 13–6. *encipher.c*

```
/***************************************************

   Encipher a file using a password selected by
   the user.

***************************************************/

#include <stdio.h>

void encipher_file(FILE *in, FILE *out, char pass[])
{
    int j;
    int flag;
    char next_char;
    int next_num;

    rewind(in);

    flag = fscanf(in, "%c", &next_char);
    j = 0;

    while (EOF != flag) {
        next_num = (int)next_char + (int)pass[j];
        fprintf(out, "%d ", next_num);

        flag = fscanf(in, "%c", &next_char);
        j = j + 1;

        if ('\0' == pass[j]) {
            j = 0;
        }
    }

    fprintf(out, "\n");
    rewind(in);
}
```

Dissection of encipher_file()

① `void encipher_file(FILE *in, FILE *out, char pass[])`

The function requires pointers to an input file and an output file, as well as a string containing the password. The files are assumed to have been opened properly.

② `next_num = (int)next_char + (int)pass[j];`

We encipher each character of the original message by adding its integer representation to that of the appropriate character of the password. The casts are used here to emphasize that the result is to be an **int**.

③ `if ('\0' == pass[j]) {`
`    j = 0;`
`}`

If the end of the password has been reached, start over with the first character of the password.

Compiling and Testing encipher_file()

Before you can test the **encipher_file()** function, you will need to write a **main()** function to do the following:

prompt for the input file
open the input file for reading
prompt for the output file
open the output file for appending
prompt for the password
read the password
call **encipher_file()**

● ▬▬▬▬ HELPFUL HINTS

- Do not attempt to use a data file without first opening it with **fopen()**. (But do not try to open a file that is already open.)

- Always check that the file pointer returned by **fopen()** is not **NULL**. A **NULL** pointer indicates that the file has not been opened properly and should not be used.

- To protect data files from accidental deletion, always open output files with mode **"a"** ("append") rather than **"w"** ("write").

- Remember that functions like **fscanf()** and **fprintf()** take file pointers, not file names, as arguments. Thus, to read an **int** from a file named **datafile**, it would be an error to write

```
fscanf("datafile", "%d", &var);              /* Wrong! */
```

Instead, you must first open the file with **fopen()**, then use the file pointer to refer to the file:

```
in = fopen("datafile", "r");
fscanf(in, "%d", &var);
```

- Do not attempt to read from a file that has been opened for writing or appending. Likewise, do not attempt to write or append to a file that has been opened for reading.
- Close files that are no longer needed. Most systems have a limit on the number of files that can be open at any one time.

● ▬▬▬▬▬   SUMMARY

Preprocessor Directive

`#include <stdio.h>`	Instructs the preprocessor to insert the contents of the standard header file *stdio.h*, containing the definition for **FILE**.

Declarations

`FILE *in;`	Declares **in** to be a pointer to a file. **FILE** must be written entirely in uppercase letters.
`FILE *out;`	Declares **out** to be a pointer to a file. **FILE** must be written entirely in uppercase letters.

File Opening

`in = fopen("infile", "r");`	Opens the file **infile** for reading; assigns a file pointer to the variable **in**.
`out = fopen("outfile", "w");`	Opens the file **outfile** for writing; assigns a file pointer to the variable **out**.
`out = fopen("outfile", "a");`	As above, but opens the file for appending.

Input/Output

```
flag = fscanf(in, "%lf", &x);
```
Reads a **double** from the file to which **in** points, stores the value in **x**, and returns an integer to **flag**.

```
fprintf(out, "%g", x);
```
Prints a **double** to the file to which **out** points.

File Rewind

```
rewind(in);
```
Resets the file position indicator to the top of the file referred to by **in**.

File Closing

```
fclose(in);
```
Closes the file referred to by **in**.

- Some operating systems allow the user to redirect the standard input and output so that programs can communicate with data files. Even on systems that do not support redirection, it is possible to write a program that can open data files, read from (or write to) the files, and close the files when it is finished.

- The simplest way to read a data file is by sequential access, in which the program begins at the top of the file and works its way to the bottom. The alternative is random access, in which the data may be read in any order.

- Programs use file pointers to refer to data files. File pointers are declared using the **FILE** data type.

- Three **FILE** pointers are declared in *stdio.h*: **stdin**, **stdout**, and **stderr**, which refer to the standard input, the standard output, and standard error, respectively. (The standard error is the place where error messages are printed, usually the terminal screen.)

- The **fopen()** function asks the operating system to open a file. If the file is opened successfully, **fopen()** returns a pointer to the file; if not, it returns a **NULL** pointer.

- **fopen()** takes two strings as arguments. The first argument is the name of the file as it is known to the operating system. The second argument is the mode, which specifies how the file is to be used.

- The **fscanf()** function reads data from a file that has been opened for reading (mode **"r"**) using **fopen()**.

- The **fprintf()** function writes data into a file that has been opened for writing (mode **"w"**) or appending (mode **"a"**) using **fopen()**.

- The **fclose()** function is used to close a file. It is important to close files that are no longer needed because some systems limit the number of files that may be open at once. (The maximum number of open data files is **FOPEN_MAX**, which is defined in *stdio.h*.)

- The file position indicator marks the next point in the file where **fscanf()** is to read or **fprintf()** is to write data. The **rewind()** function resets the file position indicator to the top of the file.

EXERCISES

1. *Define:* **a.** redirection; **b.** file pointer; **c.** file position indicator; **d.** standard input; **e.** standard output; **f.** standard error; **g.** file mode; **h.** append; **i.** null pointer.

2. *Errors.* Determine what, if anything, happens in each of the following cases:
   a. Writing to a file that has been opened for reading only.
   b. Reading from a file that has been opened for writing or appending.
   c. Rewinding a file before appending data to it.
   d. Opening the same file twice without closing it.
   e. Closing the **stdout**, then attempting to write to it.
   f. Reading and writing to the same file.
   g. Reading a file that has been closed.
   h. Writing or appending to a file that has been closed.

3. *Standard constants.* Two symbolic constants related to file input and output are defined in *stdio.h*:
   a. **FOPEN_MAX**—the maximum number of files that may be open simultaneously.
   b. **FILENAME_MAX**—the maximum length of a file name.

   Modify the *prlimits.c* program that you began in Chapter 2 so that it prints these values. Be sure to label the output appropriately.

4. Write a **main()** function that calls the **reverse_lines()** function shown in Listing 13–5.

5. *Enciphering a file.* Write a **main()** function that calls the **encipher_file()** function shown in Listing 13–6.

6. *Deciphering a file.* Write and test a function named **decipher_file()** that reverses the effect of **encipher_file()**.

7. *Reading a line from a file.* Write a function **fget_line()** that reads a line of characters from an open file into a string variable until either the variable is full or a newline character is read. This function should replace the newline character with the null character.

8. *Writing a line to a file.* Write a function **fput_line()** that prints a line of characters from a string variable to a file. This function should replace the terminating null character with a newline character.

9. *Double-spacing a file.* Write a function **fdouble_space()** that double-spaces the lines of an open input file and puts the results into an open output file. Write a **main()** function that will allow you to test **fdouble_space()**.

10. *Single-spacing a file.* Write a function **fsingle_space()** that single-spaces the lines of an open input file and puts the results into an open output file. Write a **main()** function that will allow you to test **fsingle_space()**.

11. *Adjusting file line lengths.* Write a program named ***trimfile.c*** that adjusts the lines in a file to be about *N* characters long. The program will prompt for an input file and an output file. It will get characters from the input file and print them to the output file, counting the characters as they are read in. As long as the current line is less than *N* characters long, the program will change any newline character to a space before writing to the standard output. However, as soon as the line exceeds *N* characters, the program will change the next white space it encounters to a newline character.

12. *Array functions.* Write and test the functions listed below. Note that the **main()** function should take care of opening and closing the input and output files.
    a. **fget_dbl_arr()**—reads numerical data from an open input file into a **double** array until it receives an EOF signal or the array is filled. The function should return the number of elements read.
    b. **fget_int_arr()**—reads integers from an open input file into a **int** array until it receives an **EOF** signal or the array is filled. The function should return the number of elements read.
    c. **fput_int_arr()**—writes a one-dimensional array of **int** values to an open output file.
    d. **fput_dbl_arr()**—writes a one-dimensional array of **double** values to an open output file.

13. *Two-dimensional array functions.* Write and test the functions listed below. Note that the **main()** function should take care of opening and closing the input and output files.
    a. **fget_dbl_2D()**—reads numerical data from an open input file into a two-dimensional **double** array until it receives an EOF signal or the array is filled. The first two entries in the data file should be the number of rows and columns to use in the array.
    b. **fput_dbl_2D()**—writes a two-dimensional array of **double** values to an open output file.
    c. **fget_int_2D()**—reads numerical data from an open input file into a two-dimensional **int** array until it receives an EOF signal or the array is filled. The first two entries in the data file should be the number of rows and columns to use in the array.
    d. **fput_int_2D()**—writes a two-dimensional array of **int** values to an open output file.

14. *Mail-order catalog.* The Acme Bubble Company's mail-order division sells ten different bubble-shaped items (and may add more to the line later). For each product in their catalog, they have one price for a single unit, a discounted price for a half dozen units, and an even lower price for a dozen units.

    Write a program that will be used by catalog representatives to take phone orders. The program will open a file named ***price.dat***, and read the price data into a two-dimensional array. Each row of the array will hold the prices for one particular product. (In other words, the first array index will be used as a catalog number for the product.) The first column will hold the prices for individual units, the second column will hold the prices for six-packs, and the third column will hold the prices for twelve-packs:

5.00	29.00	56.00
1.28	7.44	14.40
699.95	3600.50	6000.00
0.49	2.65	4.76
2.55	14.54	26.16
0.09	0.54	0.97
119.95	662.12	1125.61
49.95	269.73	485.51
0.98	4.55	6.60
27.00	150.00	252.00

    Thus, for product number 0, the price of one unit is $5.00; the price of a six-pack is $29.00; and the price of a twelve-pack is $56.00. Because the bubbles are prepackaged in six-packs and twelve-packs, discounts only apply to full packages. Thus, for example, the lowest price they could charge for 23 identical items would be the price for 1 dozen + that for 1/2 dozen + that for five individual items.

    After reading the price data, the program will prompt for the name of the output file that will contain the customer's bill. Then it will prompt for the catalog number and the quantity to be ordered:

Catalog number: 0 RET
Quantity: 23 RET

    Next, the program will compute the price, then print the catalog number, quantity, and price into the output file. It will continue this process (prompt for catalog number and quantity, compute price, print results to output file) until it receives an **EOF** signal. Finally, it will print the total amount due for the order.

15. *More catalog operations.* Modify the previous program so that it will also read a data file named ***stock.dat*** that contains, for each product, the numbers of individual units, six-packs, and twelve-packs that are currently in stock. If there are not enough items in stock to fill the order, the program should print the quantity available and prompt for the quantity that the customer wants

to order (assume that six-packs and twelve-packs must be sold intact). After the order has been filled, the program should revise ***stock.dat*** accordingly.

16. *Scanning for keywords.* The first step in the translation of preprocessed source code into machine language is called *scanning*. Simply put, the scanner is a program that goes through the source code and "recognizes" certain words and symbols.

    Write a simple scanner that will recognize five keywords. The name of the input file and the five keywords will be entered from the ***stdin*** by the user. The program will read the input file, word by word, until the end of the file is reached. For every word read, the program should print a numeric code on the standard output: if the word matches the first keyword, the program should print **0**; if it matches the second keyword, the program should print **1**, and so on. If no match is found, the program should print **−1**. For example, suppose the keywords are

    step   up   down   walk   left

    and that the input file contains the line

    `step up and walk down step again`

    Then the output from the program should be

    `0   1   −1   3   2   0   −1`

17. *Searching for a string.* Write a program named ***findit.c*** that searches a given file for a string and prints all line(s) in the file which contain that string. The program should prompt for the name of the file and the search string. For example, to search the file ***names*** for the string **Fred**, the user would enter

    `File: names``RET`

    `String: Fred``RET`

    The program will print any lines containing the string, even when it is part of a longer string:

    `Fred Flagstone`
    `Frederick Forsythe is the finest forklift operator in town.`
    `Jonathan Fredrickson`

    (*Hint:* Make use of **get_line()**, from the previous chapter, and **fget_line()**, described in Exercise 7.)

18. *Comparing files.* The Unix utility **diff** compares two files, line by line, and displays on the standard output any lines that are not identical in the two files. Write your own version of **diff**. Your program should prompt the user for the names of the files, and print the line numbers of any lines that are different, as well as the lines themselves. (*Hint:* Use the function **fget_line()** from Exercise 7.)

19. *Showing the end of a file.* The Unix utility **tail** displays the last ten lines of a file. This utility is especially useful for looking at large output files in which the final results are printed near the bottom of the file. Write your own version of **tail**. Your program should first prompt the user for the file name. If the file has less than ten lines, the program should display the entire file. Otherwise, it should print the last ten lines to the standard output. (*Hint #1:* Use **fget_line()**, described in Exercise 7. *Hint #2:* The program must go through the file twice, so use the function **rewind()**.)

Chapter

14.

C Shortcuts and Idioms

Until now, we have avoided many of the unique features of C that—although useful—are not often found in other languages. Indeed, most of what you have seen thus far would not appear strange to someone familiar with a language such as Fortran or Pascal. In this chapter we will examine some (by no means all) of the powerful features of C that set it apart from other languages.

The *ave.c* Program Revisited

In Chapter 6 we wrote *ave.c*, a simple program that reads **double** values from the standard input and computes their average. This program is shown again in Listing 14–1. We will show how this program might be rewritten to take advantage of some C shortcuts.

Listing 14–1. *ave.c* (Original)

```
/************************************************

    Compute the arithmetic average of double
    values taken from the standard input.

************************************************/

#include <stdio.h>

main()
{
    double next_num;
    double sum;
    double ave;
    int count;
    int flag;

    count = 0;
    sum = 0.0;

    flag = scanf("%lf", &next_num);
    while (flag != EOF) {
        sum = sum + next_num;
        count = count + 1;
        flag = scanf("%lf", &next_num);
    }

    ave = sum/(double)count;
    printf("The average is %g.\n", ave);
}
```

Declaration and Initialization

In the *ave.c* program shown in Listing 14–1, five variables are declared:

```
double next_num;
double sum;
double ave;
int count;
int flag;
```

Two of these variables, **sum** and **count**, are then initialized:

```
count = 0;
sum = 0.0;
```

C allows us to combine the declaration and initialization of a variable in one line. Thus, we can both declare and initialize **sum** and **count** this way:

```
double sum = 0.0;
int count = 0;
```

You can also combine the declaration and initialization of arrays. Suppose, for example, that you wanted to declare a four-element **double** array and fill it with the values 17.5, −6.7, −41.2, and 2.9. Here is one way to do this:

```
double list[4];
list[0] = 17.5;
list[1] = -6.7;
list[2] = -41.2;
list[3] = 2.9;
```

However, the same thing can be accomplished by the declaration

```
double list[4] = {17.5, -6.7, -41.2, 2.9};
```

The items in the list {**17.5, -6.7, -41.2, 2.9**} are called *initializers*. If you specify more array elements than initializers, the remaining elements are filled with zeroes. On the other hand, it is an error to specify an array that is too small to hold all of the initializers.

If you use initializers when declaring an array, you may omit the size of the array. The compiler will then create an array just large enough to hold all of the initializers. Thus, the previous declaration could be written this way:

```
double list[] = {17.5, -6.7, -41.2, 2.9};
```

The initialization of two-dimensional arrays is done similarly. Here is an example showing how a 4 by 3 **int** array might be declared and initialized:

```
int table[4][3] = { {3, 7, 9},
                    {2, 1, 5},
                    {4, 6, 8},
                    {6, 3, 5} };
```

Strings can also be initialized as they are declared. For example,

```
char string[29] = "This is a string initializer";
```

Note that **string[]** should be long enough to hold all of the characters in the initializer, plus the terminating null character. Often, it is more convenient to omit the string size and let the compiler figure out how many elements the string variable should have:

```
char string[] = "This is a string initializer";
```

Should you initialize variables, arrays, and strings as they are declared? Or should you separate the declaration and initialization steps? Experienced programmers disagree on this point. (We take no sides in this controversy.)

The Scanning while Loop

For our next shortcut, consider how we used a **while** loop in the **ave.c** program to read data from the standard input:

```
flag = scanf("%lf", &next_num);
while (flag != EOF) {
    sum = sum + next_num;
    count = count + 1;
    flag = scanf("%lf", &next_num);
}
```

Observe that the **int** variable **flag** receives the value returned by **scanf()**; this value is then tested by the **while** loop. Because **flag** serves no other purpose, we can skip the middleman and let the **while** loop directly test the return value from **scanf()**. We would rewrite the loop this way:

```
while (scanf("%lf", &next_num) != EOF) {
    sum = sum + next_num;
    count = count + 1;
}
```

This is certainly more compact than the original: four lines instead of six. And the new version eliminates the need for the variable **flag**, which saves some memory space. More important, the revised code more clearly expresses the intent of the programmer.

We should mention here that you can also include a **scanf()** function call as part of the condition in an **if** structure. Consider this fragment from **fact3.c** (Listing 6–4):

```
printf("This program computes the factorial.\n");
printf("Please enter a nonnegative integer: ");
flag = scanf("%d", &n);

if (1 != flag) {
   printf("Input must be an integer.\n");
}
```

The variable **flag** receives the return value from **scanf()** but is used nowhere else in the program. We can eliminate the need for this variable by putting the **scanf()** function call into the **if** condition:

```
printf("This program computes the factorial.\n");
printf("Please enter a nonnegative integer: ");

if (1 != scanf("%d", &n)) {
   printf("Input must be an integer.\n");
}
```

Compound Assignment Operators

Examine Listing 14–1 again and note how the sum is computed inside the loop:

```
sum = sum + next_num;
```

Of course, this statement updates the value of **sum** by adding the value of **next_num** to it. This kind of operation is done so often that C has a special shorthand for it:

```
sum += next_num;
```

Here, **+=** is called a *compound assignment operator*. It adds the value of **next_num** to the value stored in **sum**, just as the previous statement does.

There are five compound assignment operators that allow you to do arithmetic on a value stored in a variable: **+=, -=, *=, /=,** and **%=**. (The remainder assignment operator **%=** works only on **int** values; the others work on **int** and **double** values.) In general, if **var** is a variable and **expr** is any expression (another variable, a constant, a function call, etc.) then the following table shows how the compound assignment operators work:

Compound Assignment	Equivalent
var += expr	var = var + expr
var -= expr	var = var - expr
var *= expr	var = var * expr
var /= expr	var = var / expr
var %= expr	var = var % expr

The principal advantage offered by these new operators is that they save you keystrokes while you are writing the source code. In some cases they may also produce slightly faster executable code, but this is not guaranteed by the C standard.

Increment and Decrement Operators

The original *ave.c* program in Listing 14–1 counts each value as it is read from the standard input. Here is how the counter is updated inside the loop:

```
count = count + 1;
```

Adding 1 to the value of a variable is another common operation for which there is a special C operator. The *increment operator* is written as two plus signs (**++**) placed next to the variable. Thus, the previous statement could be replaced by

```
++count;          /* Add 1 to count */
```

Observe that there are no spaces between the plus signs. The increment operator is a *unary* operator—it works on just one variable. When placed in front of the variable name, the operator is said to be in *prefix form*. We can also place the operator after the variable name, in which case it is in *postfix form*:

```
count++;          /* Add 1 to count */
```

Either form, prefix or postfix, will increase by 1 the value stored in the variable. Nevertheless, there is a difference between the two forms. Consider the following statement:

```
save = ++i;
```

What value is stored in **save**? That depends on whether **i** is increased before or after the assignment is performed. The rule to follow is this: if the increment operator is written in prefix form, the addition occurs before the value is used. Thus, the preceding statement is equivalent to

```
i = i + 1;
save = i;
```

In contrast, if the increment operator is written in postfix form, the value is used first, then increased. Thus, the statement

```
save = i++;
```

is equivalent to

```
save = i;
i = i + 1;
```

C also has a *decrement operator*, a unary operator that subtracts 1 from the value of a variable. This operator consists of two minus signs written together (`--`). It too can be written either in prefix or postfix form:

```
--total;        /* Subtract 1 from total */
total--;        /* Subtract 1 from total */
```

It is not hard to see why the increment and decrement operators are useful. It certainly saves keystrokes to type `++count` rather than `count = count + 1`. Furthermore, on some systems `++count` may even produce slightly faster executable code, although there is no guarantee of this.

However, careless use of the increment and decrement operators can cause no end of headaches. Consider these two statements:

```
i = 1;
sum = (i++ * 2) + (i++ * 3);
```

What value is put into `sum`? Unfortunately, there is no way to know for certain—different compilers might produce different results. (The answer could be either 7 or 8—we leave it as an exercise for you to figure out why [Exercise 4].) This kind of problem occurs when the increment or decrement operation is applied to a variable that appears more than once in the same expression. You can avoid such problems by observing a simple rule:

Do not use ++ or -- in an expression that includes other operations.

The Revised *ave.c* Program

Listing 14–2 shows the *ave.c* program after it has been revised to include the shortcuts we have discussed thus far. These changes have included the following:

- *Declaration and Assignment.* We now initialize the variables **sum** and **count** as they are declared. This saves two lines of code, although some programmers would argue that it also makes the code more difficult to read.
- *Scanning* **while** *Loop.* We moved the **scanf()** function call inside the condition of the **while** loop. This allowed us to eliminate the variable **flag** and two lines of code, while making the remaining code easier to understand.
- *Compound Assignment Operator.* The revised program uses the `+=` operator to sum the data. This makes the code somewhat more concise and perhaps a bit faster.
- *Increment Operator.* We have used the increment operator to count the values as they are read and summed. Again, this makes the code more concise and perhaps a bit faster.

We made one more change to the program. Observe the last statement in the revised program:

```
printf("The average is %g.\n", sum/(double)count);
```

By computing the average as part of the **printf()** function call, we eliminate the need for the variable **ave**. Of course, if we had a need for this variable elsewhere in the program, we would not have gotten rid of it.

Listing 14–2. *ave.c* (Revised)

```
/***********************************************

    Compute the arithmetic average of double
    values taken from the standard input.
    (Revised.)

***********************************************/

#include <stdio.h>

main()
{
    double next_num;
    double sum = 0.0;
    int count = 0;

    while (scanf("%lf", &next_num) != EOF) {
        sum += next_num;
        ++count;
    }
    printf("The average is %g.\n", sum/(double)count);
}
```

● ▬▬▬▬ HELPFUL HINTS

In revising the *ave.c* program, we eliminated two variables and five lines of source code. This sort of thing can be carried too far, however. A serious criticism of the C language is that it allows, even encourages, programmers to write programs that are concise to the point of illegibility. Our advice is this:

Never sacrifice clarity for brevity.

The savings in storage space is rarely worth the cost in understanding. For the most part, computer storage is cheap; the programmer's time is not.

What about speed? Well, the revised program may run a bit faster, although it is unlikely that you would ever notice the difference. This is usually the case. Yet some programmers will go to ridiculous lengths to eke out minimal gains in efficiency, in the process producing code that is difficult to read. Our advice is

Never sacrifice clarity for efficiency, either.

● ▬▬▬▬▬ SUMMARY

Declarations and Initializations

```
double sum = 0.0;
```
Declares **sum** to be a **double** variable and assigns it the value 0.0.

```
int count = 0;
```
Declares **count** to be an **int** variable and assigns it the value 0.

Scanning Loop

```
while (scanf("%lf", &x) != EOF) {
    [body of the loop]
}
```
Calls **scanf()** to read a **double** value from the standard input and store it in the variable **x**. If this is done successfully, **scanf()** returns a 1; this makes the **while** condition true, and the body of the loop is executed. This is repeated until **scanf()** encounters an EOF signal.

Scanning Selection

```
if (scanf("%lf", &x) == 1) {
    first set of statement(s)
}
else {
    default set of statement(s)
}
```
Calls **scanf()** to read a **double** value from the standard input and store it in the variable **x**. If this is done successfully, **scanf()** returns a 1; this makes the **if** condition true, and the first set of statement(s) is executed. Otherwise, the default set of statements is executed.

Compound Assignment Operators	*Equivalent to . . .*
`var += expr`	`var = var + expr`
`var -= expr`	`var = var - expr`
`var *= expr`	`var = var * expr`
`var /= expr`	`var = var / expr`
`var %= expr`	`var = var % expr`

Increment Operators

```
save = i++;
```
Assigns value of **i** to **save**, then adds 1 to **i**.

```
save = ++i;
```
Adds 1 to **i**, then assigns the result to **save**.

Decrement Operators

save = i--;   Assigns value of **i** to **save**, then subtracts 1 from **i**.

save = --i;   Subtracts 1 from **i**, then assigns the result to **save**.

- In C, it is possible to initialize variables, arrays, and strings as they are declared.
- A common C idiom is to place the **scanf()** function in the condition controlling a **while** loop or an **if** structure. In many cases, this makes it unnecessary to declare a variable to hold the return value from **scanf()**.
- The compound assignment operators (**+=**, **-=**, ***=**, **/=**, and **%=**) are used to perform arithmetic operations (addition, subtraction, multiplication, division, and remainder) on the contents of a variable, putting the results back into the same variable. The use of these operators results in more compact code, which may also be more efficient.
- The unary increment operator (**++**) adds 1 to the value stored in a variable. If placed in front of the variable name (prefix form), the operator has the effect of incrementing the variable before its value is used. If placed after the variable name (postfix form), the operator increments the variable after its value is used.
- The unary decrement operator (**--**) subtracts 1 from the value stored in a variable. This operator, like the increment operator, can be written in either prefix or postfix form. As a prefix, the operator decrements the variable before its value is used. In postfix form, the operator decrements the variable after its value is used.

EXERCISES

1. *Define:* **a.** initializer; **b.** compound assignment operator; **c.** increment operator; **d.** decrement operator; **e.** unary operator; **f.** prefix form; **g.** postfix form.

2. *Errors.* Create a copy of the revised *ave.c* (Listing 14–2) called *errors14.c* and introduce into the new file the first error listed below. Compile the program. If the compiler catches the error, write down both the error and the error message; if not, run the executable file with test data and make a note of any unexpected results. Correct the file, then repeat the process with the next error on the list. Continue until you have tried all of the errors.

    a. Insert a space between the two parts (**+** and **+**) of the increment operator.

    b. Insert a space between the two parts (**+** and **=**) of the compound assignment operator.

    c. Interchange the two parts of the compound assignment operator, so that it becomes **=+**.

3. *Applying shortcuts.* Rewrite each of the following programs to employ the various shortcuts and idioms shown in this chapter:

   a. *fact1.c* (Listing 6–1)

   b. *fact2.c* (Listing 6–2)

   c. *fact3.c* (Listing 6–4)

   d. *sqroot.c* (Listing 6–5)

   e. *upc2.c* (Listing 9–1)

   f. *getarray.c* (Listing 9–3)

   g. *avearray.c* (Listing 9–8)

   h. *array2D.c* (Listing 10–1)

   i. *ave2D.c* (Listing 10–6)

   j. *countlds.c* (Listing 11–3)

   k. *getint.c* (Listing 11–4)

4. *Ambiguous operations.* We said that the result of the statements

   ```
   i = 1;
   sum = (i++ * 2) + (i++ * 3);
   ```

   is compiler-dependent. There are two ways that the second statement could be interpreted:

Step	Operation
1	Multiply **i** by 2
2	Add 1 to **i**
3	Multiply **i** by 3
4	Add 1 to **i**
5	Add values from Steps 1 and 3
6	Assign result of Step 5 to **sum**

Step	Operation
1	Multiply **i** by 3
2	Add 1 to **i**
3	Multiply **i** by 2
4	Add 1 to **i**
5	Add values from Steps 1 and 3
6	Assign result of Step 5 to **sum**

   What are the results of these different interpretations? Which does your compiler follow?

Operator Precedence and Associativity

Level	Description	Operator	Associativity
15	Parentheses	( )	left to right
	Array subscript	[ ]	
	Component selection	. ->	
	Postfix increment, decrement	++ --	
14	Prefix increment, decrement	++ --	right to left
	Indirection, address	* &	
	Logical NOT	!	
	Bitwise negation	~	
	Positive and negative	+ -	
	Sizeof operator	sizeof	
	Typecasts	(int) (double) etc.	
13	Multiplication, division	* / %	left to right
12	Addition, subtraction	+ -	left to right
11	Shifts	<< >>	left to right
10	Inequalities	< <= > >=	left to right
9	Equal, not equal	== !=	left to right
8	Bitwise AND	&	left to right
7	Bitwise XOR	^	left to right
6	Bitwise OR	|	left to right
5	Logical AND	&&	left to right
4	Logical OR	||	left to right
3	Ternary condition	? :	right to left
2	Assignment	= += -= *= %= /= >>= <<= &= ^= |=	right to left
1	Comma operator	,	left to right

Appendix *B*•

Standard Mathematical Functions

Except where noted, these library functions may be declared by including the header file **math.h** in your program:

```
#include <math.h>
```

A few of these functions are declared in the **stdlib.h** header file:

```
#include <stdlib.h>
```

● ▬▬▬ Trigonometric Functions

Prototype	Description
`double sin(double x);`	sine of **x**
`double cos(double x);`	cosine of **x**
`double tan(double x);`	tangent of **x**

The argument **x** must be in radians. A *range error* can occur with the tangent function if the argument is close to an odd multiple of $\pi/2$.

Inverse Trigonometric Functions

Prototype	Description
`double asin(double x);`	arc sine of x, $-1 \le x \le 1$
`double acos(double x);`	arc cosine of x, $-1 \le x \le 1$
`double atan(double x);`	arc tangent of x
`double atan2(double y, double x);`	arc tangent of y/x

These functions return the principal values of the inverse trigonometric functions, expressed in radians. The ranges of these functions are

$$-\pi/2 \le \mathbf{asin}() \le \pi/2$$

$$0 \le \mathbf{acos}() \le \pi$$

$$-\pi/2 \le \mathbf{atan}() \le \pi/2$$

$$-\pi \le \mathbf{atan2}() \le \pi$$

A *domain error* occurs with **asin()** or **acos()** if the argument x is less than -1 or greater than 1. A *domain error* occurs with **atan2()** if both x and y are zero.

Hyperbolic Functions

Prototype	Description
`double sinh(double x);`	hyperbolic sine of x
`double cosh(double x);`	hyperbolic cosine of x
`double tanh(double x);`	hyperbolic tangent of x

A *range error* can occur with either **sinh()** or **cosh()** if the argument is too large.

Square Root Function

Prototype	Description
`double sqrt(double x);`	square root of x, $x \ge 0$

A *domain error* occurs for negative arguments.

Logarithmic Functions

Prototype	Description
`double log(double x);`	natural (base-e) log of x, $x > 0$
`double log10(double x);`	common (base-10) log of x, $x > 0$

A *domain error* occurs if x is negative. A *range error* may occur for values of x near or at zero.

Exponential Function

Prototype	Description
`double exp(double x);`	exponential function, e^x

A *range error* can occur for large values of x.

Power Function

Prototype	Description
`double pow(double x, double y);`	raise x to the yth power, x^y

A *range error* can occur for large values of x and/or y. Two conditions produce a *domain error*:

1. x equals 0 and $y < 0$ (division by zero).
2. $x < 0$ and y not a whole number.

Floor and Ceiling Functions

Prototype	Description
`double floor(double x);`	largest whole number $\leq x$
`double ceil(double x);`	smallest whole number $\geq x$

Absolute Value Functions

Prototype	Description
`int abs(int n);`	absolute value of n, |n|
`long labs(long n);`	absolute value of n, |n|
`double fabs(double x);`	absolute value of x, |x|

abs() and **labs()** are integer functions, declared in the ***stdlib.h*** header file. **fabs()** is the **double** version; it is declared in ***math.h***.

Random-Number Generator

Prototype	Description
`int rand(void);`	pseudo-random **int** in the range 0 to RAND_MAX
`void srand(unsigned int s);`	initialize **rand()** using the seed **s**

rand() generates a sequence of pseudo-random integers between 0 and RAND_MAX. (RAND_MAX must be 32,767 or larger.) The sequence is determined by an integer "seed" that is initially set to 1. If the seed value is not changed, **rand()** will always generate the same sequence of numbers.

The **srand()** function changes the **rand()** seed. The new seed is passed to **srand()** as an **unsigned int**, which for the purposes of this text may be treated as a normal **int** quantity.

rand() and **srand()** are integer functions declared in ***stdlib.h***.

Matrix Algebra

A *matrix of order* $m \times n$ is a two-dimensional array having m rows and n columns. Matrices are typically designated by boldface roman letters; individual elements are designated by subscripted italic letters:

$$\mathbf{A} = [a_{ij}] = \begin{bmatrix} a_{11} & a_{12} & a_{13} & a_{14} \\ a_{21} & a_{22} & a_{23} & a_{24} \\ a_{31} & a_{32} & a_{33} & a_{34} \end{bmatrix}$$

Following the C practice of beginning indices at zero, we might represent the array $\mathbf{A}$ this way:

$$\mathbf{A} = [a_{ij}] = \begin{bmatrix} a_{00} & a_{01} & a_{02} & a_{03} \\ a_{10} & a_{11} & a_{12} & a_{13} \\ a_{20} & a_{21} & a_{22} & a_{23} \end{bmatrix}$$

Special Matrices

- **Row matrix.** A $1 \times n$ matrix is called a *row matrix* or *row vector*:

$$[47.8 \quad 55.2 \quad 10.1]$$

- **Column matrix.** An $m \times 1$ matrix is called a *column matrix* or *column vector*:

$$\begin{bmatrix} 47.8 \\ 55.2 \\ 10.1 \end{bmatrix}$$

- **Transpose.** The *transpose* of a matrix $\mathbf{A}$, denoted $\mathbf{A}^T$, is the matrix formed by interchanging the rows and columns of $\mathbf{A}$. For example,

$$\mathbf{A} = \begin{bmatrix} 1 & 2 & 3 \\ 4 & 5 & 6 \end{bmatrix} \quad \Rightarrow \quad \mathbf{A}^T = \begin{bmatrix} 1 & 4 \\ 2 & 5 \\ 3 & 6 \end{bmatrix}$$

- **Square matrix.** An $n \times n$ matrix—in other words, a matrix having the same number of rows as columns—is called a *square matrix*. For example,

$$\begin{bmatrix} 1 & 7 & 8 \\ 4 & 2 & 5 \\ 3 & 6 & 9 \end{bmatrix}.$$

- **Diagonal matrix.** Elements whose row index and column index are the same (such as a_{00}, a_{11}, a_{22}, . . . ,a_{nn}) make up the *main diagonal* of the matrix. If a square matrix contains zero elements everywhere except on the main diagonal, it is a *diagonal matrix*:

$$\begin{bmatrix} 1 & 0 & 0 \\ 0 & 2 & 0 \\ 0 & 0 & 9 \end{bmatrix}$$

- **Identity matrix.** A diagonal matrix whose diagonal elements are unity is called an *identity matrix*:

$$\begin{bmatrix} 1 & 0 & 0 \\ 0 & 1 & 0 \\ 0 & 0 & 1 \end{bmatrix}$$

- **Triangular matrix.** A square matrix in which all of the elements on one side of the diagonal are zero is a *triangular matrix*. The remaining elements may be zero or nonzero. An *upper triangular matrix* has zeroes below the diagonal, like this:

$$\begin{bmatrix} 2 & 4 & 8 & 3 \\ 0 & 4 & 7 & 0 \\ 0 & 0 & 2 & 3 \\ 0 & 0 & 0 & 2 \end{bmatrix}$$

A *lower triangular matrix* has zeroes above the diagonal, like this:

$$\begin{bmatrix} 3 & 0 & 0 & 0 \\ 1 & 5 & 0 & 0 \\ 6 & 5 & 7 & 0 \\ 4 & 9 & 9 & 3 \end{bmatrix}$$

More Useful Matrix Terms

- *Equality.* Two matrices **A** and **B** are said to be *equal* if and only if the matrices are of the same order and every element of **A** equals the corresponding element of **B**.
- *Trace.* The *trace* of a square matrix **A**, denoted tr(**A**), is the sum of the main diagonal elements of **A**.

Elementary Matrix Operations

We shall examine three elementary matrix operations: addition, subtraction, and multiplication:

- *Matrix addition.* Two matrices may be added only if they are of the same order. The sum of the $m \times n$ matrices **A** and **B** is another $m \times n$ matrix **C**. Every element of **C** is just the sum of the corresponding elements of **A** and **B**:

$$\mathbf{C} = \mathbf{A} + \mathbf{B} \quad \Rightarrow \quad c_{ij} = a_{ij} + b_{ij}$$

- *Matrix subtraction.* Two matrices may be subtracted only if they are of the same order. The difference of the $m \times n$ matrices **A** and **B** is another $m \times n$ matrix **C** whose elements are formed by subtracting the corresponding elements of **A** and **B**:

$$\mathbf{C} = \mathbf{A} - \mathbf{B} \quad \Rightarrow \quad c_{ij} = a_{ij} - b_{ij}$$

- *Matrix multiplication.* Two matrices may be multiplied only if the number of columns of the first matrix equals the number of rows of the second matrix. If **A** is an $m \times p$ matrix and **B** is a $p \times n$ matrix, their product is the $m \times n$ matrix **C** whose elements are given by

$$\mathbf{C} = \mathbf{AB} \quad \Rightarrow \quad c_{ij} = \sum_{k=0}^{p-1} a_{ik} b_{kj}$$

In general, matrix multiplication is not commutative. Hence,

$$\mathbf{AB} \neq \mathbf{BC}$$

On the other hand, the associative and distributive laws do hold for matrix multiplication:

$$(\mathbf{AB})\mathbf{C} = \mathbf{A}(\mathbf{BC})$$

$$\mathbf{A}(\mathbf{B} + \mathbf{C}) = \mathbf{AB} + \mathbf{AC}$$

$$(\mathbf{A} + \mathbf{B})\mathbf{C} = \mathbf{AC} + \mathbf{BC}$$

Systems of Equations

Perhaps the most important practical use of matrices is in the solution of systems of linear equations, which occur in almost all fields of science, engineering, and applied mathematics. The system of equations

$$
\begin{aligned}
a_{00}x_0 + a_{01}x_1 + \ldots + a_{0n}x_n &= b_0 \\
a_{10}x_0 + a_{11}x_1 + \ldots + a_{0n}x_n &= b_1 \\
&\vdots \\
a_{m0}x_0 + a_{m1}x_1 + \ldots + a_{mn}x_n &= b_m
\end{aligned}
$$

can be represented in matrix form as

$$
\begin{bmatrix}
a_{00} & a_{01} & \cdots & a_{0n} \\
a_{10} & a_{11} & \cdots & a_{1n} \\
\vdots & \vdots & \ddots & \vdots \\
a_{m0} & a_{m1} & \cdots & a_{mn}
\end{bmatrix}
\begin{bmatrix}
x_0 \\ x_1 \\ \vdots \\ x_n
\end{bmatrix}
=
\begin{bmatrix}
b_0 \\ b_1 \\ \vdots \\ b_n
\end{bmatrix}
$$

or more compactly in the form

$$\mathbf{Ax} = \mathbf{b}$$

Methods for solving equations such as this are discussed in any standard textbook on linear algebra.

ASCII and EBCDIC Character Codes

The American Standard Code for Information Interchange (ASCII) is shown in Table D–1. The standard ASCII character set encodes 128 characters, but some systems extend this to include special characters. ASCII forms the basis for an international character code known as ISO 646.

The Extended Binary-Coded Decimal Interchange Code (EBCDIC), shown in Table D–2, is used almost exclusively on IBM mainframe computers. There are 256 EBCDIC values, not all of which are currently assigned a meaning.

Abbreviations are used in the tables for certain control characters (on page A-11). Only some of these are of interest to C programmers; these are listed on the following page in boldface.

Abbreviations Used in Tables D–1 & D–2

ACK	Acknowledge		IL	Idle
BEL	**Audible bell/alert ('\a')**		IRS	Interchange record separator
BS	**Backspace ('\b')**		IUS	Interchange unit separator
BYP	Bypass		LC	Lowercase
CAN	Cancel		LF	Line feed
CC	Unit backspace		NAK	Negative acknowledge
CR	Carriage return		**NL**	**New line ('\n')**
DC1	Device control 1		**NUL**	**Null ('\0')**
DC2	Device control 2		PF	Punch off
DC3	Device control 3		PN	Punch on
DEL	Delete		RES	Restore
DLE	Data link escape		RS	Record separator
DS	Digit select		SI	Shift in
EM	End of medium		SM	Start message
ENQ	Enquire		SMM	Repeat
EOT	End of transmission		SO	Shift out
ESC	Escape		SOH	Start of heading
ETB	End of transmission block		SOS	Start of significance
ETX	End of text		**SP**	**Space (' ')**
FF	**Form feed ('\f')**		STX	Start of text
FS	File separator		SUB	Substitute
HT	**Horizontal tab ('\t')**		SYN	Synchronous idle
IFS	Interchange file separator		UC	Uppercase
IGS	Interchange group separator		**VT**	**Vertical tab ('\v')**

Appendix D ASCII and EBCDIC Character Codes

Table D–1 American Standard Code for Information Interchange (ASCII)

ASCII	Character	ASCII	Character	ASCII	Character	ASCII	Character
0	NUL	32		64	@	96	`
1	SOH	33	!	65	A	97	a
2	STX	34	"	66	B	98	b
3	ETX	35	#	67	C	99	c
4	EOT	36	$	68	D	100	d
5	ENQ	37	%	69	E	101	e
6	ACK	38	&	70	F	102	f
7	BEL	39	'	71	G	103	g
8	BS	40	(	72	H	104	h
9	HT	41	)	73	I	105	i
10	LF	42	*	74	J	106	j
11	VT	43	+	75	K	107	k
12	FF	44	,	76	L	108	l
13	CR	45	-	77	M	109	m
14	SO	46	.	78	N	110	n
15	SI	47	/	79	O	111	o
16	DLE	48	0	80	P	112	p
17	DC1	49	1	81	Q	113	q
18	DC2	50	2	82	R	114	r
19	DC3	51	3	83	S	115	s
20	DC4	52	4	84	T	116	t
21	NAK	53	5	85	U	117	u
22	SYN	54	6	86	V	118	v
23	ETB	55	7	87	W	119	w
24	CAN	56	8	88	X	120	x
25	EM	57	9	89	Y	121	y
26	SUB	58	:	90	Z	122	z
27	ESC	59	;	91	[	123	{
28	FS	60	<	92	\	124		
29	GS	61	=	93	]	125	}
30	RS	62	>	94	^	126	~
31	US	63	?	95	_	127	DEL

Table D–2 Extended Binary-Coded Decimal Interchange Code (EBCDIC)

EBCDIC	Character	EBCDIC	Character	EBCDIC	Character	EBCDIC	Character
0	NUL	32	DS	64	SP	96	–
1	SOH	33	SOS	65		97	/
2	STX	34	FS	66		98	
3	ETX	35		67		99	
4	PF	36	BYP	68		100	
5	HT	37	LF	69		101	
6	LC	38	ETB	70		102	
7	DEL	39	ESC	71		103	
8		40		72		104	
9		41		73		105	
10	SMM	42	SM	74	¢	106	|
11	VT	43		75	.	107	,
12	FF	44		76	<	108	%
13	CR	45	ENQ	77	(	109	_
14	SO	46	ACK	78	+	110	>
15	SI	47	BEL	79	OR	111	?
16	DLE	48		80	&	112	
17	DC1	49		81		113	
18	DC2	50	SYN	82		114	
19	DC3	51		83		115	
20	RES	52	PN	84		116	
21	NL	53	RS	85		117	
22	SYN	54	UC	86		118	
23	ETB	55	EOT	87		119	
24	CAN	56		88		120	
25	EM	57		89		121	`
26	CC	58		90	!	122	:
27	CU1	59		91	$	123	#
28	IFS	60	DC4	92	*	124	@
29	IGS	61	NAK	93	)	125	'
30	IRS	62		94	;	126	=
31	IUS	63	SUB	95	NOT	127	"

EBCDIC	Character	EBCDIC	Character	EBCDIC	Character	EBCDIC	Character
128		160		192	{	224	\
129	a	161	~	193	A	225	
130	b	162	s	194	B	226	S
131	c	163	t	195	C	227	T
132	d	164	u	196	D	228	U
133	e	165	v	197	E	229	V
134	f	166	w	198	F	230	W
135	g	167	x	199	G	231	X
136	h	168	y	200	H	232	Y
137	i	169	z	201	I	233	Z
138		170		202		234	
139		171		203		235	
140		172		204		236	
141		173		205		237	
142		174		206		238	
143		175		207		239	
144		176		208		240	0
145	j	177		209	J	241	1
146	k	178		210	K	242	2
147	l	179		211	L	243	3
148	m	180		212	M	244	4
149	n	181		213	N	245	5
150	o	182		214	O	246	6
151	p	183		215	P	247	7
152	q	184		216	Q	248	8
153	r	185		217	R	249	9
154		186		218		250	
155		187		219		251	
156		188		220		252	
157		189		221		253	
158		190		222		254	
159		191		223		255	

Index